MySQL Concurrency

Locking and Transactions for MySQL Developers and DBAs

Jesper Wisborg Krogh

Apress®

MySQL Concurrency: Locking and Transactions for MySQL Developers and DBAs

Jesper Wisborg Krogh
Hornsby, NSW, Australia

ISBN-13 (pbk): 978-1-4842-6651-9   ISBN-13 (electronic): 978-1-4842-6652-6
https://doi.org/10.1007/978-1-4842-6652-6

Managing Director, Apress Media LLC: Welmoed Spahr
Acquisitions Editor: Jonathan Gennick
Development Editor: Laura Berendson
Coordinating Editor: Jill Balzano

Cover image designed by Freepik (www.freepik.com)

Distributed to the book trade worldwide by Springer Science+Business Media LLC, 1 New York Plaza, Suite 4600, New York, NY 10004. Phone 1-800-SPRINGER, fax (201) 348-4505, e-mail orders-ny@springer-sbm.com, or visit www.springeronline.com. Apress Media, LLC is a California LLC and the sole member (owner) is Springer Science + Business Media Finance Inc (SSBM Finance Inc). SSBM Finance Inc is a Delaware corporation.

For information on translations, please e-mail booktranslations@springernature.com; for reprint, paperback, or audio rights, please e-mail bookpermissions@springernature.com.

Apress titles may be purchased in bulk for academic, corporate, or promotional use. eBook versions and licenses are also available for most titles. For more information, reference our Print and eBook Bulk Sales web page at http://www.apress.com/bulk-sales.

Any source code or other supplementary material referenced by the author in this book is available to readers on GitHub via the book's product page, located at www.apress.com/9781484266519. For more detailed information, please visit http://www.apress.com/source-code.

Printed on acid-free paper

To my wife Ann-Margrete – Thanks for the patience and support.

Table of Contents

About the Author

Jesper Wisborg Krogh has worked with MySQL databases since 2006 both as a SQL developer and a database administrator and for more than 8 years as part of the Oracle MySQL Support team. He currently works as a database reliability engineer for Okta. He has spoken at MySQL Connect, Oracle OpenWorld, and Oracle Developer Live on several occasions. In addition to his books, Jesper regularly blogs on MySQL topics and has authored approximately 800 documents in the Oracle Knowledge Base. He has contributed to the sys schema and four Oracle Certified Professional (OCP) exams for MySQL 5.6–8. Jesper holds a PhD in computational chemistry; lives in Sydney, Australia; and enjoys spending time outdoors walking, traveling, and reading. His areas of expertise include MySQL Cluster, MySQL Enterprise Backup (MEB), performance tuning, and the performance and sys schemas.

About the Technical Reviewer

 **Charles Bell** conducts research in emerging technologies. He is a member of the Oracle MySQL Development team and is a senior software developer for the MySQL Enterprise Backup team. He lives in a small town in rural Virginia with his loving wife. He received his Doctor of Philosophy in Engineering from Virginia Commonwealth University in 2005.

Charles is an expert in the database field and has extensive knowledge and experience in software development and systems engineering. His research interests include 3D printers, microcontrollers, three-dimensional printing, database systems, software engineering, high-availability systems, cloud, and sensor networks. He spends his limited free time as a practicing Maker, focusing on microcontroller projects and refinement of three-dimensional printers.

Acknowledgments

I would first of all like to say thank you to all of those from the Apress team that have made this book possible. In particular, I would like to shout out Jonathan Gennick who came up with the idea, Jill Balzano who coordinated the work, Laura Berendson for her work behind the scenes, and Creapzylene Roma for catching my linguistic slipups.

The knowledge shared in this book has not materialized out of nothing. Thanks to Charles Bell for providing – as always – a thorough review with constructive feedback and suggestions for improvements. Jakub Lopuszanski has been helpful with details on InnoDB locking. I would also like to thank all my colleagues over the years as they have all been part of my journey learning how MySQL works through mentorship, teaching me, asking me good questions, and general discussions. A special thank you to Edwin Desouza and Frédéric Descamps (better known as Lefred) for their assistance.

Last but not least, thanks to my wife Ann-Margrete for her patience and support while I wrote this book. Without you, it would not have been possible to write this book.

Introduction

When working with databases, locks and transactions are some of the most difficult and misunderstood topics. This book aims at improving your understanding of these two concepts, how they work, how you can investigate them, and how you can improve your workload, so it works the best with them. This is achieved through a combination of discussing monitoring, the lock and transaction theory, and a series of case studies.

MySQL is famous for its support for storage engines. However, this book exclusively covers the InnoDB storage engine, and only MySQL 8 is considered. That said, most of the discussion also applies to older versions of MySQL, and in general, it is mentioned when a feature is new in MySQL 8 or that MySQL 8 has a different behavior compared to older versions.

Book Audience

The book has been written for developers and database administrators who have experience working with MySQL and want to expand their knowledge of how locks and transactions work in the realm of MySQL concurrency.

Examples and the Book's GitHub Repository

I have tried to add as many examples and outputs from examples as possible. Some of the examples are quite short, some are quite long. In either case, I hope you are able to follow them and reproduce the effect or result demonstrated. At the same time, please do bear in mind that by nature there is often randomness involved, and the exact outcome of the examples may depend on how the tables and data have been used prior to the example. In other words, you may get different results even if you did everything right. This particularly applies to numbers that relate to lock ids, memory locations, mutexes/semaphores, timings, and the like.

Examples that are long or produce outputs that are either long or wide have been added to this book's GitHub repository. This includes some of the figures that may be hard to read with the image size that the page format allows.

Note The link to the repository can be found from the book's home page at `www.apress.com/gp/book/9781484266519`. It can also be found directly at `www.github.com/Apress/mysql-concurrency`.

To make it easier to reproduce the examples and to provide example queries that can be used to examine the issue the test demonstrates, a module written in Python for use in MySQL Shell is also included in the book's GitHub repository. The basic installation and usage instructions are covered in Chapter 1 and the full documentation in Appendix B.

The GitHub repository will also be the home of the errata for the book once that is created. I will use the errata not only to communicate errors in the book but also to provide updates when bug fixes and new features in MySQL 8 cause changes to book content. If necessary, I will also update the examples in the repository to reflect the behavior in the newer releases. For these reasons, I recommend that you keep an eye on the repository.

Book Structure

I have attempted to keep each chapter relatively self-contained with the aim that you can use the book as a reference book. The drawback of this choice is that there is some duplication of information from time to time. This is particularly evident in the case studies that repeat some of the information discussed in earlier chapters. This was a deliberate choice, and I hope it helps you to reduce the amount of page flipping to find the information you need.

The book is divided into 18 chapters and two appendixes. Chapter 1 provides an introduction, Chapters 2–4 cover monitoring of locks and transactions, Chapters 5–10 discuss locks, Chapters 11–12 contain information about transactions, and finally Chapters 13–18 go through six case studies. The appendixes contain references for monitoring locks and transactions and for the MySQL Shell module provided with the book.

- **Chapter 1, "Introduction":** This introductory chapter covers some high-level concepts as well as introduces the MySQL Shell module for reproducing the example and the test data used in this book.

- **Chapter 2, "Monitoring Locks":** This chapter covers how you can monitor locks using the Performance Schema, the `sys` schema, status counters, and InnoDB metrics. There is also information on how to use the InnoDB lock monitor and the deadlock information in the InnoDB monitor and how to obtain information about mutex and semaphore contention.

- **Chapter 3, "Monitoring InnoDB Transactions":** This chapter primarily shows how you can use the `information_schema.INNODB_TRX` view to investigate InnoDB transaction. The transaction list in the InnoDB monitor and transaction-related InnoDB metrics are also covered.

- **Chapter 4, "Transactions in the Performance Schema":** This chapter continues where the previous stopped by going through the transaction information in the Performance Schema and how you can find the statements for a transaction.

- **Chapter 5, "Lock Access Levels":** This chapter goes through shared, exclusive, and intention locks as well as shows which of these are compatible with each other.

- **Chapter 6, "High-Level Lock Types":** This chapter covers the locks that work at a higher level than records. These are mainly locks handled outside the scope of the storage engines and include user-level locks, metadata locks, flush locks, and table-level locks. The new MySQL 8 backup and log locks are also included.

- **Chapter 7, "InnoDB Locks":** This chapter goes to the record locks used by InnoDB. These include plain record locks, gab locks, predicate locks, insert intention locks, auto-increment locks, as well as mutexes and rw-lock semaphores.

- **Chapter 8, "Working with Lock Conflicts":** This chapter explains what happens when lock conflicts occur from a discussion of the contention-aware transaction scheduling (CATS) used internally to

prioritize locks and a discussion of lock compatibility to lock wait
timeouts and deadlocks.

- **Chapter 9, "Reduce Locking Issues":** This chapter covers how you
  can reduce lock contention and the effects of the contention in your
  system. Methods include reducing the transaction size and age, using
  indexes, accessing records in the same order for concurrent tasks,
  changing the transaction isolation level, and more.

- **Chapter 10, "Indexes and Foreign Keys":** This chapter considers
  the effect of indexes and foreign keys on locking in detail. Do unique
  indexes require less locks than non-unique indexes? Do foreign keys
  cause more locks? The answer is yes, and this chapter explains why
  that is the case and gives examples of the differences.

- **Chapter 11, "Transactions":** This chapter discusses what
  transactions are and how they help handle concurrent workloads.
  The chapter also covers the impact of transactions and how the group
  commit feature helps reduce the impact of persisting committed
  transactions.

- **Chapter 12, "Transaction Isolation Levels":** This chapter goes
  through the four transaction isolation levels supported by InnoDB
  with a discussion on how each level affects locking and data
  consistency.

- **Chapter 13, "Case Study: Flush Locks":** This chapter sets the
  database up, so there is flush lock contention, and then goes through
  analyzing the issue and providing a solution and discusses how to
  prevent the issue.

- **Chapter 14, "Case Study: Metadata and Schema Locks":** This
  chapter takes on another common lock issue by studying a situation
  with metadata locks.

- **Chapter 15, "Case Study: Record-Level Locks":** This chapter
  performs an investigation into InnoDB record-level locks and
  discusses how to resolve the lock issue and reduce the chance of
  encountering them.

- **Chapter 16, "Case Study: Deadlocks":** This chapter goes through an investigation of a deadlock with details of analyzing the deadlock information from the InnoDB monitor output.

- **Chapter 17, "Case Study: Foreign Keys":** This chapter covers an advanced lock scenario caused by foreign keys, involving both metadata and InnoDB record locks.

- **Chapter 18, "Case Study: Semaphores":** This chapter sets up a test case triggering semaphore contention and performs an investigation of the issue.

- **Appendix A, "References":** This appendix provides an overview of the resources for finding information related to the topics discussed in this book. The resources primarily consist of tables in the Performance Schema and views in the `sys` schema including the possible values of the `OBJECT_TYPE` and `LOCK_TYPE` columns of the `performance_schema.metadata_locks` table. Some Information Schema resources are also included, and there is a list of sections in the output from the InnoDB monitor.

- **Appendix B, "MySQL Shell Script Reproducing Lock Scenarios":** This appendix is the reference for the Python module included with the book. This includes a discussion of how to install and use the module as well as how the code is organized in case you want to extend it with your own workloads.

CHAPTER 1

Introduction

Concurrency and locking are some of the most complex topics when it comes to databases. A query that usually executes fast and without problems may suddenly take much longer or fail with an error when the conditions are "just right," so locking or contention becomes a problem. You may ask yourself why locks are around when they can cause such problems. This and the next 11 chapters will try to explain that as well as how you best deal with them. The last six chapters of the book go through six case studies putting the information together in realistic scenarios together with analysis and how to avoid or reduce the issue.

In this chapter, you will first learn why locks are important despite the problems they can cause. Then the relationship with transactions will be explained. The rest of the chapter introduces how examples are used in this book as well as the `world`, `sakila`, and `employees` databases which are used throughout this book for the examples.

Why Are Locks Needed?

It can seem like a perfect world where locking in databases is not needed. The price will however be so high that only few use cases can use that database, and it is impossible to avoid locks for a general-purpose database such as MySQL. If you do not have locking, you cannot have any concurrency. Imagine that only one connection is ever allowed to the database (you can argue that it itself is a lock and thus the system is not lock-free anyway) – that is not very useful for most applications.

Note   Often what is called a lock in MySQL is really a lock request which can be in a granted or pending state.

© Jesper Wisborg Krogh 2021
J. W. Krogh, *MySQL Concurrency*, https://doi.org/10.1007/978-1-4842-6652-6_1

When you have several connections executing queries concurrently, you need some way to ensure that the connections do not step on each other's toes. That is where locks enter the picture. You can think of locks in the same way as traffic signals in road traffic (Figure 1-1) that regulate access to the resources to avoid accidents. In a road intersection, it is necessary to ensure that two cars do not cross each other's path and collide.

Figure 1-1. *Locks in databases are similar to traffic lights*

In a database, it is necessary to ensure two queries' access to the data does not conflict. As there are different levels of controlling the access to an intersection – yielding, stop signs, and traffic lights – there are different lock types in a database.

Lock Levels

Locks in MySQL come in several flavors acting at different levels in MySQL ranging from user-level locks to record locks. At the highest level are the user-level locks which can protect whole code paths in the application and any object inside the database. In the middle there are locks that operate on the database objects. These include metadata locks that protect the metadata of the tables as well as table locks that protect all data in the table. Common for the user-level and table-level locks is that they are implemented at the SQL layer of the database. The high-level locks are discussed in Chapter 6.

At the lowest level are the locks implemented by the storage engines. By nature, these locks depend on the storage engine you use. As InnoDB is by far the most used storage engine in MySQL (and the default), this book covers the InnoDB-specific locks. InnoDB includes locks on the records, which are the easiest to understand, as well as more difficult concepts such as gap locks, next key locks, predicate locks, and insert intention locks. Additionally, there are mutexes and semaphores (this also happens at the level of the SQL layer). The InnoDB-specific locks and mutexes/semaphores are covered in Chapter 7.

Locks and Transactions

It can seem odd at first to combine the topics of locks and transactions into one book about concurrency. However, they are strongly related as you will see several examples of in this book. Some locks are held for the duration of a transaction, so it is important to understand how transactions work and how to monitor them.

The concept of transaction isolation level also plays an important role when working with locks. The isolation level influences both which locks are taken and how long a time they are held.

Chapters 3 and 4 cover how you can monitor transactions, and Chapters 11 and 12 cover how transactions work, their impact, and the transaction isolation levels.

Examples

Throughout the book there are examples that help illustrate the topic being discussed or set up a situation that you can investigate. Except for Chapters 17 and 18, all statements required to reproduce the test are listed. In general, you will need more than one connection for the examples, so the prompts for the queries have been set to indicate which connection to use for which queries when that is important. For example, `Connection 1>` means that the query should be executed by the first of your connections.

All the examples in this book have been executed in MySQL Shell. For brevity the prompt in the examples is `mysql>` except when the connection is important or when the language mode is not SQL. The examples will however also work from the old `mysql` command-line client.

Tip   If you are unfamiliar with MySQL Shell, then it is a second-generation MySQL command-line client with support for both SQL, Python, and JavaScript. It also comes with several built-in utilities including tools for managing MySQL InnoDB Cluster and traditional replication topologies. For an introduction to MySQL Shell, see the user guide at `https://dev.mysql.com/doc/mysql-shell/en/` or the book *Introducing MySQL Shell* (Apress) by Charles Bell (`www.apress.com/gp/book/9781484250822`).

Additionally, this book comes with a Python module – `concurrency_book.generate` – that can be imported into MySQL Shell and used to reproduce all but the simplest examples. The rest of this section describes how to use the MySQL Shell module. The content here is an excerpt of Appendix B which contains a longer reference for the module including how to implement your own examples.

Note   By nature, some of the data in the examples will be different for each execution. This is particularly the case for ids and memory addresses and similar. So, do not expect to get identical results for all details when you try to reproduce the examples.

Prerequisites for the concurrency_book.generate Module

The most important requirement to use the MySQL Shell module provided with this book is that you are using MySQL Shell 8.0.20 or later. This is a strict requirement as the module primarily uses the `shell.open_session()` method to create the connections needed for the test cases. This method was only introduced in release 8.0.20. The advantage of `shell.open_session()` over the `mysql.get_classic_session()` and `mysqlx.get_session()` is that `open_session()` works transparently with both the classic MySQL protocol and the new X protocol.

If you for some reason are stuck with an older version of MySQL Shell, you can update the test cases to include the protocol setting (see *Defining Workloads* in Appendix B) to explicitly specify which protocol to use.

It is also required that a connection already exists from MySQL Shell to MySQL Server as the module uses the URI of that connection when creating the additional connections required for the example.

The examples have been tested with MySQL Server 8.0.21; however, most of the examples will work with older releases and some even with MySQL 5.7. That said, it is recommended to use MySQL Server 8.0.21 or later.

Installing the concurrency_book.generate Module

To use the module, you need to download the files in the concurrency_book directory from this book's GitHub repository (the link can be found on the book's home page at www.apress.com/gp/book/9781484266519). The easiest is to clone the repository or to download the ZIP file with all the files using the menu shown in Figure 1-2.

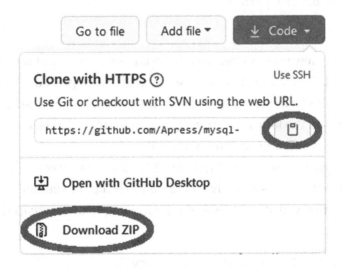

Figure 1-2. *The GitHub menu for cloning or downloading the repository*

Click on the clipboard icon to copy the URL used to clone the repository using the Git software of your system or use the *Download ZIP* link to download a ZIP file of the repository. You are free to choose any path as the location of the files as long as the structure below the concurrency_book directory is kept. For this discussion, it is assumed you have cloned the repository or unzipped the file to C:\Book\mysql-concurrency, so the generate.py file is in the directory C:\Book\mysql-concurrency\concurrency_book\.

To be able to import the module in MySQL Shell, open or create the mysqlshrc.py file. MySQL Shell searches in four places for the file. On Microsoft Windows, the paths are in the order they are searched:

1.   %PROGRAMDATA%\MySQL\mysqlsh\

2.   %MYSQLSH_HOME%\shared\mysqlsh\

3.   <mysqlsh binary path>\

4.   %APPDATA%\MySQL\mysqlsh\

On Linux and Unix

1.   /etc/mysql/mysqlsh/

2. $MYSQLSH_HOME/shared/mysqlsh/

3.   <mysqlsh binary path>/

4. $HOME/.mysqlsh/

All four paths are always searched, and if the file is found in multiple locations, each file will be executed. This means that the last found file takes precedence if the files affect the same variables. If you make changes meant for you personally, the best place to make the changes is in the fourth location. The path in step 4 can be overridden with the MYSQLSH_USER_CONFIG_HOME environment variable.

You need to ensure the mysqlshrc.py file adds the directory with the module to the Python search path, and optionally you can add an import statement to make the module available when you start MySQL Shell. An example of the mysqlshrc.py file is

```
import sys
sys.path.append('C:\\Book\\mysql-concurrency')
import concurrency_book.generate
```

The double backslashes are for Windows; on Linux and Unix, you do not need to escape the slashes that separate the path elements. If you do not include the import in the mysqlshrc.py file, you will need to execute it in MySQL Shell before you can use the module.

Getting Information

The module includes two methods that return information on how to use the module. One is the help() method which provides information on how to use the module:

```
mysql-py> concurrency_book.generate.help()
```

There is also the show() method which lists the workloads that the run() method can execute and the schemas that the load() method can load:

```
mysql-py> concurrency_book.generate.show()
```

The workloads are named after the code listings in the book, for example, the workload named "Listing 6-1" implements the example in Listing 6-1.

Before you can start executing the workloads, you need to load some test data which the module can do for you as well.

Loading Test Data

The concurrency_book.generate module supports loading the employees, sakila, and world example databases into your MySQL instance. For the employees database, you can optionally choose a version with partitions. The world database is the most important for this book followed by the sakila database. The employees database is only used for the case study in Chapter 18. Each of the three schemas is described in more detail later in this chapter.

Note   If the schema exists, it will be dropped as part of the load job. This effectively means that load() resets the schema.

You load a schema with the load() method which optionally takes the name of the schema you want to load. If you do not provide a schema name, then you will be prompted. Listing 1-1 shows an example of loading the world schema.

Listing 1-1. Loading the world schema

```
mysql-py> concurrency_book.generate.load()
Available Schema load jobs:
============================

 # Name                    Description
--------------------------------------------------------------------------
 1 employees               The employee database
 2 employees partitioned   The employee database with partitions
 3 sakila                  The sakila database
 4 world                   The world database

Choose Schema load job (# or name - empty to exit): 4
2020-07-20 21:27:15.221340  0 [INFO] Downloading https://downloads.
mysql.com/docs/world.sql.zip to C:\Users\myuser\AppData\Roaming\mysql_
concurrency_book\sample_data\world.sql.zip
2020-07-20 21:27:18.159554  0 [INFO] Processing statements in world.sql
2020-07-20 21:27:27.045219  0 [INFO] Load of the world schema completed

Available Schema load jobs:
============================

 # Name                    Description
--------------------------------------------------------------------------
 1 employees               The employee database
 2 employees partitioned   The employee database with partitions
 3 sakila                  The sakila database
 4 world                   The world database

Choose Schema load job (# or name - empty to exit):
```

The load() method downloads the file with the schema definition, if it does not already have it. The downloaded file is stored in %APPDATA\mysql_concurrency_book\ sample_data\ on Microsoft Windows and in ${HOME}/.mysql_concurrency_book/ sample_data/ on other platforms. If you want the file re-downloaded, delete it from that directory.

Tip   As only relatively low-level network routines are available in MySQL Shell's Python, downloading the employees database may fail if you have a slow or unstable connection. One option – other than installing the schema manually – is to download `https://github.com/datacharmer/test_db/archive/master.zip` and save it in the `sample_data` directory. After that, the `load()` method will pick it up and not attempt to download it again.

If you only want to load a single schema, you can specify the name as an argument to `load()`. This can be particularly useful when initiating a schema load as a command given directly on the command line when invoking MySQL Shell, for example

```
shell> mysqlsh --user=myuser --py -e "concurrency_book.generate.
load('world')"
```

When you are done loading the schemas you need, you can reply with an empty answer to exit. You are now ready to execute the workloads.

Note   If the load process crashes complaining about the file, for example, that it is not a ZIP file, then it suggests the file is corrupted or incomplete. In that case, delete the file, so it is re-downloaded, or try to download the file manually using your browser.

Executing a Workload

You execute a workload with the `run()` method. If you specify the name of the known workload, then that workload will be executed immediately. Otherwise, the available workloads are listed, and you are prompted for the workload. You can in this case specify the workload either by the number (e.g., 15 for Listing 6-1) or by the name. When using the name, the number of spaces between `Listing` and the listing number does not matter as long as there is at least one space. When you choose the workload using the prompt, you can choose another workload once the previous has completed.

After the workload has completed, for several of the workloads, you will be given a list of suggestions for investigations you can do. This can, for example, be to query the locks held by the connections used in the example. The investigations are meant as inspiration, and you are encouraged to explore the workload using your own queries. Some of the investigations are also used in the discussion of the example. Listing 1-2 shows an example of executing a workload using the prompt.

Listing 1-2. Executing a workload using the prompt

```
mysql-py> concurrency_book.generate.run()
Available workloads:
=====================

 # Name                   Description
 --------------------------------------------------------------------------
 1 Listing  2-1           Example use of the metadata_locks table
 2 Listing  2-2           Example of using the table_handles table
 3 Listing  2-3           Using the data_locks table
 ...
14 Listing  5-2           Example of obtaining exclusive locks
15 Listing  6-1           A deadlock for user-level locks
 ...

Choose workload (# or name - empty to exit): 15
Password for connections: ********
2020-07-20 20:50:41.666488  0 [INFO] Starting the workload Listing 6-1

****************************************************
*                                                  *
*   Listing 6-1. A deadlock for user-level locks   *
*                                                  *
****************************************************

-- Connection   Processlist ID   Thread ID   Event ID
-- -------------------------------------------------------
--           1            105          249          6
--           2            106          250          6
```

```
-- Connection 1
Connection 1> SELECT GET_LOCK('my_lock_1', -1);
+--------------------------+
| GET_LOCK('my_lock_1', -1) |
+--------------------------+
|                        1 |
+--------------------------+
1 row in set (0.0003 sec)

-- Connection 2
Connection 2> SELECT GET_LOCK('my_lock_2', -1);
+--------------------------+
| GET_LOCK('my_lock_2', -1) |
+--------------------------+
|                        1 |
+--------------------------+
1 row in set (0.0003 sec)

Connection 2> SELECT GET_LOCK('my_lock_1', -1);


-- Connection 1
Connection 1> SELECT GET_LOCK('my_lock_2', -1);
ERROR: 3058: Deadlock found when trying to get user-level lock; try rolling
back transaction/releasing locks and restarting lock acquisition.
```

Available investigations:
==========================

```
 # Query
------------------------------------------------------
 1 SELECT *
     FROM performance_schema.metadata_locks
    WHERE object_type = 'USER LEVEL LOCK'
          AND owner_thread_id IN (249, 250)

 2 SELECT thread_id, event_id, sql_text,
          mysql_errno, returned_sqlstate, message_text,
          errors, warnings
```

```
    FROM performance_schema.events_statements_history
   WHERE thread_id = 249 AND event_id > 6
   ORDER BY event_id
...

Choose investigation (# - empty to exit): 2
-- Investigation #2
-- Connection 3
Connection 3> SELECT thread_id, event_id, sql_text,
                   mysql_errno, returned_sqlstate, message_text,
                   errors, warnings
              FROM performance_schema.events_statements_history
             WHERE thread_id = 249 AND event_id > 6
             ORDER BY event_id\G
*************************** 1. row ***************************
       thread_id: 249
        event_id: 7
        sql_text: SELECT GET_LOCK('my_lock_1', -1)
     mysql_errno: 0
returned_sqlstate: NULL
    message_text: NULL
          errors: 0
        warnings: 0
*************************** 2. row ***************************
       thread_id: 249
        event_id: 8
        sql_text: SELECT GET_LOCK('my_lock_2', -1)
     mysql_errno: 3058
returned_sqlstate: HY000
    message_text: Deadlock found when trying to get user-level lock; try
rolling back transaction/releasing locks and restarting lock acquisition.
          errors: 1
        warnings: 0
```

```
*************************** 3. row ***************************
        thread_id: 249
         event_id: 9
         sql_text: SHOW WARNINGS
       mysql_errno: 0
returned_sqlstate: NULL
     message_text: NULL
           errors: 0
         warnings: 0
3 rows in set (0.0009 sec)

Available investigations:
=========================

 # Query
----------------------------------------------------
...

Choose investigation (# - empty to exit):

2020-07-20 20:50:46.749971  0 [INFO] Completing the workload Listing 6-1
-- Connection 1
Connection 1> SELECT RELEASE_ALL_LOCKS();
+--------------------+
| RELEASE_ALL_LOCKS() |
+--------------------+
|                  1 |
+--------------------+
1 row in set (0.0004 sec)

-- Connection 2
Connection 2> SELECT RELEASE_ALL_LOCKS();
+--------------------+
| RELEASE_ALL_LOCKS() |
+--------------------+
|                  2 |
+--------------------+
1 row in set (0.0002 sec)
```

```
2020-07-20 20:50:46.749971  0 [INFO] Disconnecting for the workload
Listing 6-1
2020-07-20 20:50:46.749971  0 [INFO] Completed the workload Listing 6-1

Available workloads:
====================

  # Name                   Description
----------------------------------------------------------------------
  1 Listing  2-1           Example use of the metadata_locks table
  2 Listing  2-2           Example of using the table_handles table
  3 Listing  2-3           Using the data_locks table
...

Choose workload (# or name - empty to exit):

mysql-py>
```

There are a few things to notice from this example. After choosing the workload, you are asked for a password. This is the password for the MySQL account that you are using. The other connection options are taken from the session.uri property in MySQL Shell, but for security reasons, the password is not stored. If you execute multiple workloads in one invocation of run(), you will only be prompted for the password once.

At the start of the execution of the workload, there is an overview of the process list ids (as from SHOW PROCESSLIST), the (Performance Schema) thread ids, and the last event ids before the start of the workload for each connection used for the workload:

```
-- Connection    Processlist ID    Thread ID    Event ID
-- ----------------------------------------------------
--            1              105          249          6
--            2              106          250          6
```

You can use these ids to execute your own investigative queries, and you can use the overview to identify listings that have been implemented as a workload in concurrency_book.generate.run().

At the end of executing the workload, this example has three queries you can execute to investigate the issue the example demonstrates. You can execute one or more of these by specifying the number of the query (one query at a time). In the code listings in this book, the output of an investigation is preceded with a comment showing which of the investigations has been executed, for example

```
-- Investigation #2
```

The number of investigations per workload varies from none to more than ten. The listings in the book do not always include the result of all of the investigations as some are left as inspiration and further examination of the issue.

Once you are done with the investigation, submit an empty answer to exit from the workload. If you do not want to execute more workloads, submit an empty answer again to exit the run() method.

If you only want to execute a single workload, you can specify the name as an argument to run(). This can be particularly useful when executing a workload as a command given directly on the command line when invoking MySQL Shell, for example

```
shell> mysqlsh --user=myuser --py -e "concurrency_book.generate.
run('Listing 6-1')"
```

The remainder of this chapter describes the three schemas used for the examples in this book.

Test Data: The world Schema

The world sample database is one of the most commonly used databases for simple tests. It consists of three tables with a few hundred to a few thousand rows. This makes it a small data set which means it can easily be used even on small test instances.

Schema

The database consists of the city, country, and countrylanguage tables. The relationship between the tables is shown in Figure 1-3.

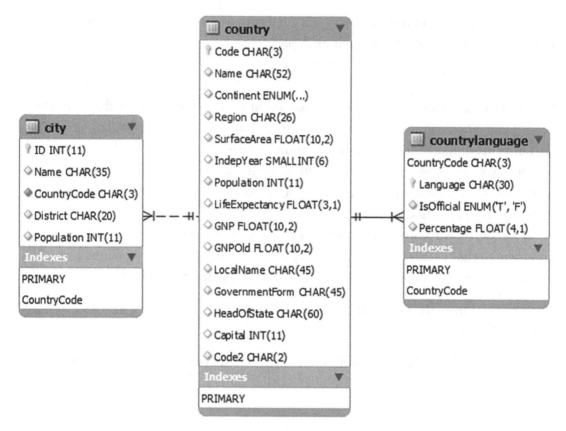

Figure 1-3. *The world database*

The country table includes information about 239 countries and serves as the parent table in foreign keys from the city and countrylanguage tables. There is a total of 4079 cities in the database and 984 combinations of country and language.

Installation

You can download a file with the table definitions and data from https://dev.mysql.com/doc/index-other.html. Oracle provides access to several example databases from that page in the section *Example Databases* as shown in Figure 1-4.

Example Databases

Title	Download DB	HTML Setup Guide	PDF Setup Guide
employee data (large dataset, includes data and test/verification suite)	GitHub	View	US Ltr | A4
world database	Gzip | Zip	View	US Ltr | A4
world_x database	TGZ | Zip	View	US Ltr | A4
sakila database	TGZ | Zip	View	US Ltr | A4
menagerie database	TGZ | Zip		

Figure 1-4. *The table with links to the example databases*

The downloaded file consists of a single file named world.sql.gz or world.sql.zip depending on whether you chose the Gzip or ZIP link. In either case, the downloaded archive contains a single file world.sql. The installation of the data is straightforward as all that is required is to execute the script.

You can source the world.sql from either MySQL Shell or the mysql command-line client. From MySQL Shell you use the \source command to load the data:

```
MySQL [localhost ssl] SQL> \source world.sql
```

If you use the legacy mysql command-line client, use the SOURCE command instead:

```
mysql> SOURCE world.sql
```

In either case, add the path to the world.sql file if it is not located in the directory where you started MySQL Shell or mysql.

If you prefer to use a GUI, then you can also load the world database using MySQL Workbench. While connected to the MySQL instance you want to load the world schema into, you click on *File* in the menu followed by *Run SQL Script* as shown in Figure 1-5.

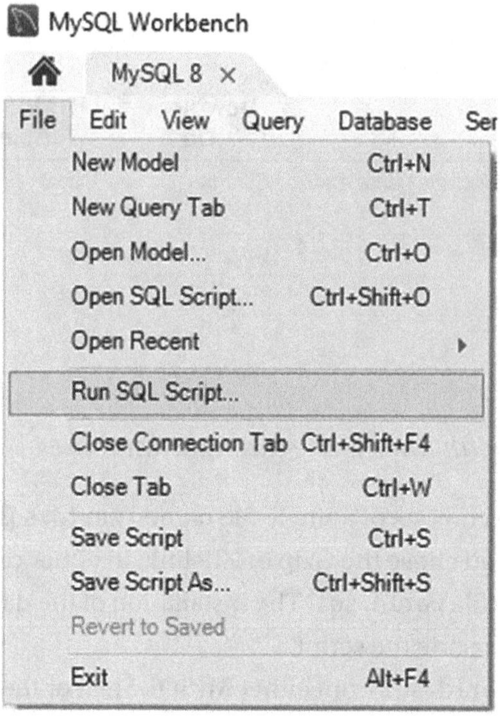

Figure 1-5. *Running an SQL script from MySQL Workbench*

This opens a file explorer where you can browse for the file. Navigate to the directory where you have saved the uncompressed `world.sql` file and choose it. The result is the dialog shown in Figure 1-6 where you can review the first part of the script and optionally set the default schema name and character set.

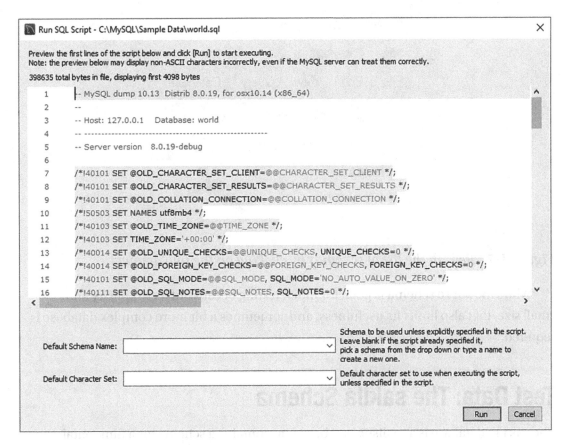

Figure 1-6. *The dialog in MySQL Workbench for reviewing the script*

In the case of the `world` schema, both the schema name and character set are included in the script, so there is no need to (and no effect of) setting those settings. Click on *Run* to execute the script. A dialog shows the progress information while MySQL executes the script. When the operation has completed, close the dialog. Optionally, you can refresh the list of schemas in the sidebar by clicking on the two arrows chasing each other as shown in Figure 1-7.

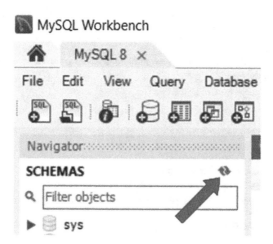

Figure 1-7. *Refresh the list of schemas by clicking on the two arrows*

While the world schema is great for much testing because of its simplicity and small size, that also limits its usefulness, and sometimes a bit more complex database is required.

Test Data: The sakila Schema

The sakila database is a realistic database that contains a schema for a film rental business with information about the films, inventory, stores, staff, and customers. It adds a full text index, a spatial index, views, and stored programs to provide a more complete example of using MySQL features. The database size is still very moderate, making it suitable for small instances.

Schema

The sakila database consists of 16 tables, seven views, three stored procedures, three stored functions, and six triggers. The tables can be split into three groups, customer data, business, and inventory. For brevity, not all columns are included in the diagrams, and most indexes are not shown. Figure 1-8 shows a complete overview of the tables, views, and stored routines.

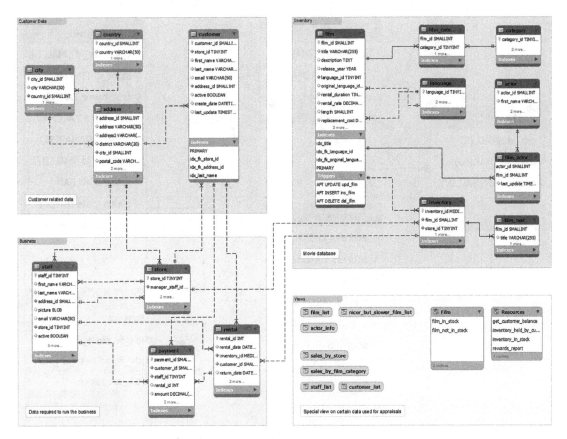

Figure 1-8. *Overview of the* sakila *database*

The tables with customer-related data (plus addresses for staff and stores) are in the area in the top-left corner. The area in the lower left includes data related to the business, and the area in the top right contains information about the films and inventory. The lower right is used for the views and stored routines.

Tip   You can view the entire diagram (though formatted differently) by opening the sakila.mwb file included with the installation in MySQL Workbench. This is also a good example of how you can use enhanced entity-relationship (EER) diagrams in MySQL Workbench to document your schema.

As there is a relatively large number of objects, they will be split into five groups (each of the table groups, views, and stored routines) when discussing the schema. The first group is the customer-related data with the tables shown in Figure 1-9.

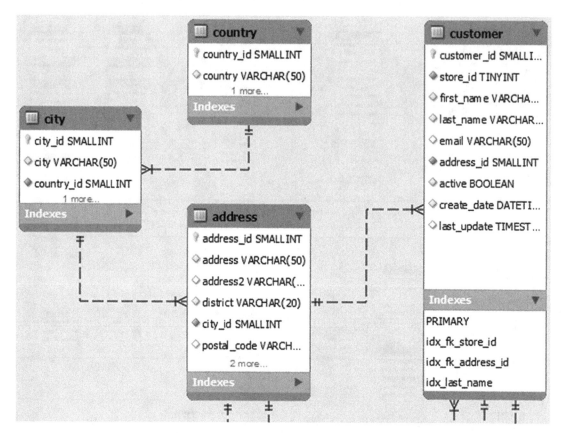

Figure 1-9. *The tables with customer data in the* sakila *database*

There are four tables with data related to the customers. The customer table is the main table, and the address information is stored in the address, city, and country tables.

There are foreign keys between the customer and business groups with a foreign key from the customer table to the store table in the business group. There are also four foreign keys from tables in the business group to the address and customer tables. The business group is shown in Figure 1-10.

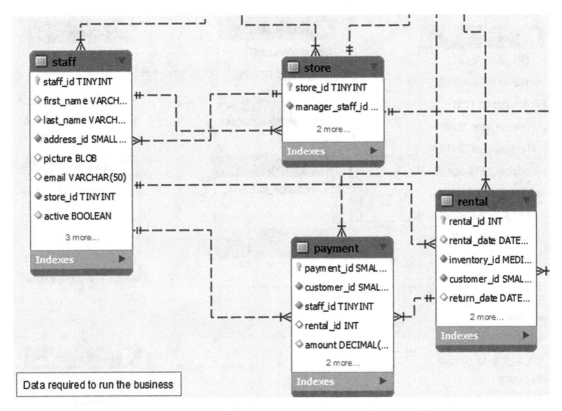

Figure 1-10. *The tables with business data in the* sakila *database*

The business tables contain information about the stores, staff, rentals, and payments. The store and staff tables have foreign keys in both directions with staff belonging to a store and a store having a manager that is part of the staff. Rentals and payments are handled by a staff member and thus indirectly linked to a store, and payments are for a rental.

The business group of tables is the one with the most relations to other groups. The staff and store tables have foreign keys to the address table, and the rental and payment tables reference the customer. Finally, the rental table has a foreign key to the inventory table which is in the inventory group. The diagram for the inventory group is shown in Figure 1-11.

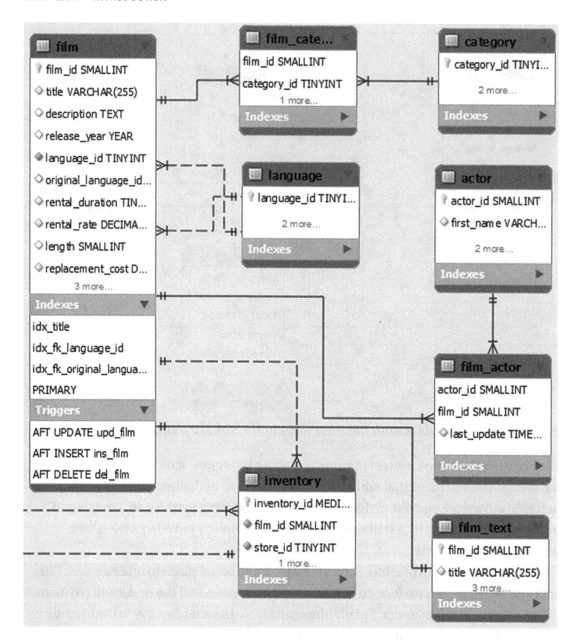

Figure 1-11. *The tables with inventory data in the* sakila *database*

The main table in the inventory group is the film table which contains the metadata about the films the stores offer. Additionally, there is the film_text table with the title and description with a full text index.

There is a many-to-many relationship between the film and the category and actor tables. Finally, there is a foreign key from the inventory table to the store table in the business group.

That covers all the tables in the sakila database, but there are also some views as shown in Figure 1-12.

Figure 1-12. *The views in the* sakila *database*

The views can be used like reports and can be divided into two categories. The film_list, nicer_but_slower_film_list, and actor_info views are related to the films stored in the database. The second category contains information related to the stores in the sales_by_store, sales_by_film_category, staff_list, and customer_list views.

To complete the database, there are also the stored functions and procedures shown in Figure 1-13.

Figure 1-13. *The stored routines in the* sakila *database*

The `film_in_stock()` and `film_not_in_stock()` procedures return a result set consisting of the inventory ids for a given film and store based on whether the film is in stock or not. The total number of inventory entries found is returned as an out parameter. The `rewards_report()` procedure generates a report based on minimum spends for the last month.

The `get_customer_balance()` function returns the balance for a given customer on a given date. The two remaining functions check the status of an inventory id with `inventory_held_by_customer()` returning customer id of the customer currently renting that item (and `NULL` if no customer is renting it), and if you want to check whether a given inventory id is in stock, you can use the `inventory_in_stock()` function.

Installation

You can download a file with the installation scripts to install the `sakila` schema from `https://dev.mysql.com/doc/index-other.html` like for the `world` database.

The downloaded file expands into a directory with three files of which two create the schema and data and the last file contains the ETL diagram in the format used by MySQL Workbench.

Note   The `sakila` database is also available with the download of the `employees` database; however, this section and the examples later in the book use the copy of the `sakila` database that is downloaded from MySQL's homepage.

The files are

- **sakila-data.sql:** The INSERT statements needed to populate the tables as well as the trigger definitions.

- **sakila-schema.sql:** The schema definition statements.

- **sakila.mwb:** The MySQL Workbench ETL diagram. This is similar to that shown in Figure 1-7 with details in Figures 1-8 to 1-12.

You install the `sakila` database by first sourcing the `sakila-schema.sql` file and then the `sakila-data.sql` file. For example, the following is using MySQL Shell:

```
MySQL [localhost+ ssl] SQL> \source sakila-schema.sql
MySQL [localhost+ ssl] SQL> \source sakila-data.sql
```

Add the path to the files if they are not located in the current directory.

Test Data: The employees Schema

The `employees` database (called employee data on the MySQL documentation download page; the name of the GitHub repository is `test_db`) was originally created by Fusheng Wang and Carlo Zaniolo and is the largest of the test data sets linked from MySQL's homepage. It comes with a choice of using nonpartitioned tables or partitioning two of the largest tables. The total size of the data files is around 180 MiB for the nonpartitioned version and 440 MiB for the partitioned version.

Schema

The `employees` database consists of six tables and two views. You can optionally install two more views, five stored functions, and two stored procedures. The tables are shown in Figure 1-14.

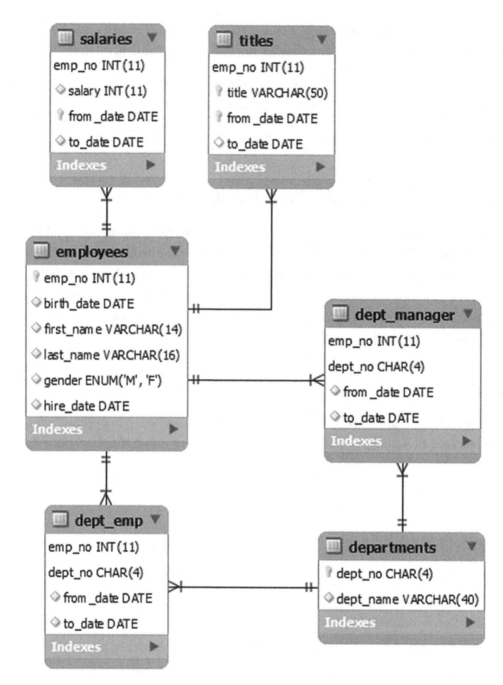

Figure 1-14. *The tables, views, and routines in the employees database*

By today's standards, it is still a relatively small amount of data in the database, but it is big enough that you can start to see lower-level contention, and for this reason, it is the schema used to cause semaphore waits in Chapter 18.

Installation

You can download a ZIP file with the files required for the installation, or you can clone the GitHub repository at `https://github.com/datacharmer/test_db`. At the time of writing, there is only a single branch named master. If you have downloaded the ZIP file, it will unzip into a directory named `test_db-master`.

There are several files. The two relevant for installing the `employees` database in MySQL 8 are `employees.sql` and `employees_partitioned.sql`. The difference is whether the `salaries` and `titles` tables are partitioned. This book uses the unpartitioned schema. (There is also `employees_partitioned_5.1.sql` which is meant for MySQL 5.1 where the partitioning scheme used in `employees_partitioned.sql` is not supported.)

The data is loaded by sourcing the `.dump` files using the `SOURCE` command which is only supported in MySQL Shell in 8.0.19 (in practice 8.0.20 due to a bug) and later. Go to the directory with the source files, and choose the `employees.sql` or `employees_partitioned.sql` file, depending on whether you want to use partitioning or not, for example

```
mysql> \source employees.sql
```

The import takes a little time and completes by showing how long it took:

```
+---------------------+
| data_load_time_diff |
+---------------------+
| 00:02:50            |
+---------------------+
1 row in set (0.0085 sec)
```

Optionally, you can load some extra views and stored routines by sourcing the `objects.sql` file:

```
mysql> \source objects.sql
```

When you load the `employees` schema using the `concurrency_book.generate.`
`load()` method, the `objects.sql` file is always included.

You are now ready to dive into the world of MySQL concurrency.

Summary

This chapter started the journey to understand MySQL concurrency of which locks and
transactions are important topics. First it was discussed why locks are needed and at
what levels they exist. Then it was covered that transactions must be included in the
discussion as some locks are held for the duration of the transaction and the transaction
isolation level influences the duration of the locks as well as the number of locks.

The rest of the chapter discussed how the examples are used in this book and
introduced the three sets of test data that is required to reproduce the test cases. To make
it easier to load the data and execute the test cases, the `concurrency_book.generate`
module for MySQL Shell was also introduced.

In the next chapter, it will be discussed how you can monitor locks.

CHAPTER 2

Monitoring Locks and Mutexes

Monitoring is essential to understanding where bottlenecks occur in your system. You need to use monitoring both to determine sources of contention and to verify that the changes you make reduce the contention.

This and the two following two chapters provide an overview of lock and mutex monitoring, InnoDB transaction monitoring, and general transaction monitoring in the Performance Schema. The remainder of the books shows examples of how you can use these monitoring resources to identify and investigate contention. Particularly Chapters 13–18 use monitoring extensively during the discussion of the case studies.

In this chapter, you will learn how you can monitor locks and mutexes. The primary resource is the Performance Schema which is covered first. Next, the ready-made reports in the sys schema are discussed. The second half of the chapter covers the status metrics, InnoDB lock monitoring, and InnoDB mutex monitoring.

Note Do not worry if you do not know what the various locks and mutexes are yet. You will learn this later with examples of using the monitoring sources discussed in this chapter.

The Performance Schema

The Performance Schema contains the source of most of the lock information available except for deadlocks. Not only can you use the lock information in the Performance Schema directly; it is also used for two lock-related views in the sys schema. Additionally, you can use the Performance Schema to investigate the low-level synchronization objects such as mutexes. First, it will be shown how metadata and table locks can be investigated.

31

© Jesper Wisborg Krogh 2021
J. W. Krogh, *MySQL Concurrency*, https://doi.org/10.1007/978-1-4842-6652-6_2

Metadata and Table Locks

Metadata locks are the most generic of the higher-level locks, and there is support for a wide range of locks ranging from the global read lock to low-level locks like for the access control list (ACL). The locks are monitored using the `metadata_locks` table which contains information about user-level locks, metadata locks, and similar. To record information, the `wait/lock/metadata/sql/mdl` Performance Schema instrument must be enabled (it is enabled by default in MySQL 8). There is an example later showing how you can enable instruments.

The `metadata_locks` table contains 11 columns which are summarized in Table 2-1.

Table 2-1. *The performance_schema.metadata_locks table*

Column Name	Description
OBJECT_TYPE	The kind of lock that is held such as GLOBAL for the global read lock and TABLE for tables and views. Appendix A includes a complete list of possible values.
OBJECT_SCHEMA	The schema the object that is locked belongs to.
OBJECT_NAME	The name of the locked object.
COLUMN_NAME	For column level locks, the column name of the locked column.
OBJECT_INSTANCE_BEGIN	The memory address of the object.
LOCK_TYPE	The lock access level such as shared, exclusive, or intention. Appendix A includes a complete list of possible values.
LOCK_DURATION	How long the lock is held for. Supported values are STATEMENT, TRANSACTION, and EXPLICIT.
LOCK_STATUS	The status of the lock. In addition to a granted and pending status, it can also show that the lock request timed out, was a victim, etc.
SOURCE	The place in the source code where the lock was requested.
OWNER_THREAD_ID	The Performance Schema thread id of the thread that requested the lock.
OWNER_EVENT_ID	The event id of the event requesting the lock.

The primary key of the table is the OBJECT_INSTANCE_BEGIN column.

Listing 2-1 shows an example of obtaining a table metadata lock and querying it in the metadata_locks table. Some of the details will be different for you.

Listing 2-1. Example use of the metadata_locks table

```
-- Connection    Processlist ID    Thread ID    Event ID
-- ----------------------------------------------------
--           1                19           59           6

-- Connection 1
mysql> START TRANSACTION;
Query OK, 0 rows affected (0.0003 sec)

mysql> SELECT * FROM world.city WHERE ID = 130;
+-----+--------+-------------+-----------------+------------+
| ID  | Name   | CountryCode | District        | Population |
+-----+--------+-------------+-----------------+------------+
| 130 | Sydney | AUS         | New South Wales |    3276207 |
+-----+--------+-------------+-----------------+------------+
1 row in set (0.0005 sec)

mysql> SELECT *
         FROM performance_schema.metadata_locks
        WHERE OBJECT_TYPE = 'TABLE'
          AND OBJECT_SCHEMA = 'world'
          AND OBJECT_NAME = 'city'
          AND OWNER_THREAD_ID = PS_CURRENT_THREAD_ID()\G
*************************** 1. row ***************************
           OBJECT_TYPE: TABLE
         OBJECT_SCHEMA: world
           OBJECT_NAME: city
           COLUMN_NAME: NULL
 OBJECT_INSTANCE_BEGIN: 2639965404080
             LOCK_TYPE: SHARED_READ
         LOCK_DURATION: TRANSACTION
           LOCK_STATUS: GRANTED
                SOURCE: sql_parse.cc:6162
```

```
      OWNER_THREAD_ID: 59
       OWNER_EVENT_ID: 10
1 row in set (0.0006 sec)

mysql> ROLLBACK;
Query OK, 0 rows affected (0.0006 sec)
```

Here you can see that it is a table level lock on the world.city table. It is a shared read lock, so other connections can obtain the same lock concurrently.

If you want to find out why a connection is waiting for its lock request to be granted, you need to query the metadata_locks table for a row where the OBJECT_TYPE, OBJECT_ SCHEMA, and OBJECT_NAME are the same as for the pending lock and the LOCK_STATUS is GRANTED. That is, to find all cases of pending locks and what is blocking them, you need a query that self-joins the table:

```sql
SELECT OBJECT_TYPE, OBJECT_SCHEMA, OBJECT_NAME,
       w.OWNER_THREAD_ID AS WAITING_THREAD_ID,
       b.OWNER_THREAD_ID AS BLOCKING_THREAD_ID
  FROM performance_schema.metadata_locks w
       INNER JOIN performance_schema.metadata_locks b
           USING (OBJECT_TYPE, OBJECT_SCHEMA, OBJECT_NAME)
 WHERE w.LOCK_STATUS = 'PENDING'
       AND b.LOCK_STATUS = 'GRANTED';
```

You can optionally join on other Performance Schema tables such as events_ statements_current to get more information about the connections involved in the lock wait. Alternatively, as it will be discussed later, for table metadata locks, you can use the sys.schema_table_lock_waits view.

A less frequently used table is table_handles which holds information about the open table handles including which table locks are currently locked. The wait/ lock/table/sql/handler Performance Schema instrument must be enabled for data to be recorded (this is the default). The information available is similar to that of the metadata_locks table, and Listing 2-2 shows an example of an explicit read lock on the world.city table. Some of the details will be different for you.

Listing 2-2. Example of using the `table_handles` table

```
-- Connection   Processlist ID   Thread ID   Event ID
-- --------------------------------------------------
--          1               21          61          6

-- Connection 1
mysql> LOCK TABLE world.city READ;
Query OK, 0 rows affected (0.0004 sec)

mysql> SELECT *
         FROM performance_schema.table_handles
        WHERE OBJECT_SCHEMA = 'world'
          AND OBJECT_NAME = 'city'
          AND OWNER_THREAD_ID = PS_CURRENT_THREAD_ID()\G
*************************** 1. row ***************************
          OBJECT_TYPE: TABLE
        OBJECT_SCHEMA: world
          OBJECT_NAME: city
OBJECT_INSTANCE_BEGIN: 2639971828776
      OWNER_THREAD_ID: 61
       OWNER_EVENT_ID: 8
        INTERNAL_LOCK: NULL
        EXTERNAL_LOCK: READ EXTERNAL
1 row in set (0.0013 sec)

mysql> UNLOCK TABLES;
Query OK, 0 rows affected (0.0004 sec)
```

The INTERNAL_LOCK column contains lock information at the SQL level such as explicit table locks on non-InnoDB tables, while the EXTERNAL_LOCK contains lock information at the storage engine level including explicit table locks for all tables.

Unlike the `metadata_locks` table, you cannot use the `table_handles` table to investigate lock contentions (but the `metadata_locks` table also includes explicit table locks like in this example, so you can use that).

The `metadata_locks` and `table_handles` tables concern the highest-level locks. The next step on the lock granularity latter is data locks which have their own tables.

Data Locks

Data locks are at the medium level between the metadata locks and the synchronization objects. What makes data locks special is that you have a large variety of lock types such as record locks, gap locks, insert intention locks, etc. that interact in complex ways as described in Chapter 7. This makes the monitoring tables for data locks particularly useful.

The data lock information is split into two tables:

- **data_locks:** This table contains details of table and records locks at the InnoDB level. It shows all locks currently held or are pending.

- **data_lock_waits:** Like the data_locks table, it shows locks related to InnoDB, but only those waiting to be granted with information on which thread is blocking the request.

You will often use these in combination to find information about lock waits.

MySQL 8 has seen a change in the way that the lock monitoring tables work. In MySQL 5.7 and earlier, the information was available in two InnoDB-specific views in the Information Schema, INNODB_LOCKS and INNODB_LOCK_WAITS. The major differences are that the Performance Schema tables are created to be storage engine agnostic and information about all locks are always made available, whereas in MySQL 5.7 and earlier, only information about locks involved in lock waits were exposed. That all locks are always available for investigation makes the MySQL 8 tables much more useful to learn about locks.

The data_locks table is the main table with detailed information about each lock. The table has 15 columns as described in Table 2-2.

Table 2-2. *The performance_schema.data_locks table*

Column Name	Description
ENGINE	The storage engine for the data. For MySQL Server, this will always be InnoDB.
ENGINE_LOCK_ID	The internal id of the lock as used by the storage engine. You should not rely on the id having a particular format.
ENGINE_TRANSACTION_ID	The transaction id specific to the storage engine. For InnoDB, you can use this id to join on the trx_id column in the information_schema.INNODB_TRX view. You should not rely on the id having a particular format, and the id may change in the duration of a transaction.

(continued)

Table 2-2. (*continued*)

Column Name	Description
THREAD_ID	The Performance Schema thread id of the thread that made the lock request.
EVENT_ID	The Performance Schema event id of the event that made the lock request. You can use this id to join with several of the events_% tables to find more information on what triggered the lock request.
OBJECT_SCHEMA	The schema the object that is subject of the lock request is in.
OBJECT_NAME	The name of the object that is subject of the lock request.
PARTITION_NAME	For locks involving partitions, the name of the partition.
SUBPARTITION_NAME	For locks involving subpartitions, the name of the subpartition.
INDEX_NAME	For locks involving indexes, the name of the index. Since everything is an index for InnoDB, the index name is always set for record level locks on InnoDB tables. If the row is locked, the value will be PRIMARY or GEN_CLUST_INDEX depending on whether you have an explicit primary key or the table used a hidden clustered index.
OBJECT_INSTANCE_BEGIN	The memory address of the lock request.
LOCK_TYPE	The level of the lock request. For InnoDB, the possible values are TABLE and RECORD.
LOCK_MODE	The locking mode used. This includes whether it is a shared or exclusive lock and the finer details of the lock, for exam ple, REC_NOT_GAP for a record lock but no gap lock.
LOCK_STATUS	Whether the lock is pending (WAITING) or has been granted (GRANTED).
LOCK_DATA	Information about the data that is locked. This can, for example, be the index value of the locked index record.

The primary key of the table is (ENGINE_LOCK_ID, ENGINE).

An example of acquiring two locks and querying the data_locks table is shown in Listing 2-3. Information such as the ids and the memory address will differ for you.

Listing 2-3. Using the data_locks table

```
-- Connection    Processlist ID    Thread ID    Event ID
-- ------------------------------------------------------
--          1               23           64           6
```

```
-- Connection 1
mysql> START TRANSACTION;
Query OK, 0 rows affected (0.0003 sec)

mysql> SELECT *
          FROM world.city
         WHERE ID = 130
           FOR SHARE;
+-----+--------+-------------+----------------+------------+
| ID  | Name   | CountryCode | District       | Population |
+-----+--------+-------------+----------------+------------+
| 130 | Sydney | AUS         | New South Wales |    3276207 |
+-----+--------+-------------+----------------+------------+
1 row in set (0.0068 sec)

mysql> SELECT *
          FROM performance_schema.data_locks
         WHERE THREAD_ID = PS_CURRENT_THREAD_ID()\G
*************************** 1. row ***************************
              ENGINE: INNODB
       ENGINE_LOCK_ID: 2639727636640:3165:2639690712184
ENGINE_TRANSACTION_ID: 284114704347296
           THREAD_ID: 64
            EVENT_ID: 10
       OBJECT_SCHEMA: world
         OBJECT_NAME: city
      PARTITION_NAME: NULL
   SUBPARTITION_NAME: NULL
          INDEX_NAME: NULL
OBJECT_INSTANCE_BEGIN: 2639690712184
           LOCK_TYPE: TABLE
```

```
          LOCK_MODE: IS
        LOCK_STATUS: GRANTED
          LOCK_DATA: NULL
*************************** 2. row ***************************
               ENGINE: INNODB
       ENGINE_LOCK_ID: 2639727636640:1926:6:131:2639690709400
ENGINE_TRANSACTION_ID: 284114704347296
            THREAD_ID: 64
             EVENT_ID: 10
        OBJECT_SCHEMA: world
          OBJECT_NAME: city
       PARTITION_NAME: NULL
    SUBPARTITION_NAME: NULL
           INDEX_NAME: PRIMARY
OBJECT_INSTANCE_BEGIN: 2639690709400
            LOCK_TYPE: RECORD
            LOCK_MODE: S,REC_NOT_GAP
          LOCK_STATUS: GRANTED
            LOCK_DATA: 130
2 rows in set (0.0018 sec)

mysql> ROLLBACK;
Query OK, 0 rows affected (0.0007 sec)
```

In this example, the query obtains an insert intention (IS) lock on the world.city table and a shared (S) record, but not gap, lock (REC NOT_GAP) on the primary key with the value 130.

The data_lock_waits table is simpler as it just includes the basic information about current cases of lock contention as shown in Table 2-3.

Table 2-3. *The* `performance_schema.data_lock_waits` *table*

Column Name	Description
ENGINE	The storage engine where the lock contention occurs.
REQUESTING_ENGINE_LOCK_ID	The ENGINE_LOCK_ID for the pending lock.
REQUESTING_ENGINE_TRANSACTION_ID	The ENGINE_TRANSACTION_ID for the pending lock.
REQUESTING_THREAD_ID	The THREAD_ID for the pending lock.
REQUESTING_EVENT_ID	The EVENT_ID for the pending lock.
REQUESTING_OBJECT_INSTANCE_BEGIN	The OBJECT_INSTANCE_BEGIN for the pending lock.
BLOCKING_ENGINE_LOCK_ID	The ENGINE_LOCK_ID for the blocking lock.
BLOCKING_ENGINE_TRANSACTION_ID	The ENGINE_TRANSACTION_ID for the blocking lock.
BLOCKING_THREAD_ID	The THREAD_ID for the blocking lock.
BLOCKING_EVENT_ID	The EVENT_ID for the blocking lock.
BLOCKING_OBJECT_INSTANCE_BEGIN	The OBJECT_INSTANCE_BEGIN for the blocking lock.

The table does not have a primary key. The primary purpose of the table is to provide a simple way to determine the pending and blocking lock requests involved in lock contention. You can then join on the `data_locks` table using the `REQUESTING_ENGINE_TRANSACTION_ID` and `BLOCKING_ENGINE_TRANSACTION_ID` columns as well as to other tables to obtain more information. A good example of this is the `sys.innodb_lock_waits` view.

This far, the Performance Schema tables that have been discussed have been for locks that are directly a result of the statements that are executed. There are also lower-level synchronization waits that are important to monitor in high-concurrency situations.

Synchronization Waits

The synchronization waits are the most difficult to monitor for several reasons. They occur very frequently, usually at a very short duration, and monitoring them has a high overhead. Instrumentation of the synchronization waits is also not enabled by default.

The synchronization waits are split into five categories:

- **cond:** Conditions used in thread to thread signals.

- **mutex:** A mutual exclusion point that protects code parts or other resources.

- **prlock:** A priority read/write lock.

- **rwlock:** A read/write lock used to limit concurrent access to specific variables, for example, for changing the gtid_mode system variable.

- **sxlock:** A shared-exclusive read/write lock. This is currently only used by InnoDB, for example, to improve the scalability of the B-tree searches.

The instrument names for the synchronization waits start with wait/synch/ followed by the name of the category, the area the wait belongs to (such as sql or innodb), and the name of the wait. For example, the mutex guarding the InnoDB double write buffer has the name wait/synch/mutex/innodb/dblwr_mutex.

You enable the instrumentation of the synchronization waits by setting the ENABLED and optionally the TIMED columns in the performance_schema.setup_instruments table for the instruments you want to monitor. Additionally, you will need to enable events_ waits_current and optionally events_waits_history and/or events_waits_history_ long in performance_schema.setup_consumers. For example, to monitor the mutex on the InnoDB double write buffer

```
mysql> UPDATE performance_schema.setup_instruments
          SET ENABLED = 'YES',
              TIMED = 'YES'
        WHERE NAME = 'wait/synch/mutex/innodb/dblwr_mutex';
Query OK, 1 row affected (0.0011 sec)

Rows matched: 1  Changed: 1  Warnings: 0

mysql> UPDATE performance_schema.setup_consumers
          SET ENABLED = 'YES'
        WHERE NAME = 'events_waits_current';
Query OK, 1 row affected (0.0005 sec)

Rows matched: 1  Changed: 1  Warnings: 0
```

In general, it is better to enable monitoring of synchronization instruments in the configuration file to ensure they are properly set up from the time MySQL starts up:

```
[mysqld]
performance_schema_instrument = wait/synch/mutex/innodb/dblwr_mutex=ON
performance_schema_consumer_events_waits_current = ON
```

Then restart MySQL.

Caution   Be very careful in enabling instrumentation of the synchronization waits and the corresponding consumers on production systems. Doing so can cause a high enough overhead that you will effectively have an outage. The more that are enabled, the higher overhead and the more likely the monitoring interferes with the measurements, so the conclusions are wrong.

You can now monitor the waits using one of the events_waits_% tables:

- **events_waits_current:** The current ongoing or last completed wait events for each existing thread. This requires the events_waits_current consumer to be enabled.

- **events_waits_history:** The last ten (the performance_schema_events_waits_history_size option) wait events for each existing thread. This requires the events_waits_history consumer to be enabled in addition to the events_waits_current consumer.

- **events_waits_history_long:** The last 10,000 (the performance_schema_events_waits_history_long_size option) events globally, including for threads that no longer exist. This requires the events_waits_history_long consumer to be enabled in addition to the events_waits_current consumer.

- **events_waits_summary_by_account_by_event_name:** The wait events grouped by the username and hostname of the accounts (also called actors in the Performance Schema).

- **events_waits_summary_by_host_by_event_name:** The wait events grouped by the hostname of the account triggering the event and event name.

- **events_waits_summary_by_instance:** The wait events grouped by the event name as well as the memory address (OBJECT_INSTANCE_BEGIN) of the object. This is useful for events with more than one instance to monitor whether the waits are evenly distributed among the instances. An example is the table cache mutex (wait/synch/mutex/sql/LOCK_table_cache) which has one object per table cache instance (table_open_cache_instances).

- **events_waits_summary_by_thread_by_event_name:** The wait events for currently existing threads grouped by the thread id and event name.

- **events_waits_summary_by_user_by_event_name:** The wait events grouped by the username of the account triggering the event and event name.

- **events_waits_summary_global_by_event_name:** The wait events grouped by the event names. This table is useful to get an overview of how much time is spent waiting for a given type of event.

Given how short lived a synchronization wait normally is and how frequently they are encountered, the summary tables are usually the most useful for investigating waits using the Performance Schema. That said, since the relevant wait instruments are not enabled by default and they have relatively high overhead when monitoring them, usually the semaphore section of the InnoDB monitor or the SHOW ENGINE INNODB MUTEX statement as described later in this chapter is used for InnoDB mutexes and semaphores. The exception is when you want to investigate a specific contention issue.

Another useful way to use the Performance Schema for lock analysis is to query for the errors that statements are encountering.

Statement and Error Tables

The Performance Schema includes several tables that can be used to investigate the errors that are encountered. Since a failure to obtain a lock either due to a timeout or a deadlock triggers an error, you can query for lock-related errors to determine which statements, accounts, and so on that are most affected by lock contention.

At the individual statement level, you can use the events_statements_current, events_statements_history, and events_statements_history_long to see whether any error or a specific error has occurred. The first two of the tables are enabled by default, whereas the events_statements_history_long table requires that you enable the events_statements_history_long consumer. Listing 2-4 shows an example of a lock wait timeout and how it shows up in the events_statements_history table.

Listing 2-4. Example of a lock error in the statement tables

```
-- Connection    Processlist ID    Thread ID    Event ID
-- ----------------------------------------------------------
--            1                63          179           6
--            2                64          180           6

-- Connection 1
Connection 1> START TRANSACTION;
Query OK, 0 rows affected (0.0003 sec)

Connection 1> UPDATE world.city
                SET Population = Population + 1
              WHERE ID = 130;
Query OK, 1 row affected (0.0011 sec)

Rows matched: 1  Changed: 1  Warnings: 0

-- Connection 2
Connection 2> SET SESSION innodb_lock_wait_timeout = 1;
Query OK, 0 rows affected (0.0003 sec)

Connection 2> START TRANSACTION;
Query OK, 0 rows affected (0.0002 sec)

Connection 2> UPDATE world.city
                SET Population = Population + 1
              WHERE ID = 130;
ERROR: 1205: Lock wait timeout exceeded; try restarting transaction
```

```
Connection 2> SELECT thread_id, event_id,
                     FORMAT_PICO_TIME(lock_time) AS lock_time,
                     sys.format_statement(SQL_TEXT) AS statement,
                     digest, mysql_errno,
                     returned_sqlstate, message_text, errors
                FROM performance_schema.events_statements_history
               WHERE thread_id = PS_CURRENT_THREAD_ID()
                 AND mysql_errno > 0\G
*************************** 1. row ***************************
        thread_id: 180
         event_id: 10
        lock_time: 271.00 us
        statement: UPDATE world.city    SET Popul ... Population + 1  WHERE
                   ID = 130
           digest: 3e9795ad6fc0f4e3a4b4e99f33fbab2dc7b40d0761a8adbc60abfab
           02326108d
      mysql_errno: 1205
returned_sqlstate: HY000
     message_text: Lock wait timeout exceeded; try restarting transaction
           errors: 1
1 row in set (0.0016 sec)

-- Connection 1
Connection 1> ROLLBACK;
Query OK, 0 rows affected (0.0472 sec)

-- Connection 2
Connection 2> ROLLBACK;
Query OK, 0 rows affected (0.0003 sec)
```

There are a few things worth noting from the example. The first thing is that the lock time is only 271 microseconds despite that it took a full second before the lock wait timeout occurred. That is, waiting for a record lock inside InnoDB is not adding to the lock time reported by the Performance Schema, so you cannot use that to investigate record level lock contention.

The second thing is that the `mysql_errno`, `returned_sqlstate`, and `message_text` include the same error information as it returned to the client which makes it useful for querying as it is also done in this case. Third, the `errors` column contains a count of the number of errors encountered. While the count doesn't say anything about the nature of the error, it is useful as unlike the columns with the specifics of the error, the error counter is also present in the statement summary tables, so you can use it to find which statements encounter an error of any kind.

Tip   It can be useful to log encountered errors in the application. You can then, for example, analyze the application logs with a service like Splunk to generate reports showing which errors are encountered and when they are a problem.

A group of summary tables of special interest in this context consists of the tables that summarize errors. There are five such tables grouped by the account, host, thread, user, and global, respectively:

```
mysql> SHOW TABLES FROM performance_schema LIKE '%error%';
+--------------------------------------------+
| Tables_in_performance_schema (%error%)     |
+--------------------------------------------+
| events_errors_summary_by_account_by_error  |
| events_errors_summary_by_host_by_error     |
| events_errors_summary_by_thread_by_error   |
| events_errors_summary_by_user_by_error     |
| events_errors_summary_global_by_error      |
+--------------------------------------------+
5 rows in set (0.0012 sec)
```

For example, to retrieve the statistics for lock wait timeouts and deadlocks

```
mysql> SELECT *
         FROM performance_schema.events_errors_summary_global_by_error
         WHERE error_name IN ('ER_LOCK_WAIT_TIMEOUT', 'ER_LOCK_DEADLOCK')\G
```

```
*************************** 1. row ***************************
     ERROR_NUMBER: 1205
       ERROR_NAME: ER_LOCK_WAIT_TIMEOUT
        SQL_STATE: HY000
 SUM_ERROR_RAISED: 4
SUM_ERROR_HANDLED: 0
       FIRST_SEEN: 2020-06-28 11:33:10
        LAST_SEEN: 2020-06-28 11:49:30
*************************** 2. row ***************************
     ERROR_NUMBER: 1213
       ERROR_NAME: ER_LOCK_DEADLOCK
        SQL_STATE: 40001
 SUM_ERROR_RAISED: 3
SUM_ERROR_HANDLED: 0
       FIRST_SEEN: 2020-06-27 12:06:38
        LAST_SEEN: 2020-06-27 12:54:27
2 rows in set (0.0048 sec)
```

While this does not help you identify which statements encounter the errors, it can help you monitor the frequency you encounter the errors and, in that way, determine whether lock errors become more frequent.

Tip The events_errors_summary_global_by_error is populated with all known errors from the time MySQL is started even if the error has not yet been encountered. So, you can safely query for specific errors at all time including using the table to look up the error number from the name.

The data in the Performance Schema tables is the raw data, either as individual events or aggregated. Often when you investigate lock issues or monitor for lock issues, it is more interesting to determine if there are any lock waits or to obtain a report of the wait events where most time is spent. For that information, you need to use the sys schema.

The sys Schema

The sys schema can be considered a collection of views that serve as reports on the Performance Schema and Information Schema as well as various utility functions and procedures. For this discussion the focus is on the two views that take the information in the Performance Schema tables and return the lock pairs where one lock cannot be granted because of the other lock. Thus, they show where there are problems with lock waits. The two views are innodb_lock_waits and schema_table_lock_waits.

The innodb_lock_waits view uses the data_locks and data_lock_waits view in the Performance Schema to return all cases of lock waits for InnoDB record locks. It shows information such as what lock the connection is trying to obtain and which connections and queries are involved. The view also exists as x$innodb_lock_waits, if you need the information without formatting.

The schema_table_lock_waits view works in a similar way but uses the metadata_locks table to return lock waits related to schema objects. The information is also available unformatted in the x$schema_table_lock_waits view.

Tip   Several views also exist where x$ is prepended to the view name. This view contains the same information as the view without x$ in the name except all the data is unformatted. This makes the data more suitable for scripts and programs that process the information.

Chapters 13–17 include examples of using both views to investigate lock issues.

For a high-level view of the contention, you can also use the status counters and InnoDB metrics.

Status Counters and InnoDB Metrics

There are several status counters and InnoDB metrics that provide information about locking. These are mostly used at the global (instance) level and can be useful to detect an overall increase in lock issues.

Querying the Data

There are two sources for status counters and InnoDB metrics. The global status counters can be found in the performance_schema.global_status table or with the SHOW GLOBAL STATUS statement. The InnoDB metrics are found in the information_schema.INNODB_METRICS view.

The InnoDB metrics are similar to the global status variables and can provide some valuable information on status of InnoDB. The NAME column can be used to query the metric by name. At the time of writing, there are 313 visible metrics of which 74 are enabled by default. There is also one hidden metric which is the latch metric that controls whether mutex wait statistics are collected. The metrics are grouped into subsystems (the SUBSYSTEM column), and for each metric there is a description of what the metric measures in the COMMENT column, and the type of metric (counter, value, etc.) can be seen in the TYPE column.

A great way to monitor all of these metrics together is to use the sys.metrics view. Listing 2-5 shows an example of retrieving the metrics.

Listing 2-5. Lock metrics

```
-- Connection   Processlist ID   Thread ID   Event ID
-- ----------------------------------------------------
--          1               27          69          6

-- Connection 1
mysql> SELECT Variable_name,
              Variable_value AS Value,
              Enabled
         FROM sys.metrics
        WHERE Variable_name LIKE 'innodb_row_lock%'
           OR Variable_name LIKE 'Table_locks%'
           OR Variable_name LIKE 'innodb_rwlock_%'
           OR Type = 'InnoDB Metrics - lock';
```

Variable_name	Value	Enabled
innodb_row_lock_current_waits	**0**	**YES**
innodb_row_lock_time	**2163**	**YES**
innodb_row_lock_time_avg	**721**	**YES**
innodb_row_lock_time_max	**2000**	**YES**
innodb_row_lock_waits	**3**	**YES**
table_locks_immediate	330	YES
table_locks_waited	0	YES
lock_deadlock_false_positives	0	YES
lock_deadlock_rounds	37214	YES
lock_deadlocks	**1**	**YES**
lock_rec_grant_attempts	1	YES
lock_rec_lock_created	0	NO
lock_rec_lock_removed	0	NO
lock_rec_lock_requests	0	NO
lock_rec_lock_waits	0	NO
lock_rec_locks	0	NO
lock_rec_release_attempts	24317	YES
lock_row_lock_current_waits	0	YES
lock_schedule_refreshes	37214	YES
lock_table_lock_created	0	NO
lock_table_lock_removed	0	NO
lock_table_lock_waits	0	NO
lock_table_locks	0	NO
lock_threads_waiting	0	YES
lock_timeouts	**1**	**YES**
innodb_rwlock_s_os_waits	12248	YES
innodb_rwlock_s_spin_rounds	19299	YES
innodb_rwlock_s_spin_waits	6811	YES
innodb_rwlock_sx_os_waits	171	YES
innodb_rwlock_sx_spin_rounds	5239	YES
innodb_rwlock_sx_spin_waits	182	YES

```
| innodb_rwlock_x_os_waits      | 26283  | YES     |
| innodb_rwlock_x_spin_rounds   | 774745 | YES     |
| innodb_rwlock_x_spin_waits    | 12666  | YES     |
+------------------------------+--------+---------+
34 rows in set (0.0174 sec)
```

The innodb_row_lock_% , lock_deadlocks, and lock_timeouts metrics are the
most interesting. The row lock metrics show how many locks are currently waiting and
statistics for the amount of time in milliseconds spent on waiting to acquire InnoDB
record locks. The lock_deadlocks and lock_timeouts metrics show the number of
deadlocks and lock wait timeouts that have been encountered, respectively.

If you encounter InnoDB mutex or semaphore contention, then the innodb_
rwlock_% metrics are useful to monitor the rate the waits happen and how many rounds
that are spent waiting.

As you can see, not all of the metrics are enabled by default (these are all InnoDB
metrics), so let's investigate how it is possible to enable and disable the metrics that
come from the INNODB_METRICS view.

Configuring the InnoDB Metrics

The InnoDB metrics can be configured, so you can choose which are enabled, and you
can reset the statistics. You enable, disable, and reset the metrics using global system
variables:

- **innodb_monitor_disable:** Disable one or more metrics.

- **innodb_monitor_enable:** Enable one or more metrics.

- **innodb_monitor_reset:** Reset the counter for one or more metrics.

- **innodb_monitor_reset_all:** Reset all statistics including the counter,
  minimum, and maximum values for one or more metrics.

The metrics can be turned on and off as needed with the current status found in the
STATUS column of the INNODB_METRICS view. You specify the name of the metric or the
name of the subsystem prepended with module_ as the value to the innodb_monitor_
enable or innodb_monitor_disable variable, and you can use % as a wild card. The
value all works as a special value to affect all metrics.

51

Note   When you specify a module, it will only work as expected if there is no metric matching the module. Examples where you cannot specify the module are `module_cpu`, `module_page_track`, and `module_dblwr`.

Listing 2-6 shows an example of enabling and using all the metrics matching `icp%` (which happens to be the metrics in the `icp` – index condition pushdown – subsystem). After querying the metrics, they are disabled again using the subsystem as the argument. The values of `COUNT` depend on the workload you have at the time of the query.

Listing 2-6. Using the `INNODB_METRICS` view

```
-- Connection   Processlist ID   Thread ID   Event ID
-- -------------------------------------------------
--           1               32          74          6
-- Connection 1
mysql> SET GLOBAL innodb_monitor_enable = 'icp%';
Query OK, 0 rows affected (0.0003 sec)

mysql> SELECT NAME, SUBSYSTEM, COUNT, MIN_COUNT,
              MAX_COUNT, AVG_COUNT,
              STATUS, COMMENT
        FROM information_schema.INNODB_METRICS
             WHERE SUBSYSTEM = 'icp'\G
*************************** 1. row ***************************
     NAME: icp_attempts
SUBSYSTEM: icp
    COUNT: 0
MIN_COUNT: NULL
MAX_COUNT: NULL
AVG_COUNT: 0
   STATUS: enabled
  COMMENT: Number of attempts for index push-down condition checks
```

```
*************************** 2. row ***************************
      NAME: icp_no_match
 SUBSYSTEM: icp
     COUNT: 0
 MIN_COUNT: NULL
 MAX_COUNT: NULL
 AVG_COUNT: 0
    STATUS: enabled
   COMMENT: Index push-down condition does not match
*************************** 3. row ***************************
      NAME: icp_out_of_range
 SUBSYSTEM: icp
     COUNT: 0
 MIN_COUNT: NULL
 MAX_COUNT: NULL
 AVG_COUNT: 0
    STATUS: enabled
   COMMENT: Index push-down condition out of range
*************************** 4. row ***************************
      NAME: icp_match
 SUBSYSTEM: icp
     COUNT: 0
 MIN_COUNT: NULL
 MAX_COUNT: NULL
 AVG_COUNT: 0
    STATUS: enabled
   COMMENT: Index push-down condition matches
4 rows in set (0.0011 sec)

mysql> SET GLOBAL innodb_monitor_disable = 'module_icp';
Query OK, 0 rows affected (0.0004 sec)
```

First, the metrics are enabled using the innodb_monitor_enable variable; then the values are retrieved. In addition to the values shown, there is also a set of columns with the _RESET suffix which are reset when you set the innodb_monitor_reset (only the counter) or innodb_monitor_reset_all system variable. Finally, the metrics are disabled again.

Caution   The metrics have varying overheads, so you are recommended to test with your workload before enabling metrics in production.

InnoDB Lock Monitor and Deadlock Logging

InnoDB has for a long time had its own lock monitor with the lock information returned in the InnoDB monitor output. By default, the InnoDB monitor includes information about the latest deadlock as well as locks involved in lock waits. By enabling the innodb_ status_output_locks option (disabled by default), all locks will be listed; this is similar to what you have in the Performance Schema data_locks table.

To demonstrate the deadlock and transaction information, you can create a deadlock using the steps in Listing 2-7.

Listing 2-7. An example of creating a deadlock

```
-- Connection    Processlist ID    Thread ID    Event ID
-- ---------------------------------------------------
--            1                19           66           6
--            2                20           67           6

-- Connection 1
Connection 1> START TRANSACTION;
Query OK, 0 rows affected (0.0003 sec)

Connection 1> UPDATE world.city
                 SET Population = Population + 1
              WHERE ID = 130;
Query OK, 1 row affected (0.0008 sec)

Rows matched: 1  Changed: 1  Warnings: 0

-- Connection 2
Connection 2> START TRANSACTION;
Query OK, 0 rows affected (0.0002 sec)
```

```
Connection 2> UPDATE world.city
              SET Population = Population + 1
            WHERE ID = 3805;
Query OK, 1 row affected (0.0008 sec)

Rows matched: 1  Changed: 1  Warnings: 0

Connection 2> UPDATE world.city
              SET Population = Population + 1
            WHERE ID = 130;
-- Connection 1
Connection 1> UPDATE world.city
              SET Population = Population + 1
            WHERE ID = 3805;
2020-06-27 12:54:26.833760  1 [ERROR] mysqlsh.DBError ...
```

**ERROR: 1213: Deadlock found when trying to get lock; try restarting
transaction**

```
-- Connection 2
Query OK, 1 row affected (0.1013 sec)

Rows matched: 1  Changed: 1  Warnings: 0
```

You generate the InnoDB lock monitor output using the SHOW ENGINE INNODB
STATUS statement. Listing 2-8 shows an example of enabling all lock information and
generating the monitor output after executing the statements in Listing 2-7. (The
statements used in Listing 2-8 are included as an investigation for the Listing 2-7
workload in the concurrency_book Python module.) The complete InnoDB monitor
output is also available from this book's GitHub repository in the file listing_2_8.txt.

Listing 2-8. The InnoDB monitor output

```
-- Investigation #1
-- Connection 3
Connection 3> SET GLOBAL innodb_status_output_locks = ON;
Query OK, 0 rows affected (0.0005 sec)

-- Investigation #3
Connection 3> SHOW ENGINE INNODB STATUS\G
```

```
*************************** 1. row ***************************
   Type: InnoDB
   Name:
 Status:
======================================
2020-06-27 12:54:29 0x7f00 INNODB MONITOR OUTPUT
======================================
Per second averages calculated from the last 50 seconds
-----------------
BACKGROUND THREAD
-----------------
srv_master_thread loops: 2532 srv_active, 0 srv_shutdown, 1224 srv_idle
srv_master_thread log flush and writes: 0
----------
SEMAPHORES
----------
OS WAIT ARRAY INFO: reservation count 7750
OS WAIT ARRAY INFO: signal count 6744
RW-shared spins 3033, rounds 5292, OS waits 2261
RW-excl spins 1600, rounds 25565, OS waits 1082
RW-sx spins 2167, rounds 61634, OS waits 1874
Spin rounds per wait: 1.74 RW-shared, 15.98 RW-excl, 28.44 RW-sx
------------------------
LATEST DETECTED DEADLOCK
------------------------
2020-06-27 12:54:26 0x862c
*** (1) TRANSACTION:
TRANSACTION 296726, ACTIVE 0 sec starting index read
mysql tables in use 1, locked 1
LOCK WAIT 3 lock struct(s), heap size 1136, 2 row lock(s), undo log entries
1
MySQL thread id 20, OS thread handle 29332, query id 56150 localhost ::1
root updating
UPDATE world.city
   SET Population = Population + 1
 WHERE ID = 130
```

*** (1) HOLDS THE LOCK(S):
RECORD LOCKS space id 259 page no 34 n bits 248 index PRIMARY of table
`world`.`city` trx id 296726 lock_mode X locks rec but not gap
Record lock, heap no 66 PHYSICAL RECORD: n_fields 7; compact format; info
bits 0
 0: len 4; hex 80000edd; asc   ;;
 1: len 6; hex 000000048716; asc   ;;
 2: len 7; hex 020000015f2949; asc   _)I;;
 3: len 30; hex 53616e204672616e636973636f2020202020202020202020202020
    2020; asc San Francisco   ; (total 35 bytes);
 4: len 3; hex 555341; asc USA;;
 5: len 20; hex 43616c69666f726e69612020202020202020202020; asc
California   ;;
 6: len 4; hex 800bda1e; asc   ;;

*** (1) WAITING FOR THIS LOCK TO BE GRANTED:
RECORD LOCKS space id 259 page no 7 n bits 248 index PRIMARY of table
`world`.`city` trx id 296726 lock_mode X locks rec but not gap waiting
Record lock, heap no 44 PHYSICAL RECORD: n_fields 7; compact format; info
bits 0
 0: len 4; hex 80000082; asc   ;;
 1: len 6; hex 000000048715; asc   ;;
 2: len 7; hex 01000000d81fcd; asc   ;;
 3: len 30; hex 5379646e657920202020202020202020202020202020202020202020
    20; asc Sydney   ; (total 35 bytes);
 4: len 3; hex 415553; asc AUS;;
 5: len 20; hex 4e657720536f7574682057616c65732020202020; asc New South
    Wales   ;;
 6: len 4; hex 8031fdb0; asc 1 ;;

*** (2) TRANSACTION:
TRANSACTION 296725, ACTIVE 0 sec starting index read
mysql tables in use 1, locked 1
LOCK WAIT 3 lock struct(s), heap size 1136, 2 row lock(s), undo log entries 1
MySQL thread id 19, OS thread handle 6576, query id 56151 localhost ::1
root updating

```
UPDATE world.city
   SET Population = Population + 1
 WHERE ID = 3805
```

*** (2) HOLDS THE LOCK(S):
RECORD LOCKS space id 259 page no 7 n bits 248 index PRIMARY of table
`world`.`city` trx id 296725 lock_mode X locks rec but not gap
Record lock, heap no 44 PHYSICAL RECORD: n_fields 7; compact format; info
bits 0
 0: len 4; hex 80000082; asc   ;;
 1: len 6; hex 000000048715; asc   ;;
 2: len 7; hex 01000000d81fcd; asc   ;;
 3: len 30; hex 5379646e6579202020202020202020202020202020202020202020
    2020; asc Sydney   ; (total 35 bytes);
 4: len 3; hex 415553; asc AUS;;
 5: len 20; hex 4e657720536f7574682057616c65732020202020; asc New South
    Wales   ;;
 6: len 4; hex 8031fdb0; asc 1 ;;

*** (2) WAITING FOR THIS LOCK TO BE GRANTED:
RECORD LOCKS space id 259 page no 34 n bits 248 index PRIMARY of table
`world`.`city` trx id 296725 lock_mode X locks rec but not gap waiting
Record lock, heap no 66 PHYSICAL RECORD: n_fields 7; compact format; info
bits 0
 0: len 4; hex 80000edd; asc   ;;
 1: len 6; hex 000000048716; asc   ;;
 2: len 7; hex 020000015f2949; asc   _)I;;
 3: len 30; hex 53616e204672616e636973636f20202020202020202020202020
    2020; asc San Francisco   ; (total 35 bytes);
 4: len 3; hex 555341; asc USA;;
 5: len 20; hex 43616c69666f726e69612020202020202020202020; asc
    California   ;;
 6: len 4; hex 800bda1e; asc   ;;
```
```

```
*** WE ROLL BACK TRANSACTION (2)
------------
```

TRANSACTIONS

```
------------
Trx id counter 296728
Purge done for trx's n:o < 296728 undo n:o < 0 state: running but idle
History list length 1
LIST OF TRANSACTIONS FOR EACH SESSION:
---TRANSACTION 283598406541472, not started
0 lock struct(s), heap size 1136, 0 row lock(s)
---TRANSACTION 283598406540640, not started
0 lock struct(s), heap size 1136, 0 row lock(s)
---TRANSACTION 283598406539808, not started
0 lock struct(s), heap size 1136, 0 row lock(s)
---TRANSACTION 283598406538976, not started
0 lock struct(s), heap size 1136, 0 row lock(s)
---TRANSACTION 296726, ACTIVE 3 sec
3 lock struct(s), heap size 1136, 2 row lock(s), undo log entries 2
MySQL thread id 20, OS thread handle 29332, query id 56150 localhost ::1
root
TABLE LOCK table `world`.`city` trx id 296726 lock mode IX
RECORD LOCKS space id 259 page no 34 n bits 248 index PRIMARY of table
`world`.`city` trx id 296726 lock_mode X locks rec but not gap
Record lock, heap no 66 PHYSICAL RECORD: n_fields 7; compact format; info
bits 0
 0: len 4; hex 80000edd; asc     ;;
 1: len 6; hex 000000048716; asc        ;;
 2: len 7; hex 020000015f2949; asc     _)I;;
 3: len 30; hex 53616e204672616e636973636f202020202020202020202020202020
    2020; asc San Francisco               ; (total 35 bytes);
 4: len 3; hex 555341; asc USA;;
 5: len 20; hex 43616c69666f726e69612020202020202020202020; asc
    California          ;;
 6: len 4; hex 800bda1e; asc     ;;
```

```
RECORD LOCKS space id 259 page no 7 n bits 248 index PRIMARY of table
`world`.`city` trx id 296726 lock_mode X locks rec but not gap
Record lock, heap no 44 PHYSICAL RECORD: n_fields 7; compact format; info
bits 0
 0: len 4; hex 80000082; asc     ;;
 1: len 6; hex 000000048716; asc       ;;
 2: len 7; hex 020000015f296c; asc     _)l;;
 3: len 30; hex 5379646e6579202020202020202020202020202020202020202020202020
    2020; asc Sydney                      ; (total 35 bytes);
 4: len 3; hex 415553; asc AUS;;
 5: len 20; hex 4e657720536f7574682057616c65732020202020; asc New South
    Wales       ;;
 6: len 4; hex 8031fdb0; asc  1  ;;
...

-- Investigation #2
Connection 3> SET GLOBAL innodb_status_output_locks = OFF;
Query OK, 0 rows affected (0.0005 sec)
```

Appendix A includes an overview of the sections that the report consists of.

Near the top is the section LATEST DETECTED DEADLOCK which includes details of the transactions and locks involved in the latest deadlock and when it occurred. If no deadlocks have occurred since the last restart of MySQL, this section is omitted. Chapter 16 includes an example of investigating deadlocks.

Note   The deadlock section in the InnoDB monitor output only includes information for deadlocks involving InnoDB record locks. For deadlocks involving non-InnoDB locks such as user-level locks, there is no equivalent information.

A little further down the output, there is the section TRANSACTIONS which lists the InnoDB transactions. Do note that transactions that are not holding any locks (e.g., pure SELECT queries) are not included. In the example, there is an intention exclusive lock held on the world.city table and exclusive locks on the rows with the primary key equal to 3805 (the 80000edd in the record lock information for the first field means the row with the value 0xedd, which is the same as 3805 in decimal notation) and 130 (80000082).

Tip   Nowadays, the lock information in the InnoDB monitor output is better obtained from the `performance_schema.data_locks` and `performance_schema.data_lock_waits` tables. The deadlock information is however still very useful.

You can request the monitor output to be dumped every 15 seconds to stderr by enabling the `innodb_status_output` option. Do note that the output is quite large, so be prepared for your error log to grow quickly if you enable it. The InnoDB monitor output can also easily end up hiding messages about more serious issues. InnoDB also enables outputting the monitor output to the error log automatically when certain conditions apply such as when InnoDB has difficulties finding free blocks in the buffer pool or there are long semaphore waits.

If you want to ensure you record all deadlocks, you can enable the `innodb_print_all_deadlocks` option. This causes deadlock information like that in the InnoDB monitor output to be printed to the error log every time a deadlock occurs. This can be useful, if you need to investigate deadlocks, but it is recommended only to enable it on demand to avoid the error log to become very large and potentially hide other problems.

Caution   Be careful if you enable regular outputs of the InnoDB monitor or information about all deadlocks. The information may easily hide important messages logged to the error log.

The top of the InnoDB monitor output includes information about semaphore waits which is the last monitoring category to discuss.

InnoDB Mutexes and Semaphores

InnoDB uses mutual exclusion objects (better known as mutexes)[1] and semaphores to guard code paths, for example, to avoid race conditions when updating the buffer pool. There are three resources available for monitoring mutexes in MySQL of which two have already been encountered. The most generic tool is the synchronization waits

---

[1]https://en.wikipedia.org/wiki/Mutual_exclusion

in the Performance Schema; however, they are not enabled by default and can cause performance problems to have enabled. This section focuses on the two other resources that are specific to InnoDB.

Note   In InnoDB monitoring there is no clear distinction between mutexes and semaphores.

As seen in the previous section, the InnoDB monitor output contains a semaphores section which shows some general statistics as well as currently waiting semaphores. Listing 2-9 shows an example of the semaphores section with ongoing waits. (It is not trivial to generate semaphore waits on demand, so reproduction steps have not been included. See Chapter 18 for an example of a workload that is likely to cause semaphore waits.)

Listing 2-9. The InnoDB monitor semaphores section

```
----------
SEMAPHORES
----------
OS WAIT ARRAY INFO: reservation count 831
--Thread 28544 has waited at buf0buf.cc line 4637 for 0 seconds the
semaphore:
Mutex at 000001F1AD24D5E8, Mutex BUF_POOL_LRU_LIST created buf0buf.cc:1228,
lock var 1

--Thread 10676 has waited at buf0flu.cc line 1639 for 1 seconds the
semaphore:
Mutex at 000001F1AD24D5E8, Mutex BUF_POOL_LRU_LIST created buf0buf.cc:1228,
lock var 1

--Thread 10900 has waited at buf0lru.cc line 1051 for 0 seconds the
semaphore:
Mutex at 000001F1AD24D5E8, Mutex BUF_POOL_LRU_LIST created buf0buf.cc:1228,
lock var 1

--Thread 28128 has waited at buf0buf.cc line 2797 for 1 seconds the
semaphore:
```

Mutex at 000001F1AD24D5E8, Mutex BUF_POOL_LRU_LIST created buf0buf.cc:1228, lock var 1

--Thread 33584 has waited at buf0buf.cc line 2945 for 0 seconds the semaphore:
Mutex at 000001F1AD24D5E8, Mutex BUF_POOL_LRU_LIST created buf0buf.cc:1228, lock var 1

OS WAIT ARRAY INFO: signal count 207
RW-shared spins 51, rounds 86, OS waits 35
RW-excl spins 39, rounds 993, OS waits 35
RW-sx spins 30, rounds 862, OS waits 25
Spin rounds per wait: 1.69 RW-shared, 25.46 RW-excl, 28.73 RW-sx

In this case the first wait is in buf0buf.cc line 4637 which refers to the source code file name and line number where the mutex is requested. The line number depends on the release number you are using, and the compiler/platform can even make line number change by one. The buf0buf.cc refers to which contains the following code in MySQL 8.0.21 around line 4637 (the line number is prefixed each line):

4577 /** Inits a page for read to the buffer buf_pool. If the page is
4578 (1) already in buf_pool, or
4579 (2) if we specify to read only ibuf pages and the page is not an ibuf page, or
4580 (3) if the space is deleted or being deleted,
4581 then this function does nothing.
4582 Sets the io_fix flag to BUF_IO_READ and sets a non-recursive exclusive lock
4583 on the buffer frame. The io-handler must take care that the flag is cleared
4584 and the lock released later.
4585 @param[out]   err   DB_SUCCESS or DB_TABLESPACE_DELETED
4586 @param[in]   mode   BUF_READ_IBUF_PAGES_ONLY, ...
4587 @param[in]   page_id   page id
4588 @param[in]   page_size   page size
4589 @param[in]   unzip   TRUE=request uncompressed page

```
4590 @return pointer to the block or NULL */
4591 buf_page_t *buf_page_init_for_read(dberr_t *err, ulint mode,
4592                                     const page_id_t &page_id,
4593                                     const page_size_t &page_size, ibool
                                        unzip) {
...
4637     mutex_enter(&buf_pool->LRU_list_mutex);
...
```

The function is trying to read a page into the buffer pool and in line 4637 requests the mutex on the LRU list of the buffer pool. This mutex was created in buf0buf.cc:1228 (also seen from the semaphores section). It is the same mutex that all the waits are for, but in different parts of the source. So, this means that there is contention maintaining the least recently used list of the InnoDB buffer pool. (The waits in this case were created by having innodb_buffer_pool_size = 5M while executing concurrent queries on an almost 2 GiB large table.)

Thus, it is in general necessary to reference the source code when investigating semaphore waits. That said, the file name is a good hint in what part of the code the contention is, for example, buf0buf.cc is related to the buffer pool, and buf0flu.cc is related to the buffer pool flushing algorithm.

The semaphores section is useful to see the waits that are ongoing, but it is of little use when monitoring over time. For that the InnoDB mutex monitor is a better option. You access the mutex monitor using the SHOW ENGINE INNODB MUTEX statement:

```
mysql> SHOW ENGINE INNODB MUTEX;
+--------+------------------------------+------------+
| Type   | Name                         | Status     |
+--------+------------------------------+------------+
| InnoDB | rwlock: dict0dict.cc:2455    | waits=748  |
| InnoDB | rwlock: dict0dict.cc:2455    | waits=171  |
| InnoDB | rwlock: fil0fil.cc:3206      | waits=38   |
| InnoDB | rwlock: sync0sharded_rw.h:72 | waits=1    |
| InnoDB | rwlock: sync0sharded_rw.h:72 | waits=1    |
| InnoDB | rwlock: sync0sharded_rw.h:72 | waits=1    |
| InnoDB | sum rwlock: buf0buf.cc:778   | waits=2436 |
+--------+------------------------------+------------+
7 rows in set (0.0111 sec)
```

The file name and line number refers to where the mutex is created. The mutex monitor is not the most user-friendly tool in MySQL as each mutex may be present multiple times and the waits cannot be summed without parsing the output. However, it is enabled by default, so you can use it at any time.

Note   SHOW ENGINE INNODB MUTEX only includes mutexes and rw-lock semaphores that has had at least one OS wait.

The collection of mutex information is enabled and disabled using the latch InnoDB metric (which is hidden, so you cannot see the current value). There is usually no reason to disable the latch metric.

Summary

In this chapter the resources available for monitoring and investigating locks have been introduced. First the Performance Schema tables were considered. There are dedicated tables for querying the current metadata and data lock requests with information about the object that is the target of the lock, whether it is a shared or exclusive lock and whether the lock request has been granted. At the lowest level, there are also tables that allow you to investigate synchronization waits; however, these are not enabled by default and have a significant overhead. At the opposite end of the granularity scale, the statement tables and error summary tables can be used to investigate which statements encounter errors and the frequency of errors.

Second, the sys schema can also be useful particularly to investigate lock waits issues with the innodb_lock_waits view providing information about ongoing InnoDB data lock waits and schema_table_lock_waits about ongoing table metadata lock waits.

Third, at the highest level, the status counters and InnoDB metrics give an overview of the activity on the instance including the use of locks and failure to obtain locks. If you want more information about InnoDB locks, then the lock monitor provides similar information to the data lock tables in the Performance Schema, but in a less readily usable format, and the InnoDB monitor includes details of the latest occurred deadlock. The InnoDB monitor also includes information about semaphore waits, and finally the InnoDB mutex monitor provides statistics about mutex waits.

Another useful way to get information about the lock usage is to look at the transaction information. This will be considered in the next chapter.

CHAPTER 3

Monitoring InnoDB Transactions

In the previous chapter, you learned how to find information about locks at a relatively low level. It is also important to include information at a higher level as locks have a duration up to the completion of the transaction. (Exceptions are user locks and explicit table locks which can last for longer.) In MySQL Server, transactions mean InnoDB, and this chapter focuses on monitoring InnoDB transactions.

First the INNODB_TRX view in the Information Schema will be covered. This is often the most important resource when it comes to investigating ongoing transactions. Another source of information about transactions is the InnoDB monitor which you also encountered in the previous chapter. Finally, the metrics in the INNODB_METRICS and the sys.metrics views are discussed.

Information Schema INNODB_TRX

The INNODB_TRX view in the Information Schema is the most dedicated source of information about InnoDB transactions. It includes information such as when the transaction started, how many rows have been modified, and how many locks are held. The INNODB_TRX view is also used by the sys.innodb_lock_waits view to provide some information about the transactions involved in lock wait issues. Table 3-1 summarizes the columns in the table.

© Jesper Wisborg Krogh 2021
J. W. Krogh, *MySQL Concurrency*, https://doi.org/10.1007/978-1-4842-6652-6_3

Table 3-1. *The columns in the* information_schema.INNODB_TRX *view*

Column/Data Type	Description
trx_id varchar(18)	The transaction id. This can be useful when referring to the transaction or comparing with the output of the InnoDB monitor. Otherwise, the id should be treated purely internal and not be given any significance. The id is only assigned to transactions that have modified data or locked rows; a transaction that only has executed read-only SELECT statements will have a dummy id like 421124985258256 which will change if the transaction starts to modify or lock records.
trx_state varchar(13)	The state of the transaction. This can be one of RUNNING, LOCK WAIT, ROLLING BACK, and COMMITTING.
trx_started datetime	When the transaction was started using the system time zone.
trx_requested_ lock_id varchar(105)	When the trx_state is LOCK WAIT, this column shows the id of the lock that the transaction is waiting for.
trx_wait_started datetime	When the trx_state is LOCK WAIT, this column shows when the lock wait started using the system time zone.
trx_weight bigint unsigned	A measure of how much work has been done by the transaction in terms of rows modified and locks held. This is the weight that is used to determine which transaction is rolled back in case of a deadlock. The higher the weight, the more work has been done.
trx_mysql_thread_id bigint unsigned	The connection id (the same as the PROCESSLIST_ID column in the Performance Schema threads table) of the connection executing the transaction.
trx_query varchar(1024)	The query currently executed by the transaction. If the transaction is idle, the query is NULL.
trx_operation_state varchar(64)	The current operation performed by the transaction. This may be NULL even when a query is executing.
trx_tables_in_use bigint unsigned	The number of tables the transaction has used.

(continued)

Table 3-1. (*continued*)

Column/Data Type	Description
trx_tables_locked bigint unsigned	The number of tables the transaction holds row locks in.
trx_lock_structs bigint unsigned	The number of lock structures created by the transaction.
trx_lock_memory_ bytes bigint unsigned	The amount of memory in bytes used by the locks held by the transaction.
trx_rows_locked bigint unsigned	The number of record locks held by the transaction. While called row locks, it also includes index locks.
trx_rows_modified bigint unsigned	The number of rows modified by the transaction.
trx_concurrency_ tickets bigint unsigned	When innodb_thread_concurrency is not 0, a transaction is assigned innodb_concurrency_tickets tickets that it can use before it must allow another transaction to perform work. One ticket corresponds to accessing one row. This column shows how many tickets are left.
trx_isolation_level varchar(16)	The transaction isolation level used for the transaction.
trx_unique_checks int	Whether the unique_checks variable is enabled for the connection.
trx_foreign_key_ checks int	Whether the foreign_key_checks variable is enabled for the connection.
trx_last_foreign_ key_error varchar(256)	The error message of the last (if any) foreign key error encountered by the transaction.
trx_adaptive_hash_ latched int	Whether the transaction has locked a part of the adaptive hash index. There is a total of innodb_adaptive_hash_index_parts parts. This column is effectively a Boolean value.

(*continued*)

Table 3-1. (*continued*)

Column/Data Type	Description
trx_adaptive_hash_ timeout bigint unsigned	Whether to keep the lock on the adaptive hash index across multiple queries. If there is only one part for the adaptive hash index and there is no contention, then the timeout counts down, and the lock is released when the timeout reaches 0. When there is contention or there are multiple parts, the lock is always released after each query, and the timeout value is 0.
trx_is_read_only int	Whether the transaction is a read-only transaction. A transaction can be read-only either by declaring it explicitly or for single-statement transactions with autocommit enabled where InnoDB can detect that the query will only read data.
trx_autocommit_non_ locking int	When the transaction is a single-statement non-locking SELECT and the autocommit option is enabled, this column is set to 1. When both this column and trx_is_read_only are 1, InnoDB can optimize the transaction to reduce the overhead.
trx_schedule_weight bigint unsigned	The transaction weight that is assigned to the transaction by the Contention-Aware Transaction Scheduling (CATS) algorithm (see Chapter 8). The value only has a meaning for transactions in the LOCK WAIT state. This column was added in 8.0.20.

The information available from the INNODB_TRX view makes it possible to determine which transactions have the greatest impact. Listing 3-1 shows an example of starting two transactions that can be investigated.

Listing 3-1. Example transactions

```
-- Connection   Processlist ID   Thread ID   Event ID
-- ----------------------------------------------------
--          1               53         163          6
--          2               54         164          6

-- Connection 1
Connection 1> START TRANSACTION;
Query OK, 0 rows affected (0.0002 sec)
```

```
Connection 1> UPDATE world.city SET Population = Population + MOD(ID, 2) +
SLEEP(0.01);

-- Connection 2
Connection 2> SET SESSION autocommit = ON;
Query OK, 0 rows affected (0.0004 sec)

Connection 2> SELECT COUNT(*) FROM world.city WHERE ID > SLEEP(0.01);
```

The transactions will run for 40–50 seconds. While they are executing, you can query the INNODB_TRX view like it is shown in Listing 3-2 (the exact data depends on the ids in your test and when you query the INNODB_TRX view).

Listing 3-2. Example output of the INNODB_TRX view

```
-- Investigation #1
-- Connection 3
Connection 3> SELECT *
                FROM information_schema.INNODB_TRX
                WHERE trx_mysql_thread_id IN (53, 54)\G
*************************** 1. row ***************************
                  trx_id: 296813
               trx_state: RUNNING
             trx_started: 2020-06-27 17:46:10
     trx_requested_lock_id: NULL
         trx_wait_started: NULL
              trx_weight: 1023
       trx_mysql_thread_id: 53
               trx_query: UPDATE world.city SET Population = Population +
               MOD(ID, 2) + SLEEP(0.01)
      trx_operation_state: NULL
        trx_tables_in_use: 1
        trx_tables_locked: 1
         trx_lock_structs: 14
   trx_lock_memory_bytes: 1136
          trx_rows_locked: 2031
        trx_rows_modified: 1009
```

```
       trx_concurrency_tickets: 0
            trx_isolation_level: REPEATABLE READ
              trx_unique_checks: 1
         trx_foreign_key_checks: 1
     trx_last_foreign_key_error: NULL
       trx_adaptive_hash_latched: 0
       trx_adaptive_hash_timeout: 0
                trx_is_read_only: 0
    trx_autocommit_non_locking: 0
           trx_schedule_weight: NULL
*************************** 2. row ***************************
                         trx_id: 283598406543136
                      trx_state: RUNNING
                    trx_started: 2020-06-27 17:46:10
          trx_requested_lock_id: NULL
               trx_wait_started: NULL
                     trx_weight: 0
           trx_mysql_thread_id: 54
                      trx_query: SELECT COUNT(*) FROM world.city WHERE ID >
                                 SLEEP(0.01)
            trx_operation_state: NULL
             trx_tables_in_use: 1
              trx_tables_locked: 0
              trx_lock_structs: 0
         trx_lock_memory_bytes: 1136
                trx_rows_locked: 0
              trx_rows_modified: 0
       trx_concurrency_tickets: 0
            trx_isolation_level: REPEATABLE READ
              trx_unique_checks: 1
         trx_foreign_key_checks: 1
     trx_last_foreign_key_error: NULL
       trx_adaptive_hash_latched: 0
       trx_adaptive_hash_timeout: 0
                trx_is_read_only: 1
```

trx_autocommit_non_locking: 1
       trx_schedule_weight: NULL
2 rows in set (0.0008 sec)

The first row shows an example of a transaction that modifies data. At the time the information is retrieved, 1009 rows have been modified, and there are around twice as many record locks. You can also see that the transaction is still actively executing a query (an UPDATE statement).

The second row is an example of a SELECT statement executed with autocommit enabled. Since autocommitting is enabled, there can only be one statement in the transaction (an explicit START TRANSACTION disables autocommitting). The trx_query column shows it is a SELECT COUNT(*) query without any lock clauses, so it is a read-only statement. This means that InnoDB can skip some things such as preparing to hold lock and undo information for the transaction which reduces the overhead of the transaction. The trx_autocommit_non_locking column is set to 1 to reflect that.

Which transactions you should be worried about depends on the expected workload on your system. If you have an OLAP workload, it is expected that there will be relatively long-running SELECT queries. For a pure OLTP workload, any transaction running for more than a second and modifying more than a handful of rows may be a sign of problems. For example, to find transactions that are older than 10 seconds, you can use the following query:

```
SELECT *
  FROM information_schema.INNODB_TRX
 WHERE trx_started < NOW() - INTERVAL 10 SECOND;
```

You can optionally join on other tables such as threads and events_statements_current in the Performance Schema. An example of this is shown in Listing 3-3.

Listing 3-3. Querying details of old transactions

```
-- Investigation #3
Connection 3> SELECT thd.thread_id, thd.processlist_id,
                     trx.trx_id, stmt.event_id, trx.trx_started,
                     TO_SECONDS(NOW()) -
                             TO_SECONDS(trx.trx_started
                             ) AS age_seconds,
```

```
                       trx.trx_rows_locked, trx.trx_rows_modified,
                       FORMAT_PICO_TIME(stmt.timer_wait) AS latency,
                       stmt.rows_examined, stmt.rows_affected,
                       sys.format_statement(SQL_TEXT) as statement
                  FROM information_schema.INNODB_TRX trx
                       INNER JOIN performance_schema.threads thd
                              ON thd.processlist_id = trx.trx_mysql_
                              thread_id
                       INNER JOIN performance_schema.events_statements_
                       current stmt
                            USING (thread_id)
                 WHERE trx_started < NOW() - INTERVAL 10 SECOND\G
*************************** 1. row ***************************
        thread_id: 163
   processlist_id: 53
           trx_id: 296813
         event_id: 9
      trx_started: 2020-06-27 17:46:10
      age_seconds: 25
  trx_rows_locked: 2214
trx_rows_modified: 1100
          latency: 25.24 s
    rows_examined: 2201
    rows_affected: 0
        statement: UPDATE world.city SET Populati ... ion + MOD(ID, 2) +
        SLEEP(0.01)
*************************** 2. row ***************************
        thread_id: 164
   processlist_id: 54
           trx_id: 283598406543136
         event_id: 8
      trx_started: 2020-06-27 17:46:10
      age_seconds: 25
  trx_rows_locked: 0
trx_rows_modified: 0
```

```
      latency: 25.14 s
 rows_examined: 0
 rows_affected: 0
      statement: SELECT COUNT(*) FROM world.city WHERE ID > SLEEP(0.01)
  2 rows in set (0.0021 sec)
```

You can join to the tables and choose the columns of relevance for your investigation.

Related to the INNODB_TRX view is the transaction list in the InnoDB monitor.

InnoDB Monitor

The InnoDB monitor is a kind of Swiss army knife of InnoDB information and also includes information about transactions. The TRANSACTIONS section in the output from the InnoDB monitor is dedicated to transactional information. This information does include not only a list of transactions but also the history list length. Listing 3-4 shows an excerpt of the InnoDB monitor with the example of the transaction section taken just after the previous output from the INNODB_TRX view.

Listing 3-4. Transaction information from the InnoDB monitor

```
-- Investigation #4
Connection 3> SHOW ENGINE INNODB STATUS\G
*************************** 1. row ***************************
  Type: InnoDB
  Name:
Status:
=====================================
2020-06-27 17:46:36 0x5784 INNODB MONITOR OUTPUT
=====================================
Per second averages calculated from the last 20 seconds
...
```

```
------------
TRANSACTIONS
------------
Trx id counter 296814
Purge done for trx's n:o < 296813 undo n:o < 0 state: running but idle
History list length 1
LIST OF TRANSACTIONS FOR EACH SESSION:
---TRANSACTION 283598406541472, not started
0 lock struct(s), heap size 1136, 0 row lock(s)
---TRANSACTION 283598406540640, not started
0 lock struct(s), heap size 1136, 0 row lock(s)
---TRANSACTION 283598406539808, not started
0 lock struct(s), heap size 1136, 0 row lock(s)
---TRANSACTION 283598406538976, not started
0 lock struct(s), heap size 1136, 0 row lock(s)
---TRANSACTION 296813, ACTIVE 26 sec fetching rows
mysql tables in use 1, locked 1
15 lock struct(s), heap size 1136, 2333 row lock(s), undo log entries 1160
MySQL thread id 53, OS thread handle 23748, query id 56574 localhost ::1
root User sleep
UPDATE world.city SET Population = Population + MOD(ID, 2) + SLEEP(0.01)
...
```

The top of the TRANSACTIONS section shows the current value of the transaction id counter followed by information of what has been purged from the undo logs. It shows that the undo logs for transaction ids less than 296813 have been purged. The further this purge is behind, the larger the history list length (in the third line of the section) is. Reading the history list length from the InnoDB monitor output is the traditional way to get the length of the history list. In the next section, it will be shown how to get the value in a better way when used for monitoring purposes.

The rest of the section is a list of transactions. Notice that while the output is generated with the same two active transactions as were found in INNODB_TRX, the transaction list only includes one active transaction (the one for the UPDATE statement). In MySQL 5.7 and later, read-only non-locking transactions are not included in the InnoDB monitor transaction list. For this reason, it is better to use the INNODB_TRX view, if you need to include all active transactions.

As mentioned, there is an alternative way to get the history list length. You need to use the InnoDB metrics for this.

INNODB_METRICS and sys.metrics

The InnoDB monitor report is useful for a database administrator to get an overview of what is going on in InnoDB, but for monitoring it is not as useful as it requires parsing to get out the data in a way monitoring can use it. You saw earlier in the chapter how the information about the transactions can be obtained from the information_schema. INNODB_TRX view, but how about metrics such as the history list length?

The InnoDB metric system includes several metrics that show information about the transactions in the information_schema.INNODB_METRICS view. These metrics are all located in the transaction subsystem. Listing 3-5 shows a list of the transaction metrics, whether they are enabled by default, and a brief comment explaining what the metric measures.

Listing 3-5. InnoDB metrics related to transactions

```
-- Connection    Processlist ID   Thread ID   Event ID
-- ----------------------------------------------------
--          1               56         166          6

-- Connection 1
Connection 1> SELECT NAME, COUNT, STATUS, COMMENT
                FROM information_schema.INNODB_METRICS
                WHERE SUBSYSTEM = 'transaction'\G
*************************** 1. row ***************************
   NAME: trx_rw_commits
  COUNT: 0
 STATUS: disabled
COMMENT: Number of read-write transactions  committed
*************************** 2. row ***************************
   NAME: trx_ro_commits
  COUNT: 0
 STATUS: disabled
COMMENT: Number of read-only transactions committed
```

```
*************************** 3. row ***************************
   NAME: trx_nl_ro_commits
  COUNT: 0
 STATUS: disabled
COMMENT: Number of non-locking auto-commit read-only transactions committed
*************************** 4. row ***************************
   NAME: trx_commits_insert_update
  COUNT: 0
 STATUS: disabled
COMMENT: Number of transactions committed with inserts and updates
*************************** 5. row ***************************
   NAME: trx_rollbacks
  COUNT: 0
 STATUS: disabled
COMMENT: Number of transactions rolled back
*************************** 6. row ***************************
   NAME: trx_rollbacks_savepoint
  COUNT: 0
 STATUS: disabled
COMMENT: Number of transactions rolled back to savepoint
*************************** 7. row ***************************
   NAME: trx_rollback_active
  COUNT: 0
 STATUS: disabled
COMMENT: Number of resurrected active transactions rolled back
*************************** 8. row ***************************
   NAME: trx_active_transactions
  COUNT: 0
 STATUS: disabled
COMMENT: Number of active transactions
*************************** 9. row ***************************
   NAME: trx_on_log_no_waits
  COUNT: 0
 STATUS: disabled
COMMENT: Waits for redo during transaction commits
```

```
*************************** 10. row ***************************
   NAME: trx_on_log_waits
  COUNT: 0
 STATUS: disabled
COMMENT: Waits for redo during transaction commits
*************************** 11. row ***************************
   NAME: trx_on_log_wait_loops
  COUNT: 0
 STATUS: disabled
COMMENT: Waits for redo during transaction commits
*************************** 12. row ***************************
   NAME: trx_rseg_history_len
  COUNT: 9
 STATUS: enabled
COMMENT: Length of the TRX_RSEG_HISTORY list
*************************** 13. row ***************************
   NAME: trx_undo_slots_used
  COUNT: 0
 STATUS: disabled
COMMENT: Number of undo slots used
*************************** 14. row ***************************
   NAME: trx_undo_slots_cached
  COUNT: 0
 STATUS: disabled
COMMENT: Number of undo slots cached
*************************** 15. row ***************************
   NAME: trx_rseg_current_size
  COUNT: 0
 STATUS: disabled
COMMENT: Current rollback segment size in pages
15 rows in set (0.0012 sec)
```

The most important of these metrics is trx_rseg_history_len which is the history list length. This is also the only metric that is enabled by default. The metrics related to commits and rollbacks can be used to determine how many read-write, read-only, and non-locking read-only transactions you have and how often they are committed and rolled back. Many rollbacks suggest there is a problem. If you suspect the redo log is a bottleneck, the `trx_on_log_%` metrics can be used to get a measure of how much transactions are waiting for the redo log during transaction commits.

Tip   You enable InnoDB metrics with the `innodb_monitor_enable` option and disable them with `innodb_monitor_disable`. This can be done dynamically.

An alternative and convenient way to query the InnoDB metrics is to use the `sys.metrics` view which also includes the global status variables. Listing 3-6 shows an example of using the `sys.metrics` view to obtain the current values and whether the metric is enabled.

Listing 3-6. Using the `sys.metrics` view to get the transaction metrics

```
-- Connection    Processlist ID    Thread ID    Event ID
-- ------------------------------------------------------
--          1                52          125            6

-- Connection 1
Connection 1> SELECT Variable_name AS Name,
                     Variable_value AS Value,
                     Enabled
                FROM sys.metrics
               WHERE Type = 'InnoDB Metrics - transaction';
+----------------------------+-------+---------+
| Name                       | Value | Enabled |
+----------------------------+-------+---------+
| trx_active_transactions    | 0     | NO      |
| trx_commits_insert_update  | 0     | NO      |
| trx_nl_ro_commits          | 0     | NO      |
| trx_on_log_no_waits        | 0     | NO      |
| trx_on_log_wait_loops      | 0     | NO      |
| trx_on_log_waits           | 0     | NO      |
| trx_ro_commits             | 0     | NO      |
| trx_rollback_active        | 0     | NO      |
| trx_rollbacks              | 0     | NO      |
```

```
| trx_rollbacks_savepoint   | 0     | NO      |
| trx_rseg_current_size     | 0     | NO      |
| trx_rseg_history_len      | 16    | YES     |
| trx_rw_commits            | 0     | NO      |
| trx_undo_slots_cached     | 0     | NO      |
| trx_undo_slots_used       | 0     | NO      |
+---------------------------+-------+---------+
15 rows in set (0.0089 sec)
```

This shows that the history list length is 16 which is a good low value, so there is next to none overhead from the undo logs. The rest of the metrics are disabled.

Summary

This chapter has covered how you can obtain information about InnoDB transactions. The primary source of detailed information is the INNODB_TRX view in the Information Schema which includes details such as when the transaction was started, the number of locked and modified rows, etc. You can optionally join on the Performance Schema tables to get more information about the transaction.

You can also use the InnoDB monitor to get information about locking transactions; however, in general, it is preferred to use the INNODB_TRX view. If you are looking for higher-level aggregate statistics, you can use the information_schema.INNODB_METRICS view or alternatively the sys.metrics view. The most commonly used metric is trx_rseg_history_len which shows the history list length.

Thus far, the discussion of transaction information has been about aggregate statistics either for all transactions or individual transactions. If you want to go deeper into what work a transaction has done, you need to use the Performance Schema as discussed in the next chapter.

CHAPTER 4

Transactions in the Performance Schema

The Performance Schema supports transaction monitoring in MySQL 5.7 and later, and it is enabled by default in MySQL 8. There are not many transaction details other than related to XA transactions and savepoints available in the Performance Schema that cannot be obtained from the INNODB_TRX view in the Information Schema. However, the Performance Schema transaction events have the advantage that you can combine them with other event types such as statements to get information about the work done by a transaction. This is the main focus of this chapter. Additionally, the Performance Schema offers summary tables with aggregate statistics.

Transaction Events and Their Statements

The main tables for investigating transactions in the Performance Schema are the transaction event tables. There are three tables for recording current or recent transactions: events_transactions_current, events_transactions_history, and events_transactions_history_long. They have the columns as summarized in Table 4-1.

© Jesper Wisborg Krogh 2021
J. W. Krogh, *MySQL Concurrency*, https://doi.org/10.1007/978-1-4842-6652-6_4

Table 4-1. *The columns of the non-summary transaction event tables*

Column/Data Type	Description
THREAD_ID bigint unsigned	The Performance Schema thread id of the connection executing the transaction.
EVENT_ID bigint unsigned	The event id for the event. You can use the event id to order the events for a thread or as a foreign key together with the thread id between event tables.
END_EVENT_ID bigint unsigned	The event id when the transaction completed. If the event id is NULL, the transaction is still ongoing.
EVENT_NAME varchar(128)	The transaction event name. Currently this column always has the value transaction.
STATE enum	The state of the transaction. Possible values are ACTIVE, COMMITTED, and ROLLED BACK.
TRX_ID bigint unsigned	This is currently unused and will always be NULL.
GTID varchar(64)	The GTID for the transaction. When the GTID is automatically determined (the usual), AUTOMATIC is returned. This is the same as the gtid_next variable for the connection executing the transaction.
XID_FORMAT_ID int	For XA transactions, the format id.
XID_GTRID varchar(130)	For XA transactions, the gtrid value.
XID_BQUAL varchar(130)	For XA transactions, the bqual value.
XA_STATE varchar(64)	For a XA transaction, the state of the transaction. This can be ACTIVE, IDLE, PREPARED, ROLLED BACK, or COMMITTED.
SOURCE varchar(64)	The source code file and line number where the event was recorded.
TIMER_START bigint unsigned	The time in picoseconds when the event started.

(*continued*)

Table 4-1. (*continued*)

Column/Data Type	Description
TIMER_END bigint unsigned	The time in picoseconds when the event completed. If the transaction has not completed yet, the value corresponds to the current time.
TIMER_WAIT bigint unsigned	The total time in picoseconds it took to execute the event. If the event has not completed yet, the value corresponds to how long the transaction has been active.
ACCESS_MODE enum	Whether the transaction is in read-only (READ ONLY) or in read-write (READ WRITE) mode.
ISOLATION_LEVEL varchar(64)	The transaction isolation level for the transaction.
AUTOCOMMIT enum	Whether the transaction is autocommitting based on the autocommit option and whether an explicit transaction has been started. Possible values are NO and YES.
NUMBER_OF_ SAVEPOINTS bigint unsigned	The number of savepoints created in the transaction.
NUMBER_OF_ROLLBACK_ TO_SAVEPOINT bigint unsigned	The number of times the transaction has rolled back to a savepoint.
NUMBER_OF_RELEASE_ SAVEPOINT bigint unsigned	The number of times the transaction has released a savepoint.
OBJECT_INSTANCE_ BEGIN bigint unsigned	This field is currently unused and always set to NULL.
NESTING_EVENT_ID bigint unsigned	The event id of the event that triggered the transaction.
NESTING_EVENT_TYPE enum	The event type of the event that triggered the transaction.

If you are working with XA transactions, the transaction event tables are great when you need to recover a transaction as the format id, gtrid, and bqual values are directly available from the tables, unlike for the XA RECOVER statement where you have to parse the output. In the same way, if you work with savepoints, you can get statistics on the savepoint usage. Otherwise, the information is very similar to what is available in the information_schema.INNODB_TRX view.

For an example of using the events_transactions_current table, you can start two transactions as shown in Listing 4-1.

Listing 4-1. Example transactions

```
-- Connection    Processlist ID    Thread ID    Event ID
-- --------------------------------------------------------
--             1               57          140           6
--             2               58          141           6

-- Connection 1
Connection 1> START TRANSACTION;
Query OK, 0 rows affected (0.0004 sec)

Connection 1> UPDATE world.city SET Population = 5200000 WHERE ID = 130;

Connection 1> UPDATE world.city SET Population = 4900000 WHERE ID = 131;

Connection 1> UPDATE world.city SET Population = 2400000 WHERE ID = 132;

Connection 1> UPDATE world.city SET Population = 2000000 WHERE ID = 133;

-- Connection 2
Connection 2> XA START 'abc', 'def', 1;

Connection 2> UPDATE world.city SET Population = 900000 WHERE ID = 3805;
```

The first transaction is a normal transaction that updates the population of several cities, and the second transaction is an XA transaction. Listing 4-2 shows an example output of the events_transactions_current table listing the currently active transactions.

Listing 4-2. Using the events_transactions_current table

```
-- Investigation #1
-- Connection 3
Connection 3> SELECT *
                FROM performance_schema.events_transactions_current
              WHERE state = 'ACTIVE'\G
*************************** 1. row ***************************
                    THREAD_ID: 140
                     EVENT_ID: 8
                 END_EVENT_ID: NULL
                   EVENT_NAME: transaction
                        STATE: ACTIVE
                       TRX_ID: NULL
                         GTID: AUTOMATIC
                XID_FORMAT_ID: NULL
                    XID_GTRID: NULL
                    XID_BQUAL: NULL
                     XA_STATE: NULL
                       SOURCE: transaction.cc:209
                  TIMER_START: 72081362554600000
                    TIMER_END: 72161455792800000
                   TIMER_WAIT: 80093238200000
                  ACCESS_MODE: READ WRITE
              ISOLATION_LEVEL: REPEATABLE READ
                   AUTOCOMMIT: NO
         NUMBER_OF_SAVEPOINTS: 0
NUMBER_OF_ROLLBACK_TO_SAVEPOINT: 0
   NUMBER_OF_RELEASE_SAVEPOINT: 0
          OBJECT_INSTANCE_BEGIN: NULL
              NESTING_EVENT_ID: 7
            NESTING_EVENT_TYPE: STATEMENT
*************************** 2. row ***************************
                    THREAD_ID: 141
                     EVENT_ID: 8
                 END_EVENT_ID: NULL
```

```
              EVENT_NAME: transaction
                   STATE: ACTIVE
                  TRX_ID: NULL
                    GTID: AUTOMATIC
           XID_FORMAT_ID: 1
               XID_GTRID: abc
               XID_BQUAL: def
                XA_STATE: ACTIVE
                  SOURCE: transaction.cc:209
             TIMER_START: 72081766957700000
               TIMER_END: 72161455799300000
              TIMER_WAIT: 79688841600000
             ACCESS_MODE: READ WRITE
         ISOLATION_LEVEL: REPEATABLE READ
              AUTOCOMMIT: NO
      NUMBER_OF_SAVEPOINTS: 0
NUMBER_OF_ROLLBACK_TO_SAVEPOINT: 0
   NUMBER_OF_RELEASE_SAVEPOINT: 0
      OBJECT_INSTANCE_BEGIN: NULL
        NESTING_EVENT_ID: 7
      NESTING_EVENT_TYPE: STATEMENT
2 rows in set (0.0007 sec)
```

The transaction in row 1 is a regular transaction, whereas the transaction in row 2 is an XA transaction. Both transactions were started by a statement which can be seen from the nesting event type. If you want to find the statement that triggered the transaction, you can use that to query the events_statements_history table like

```
-- Investigation #2
Connection 3> SELECT sql_text
              FROM performance_schema.events_statements_history
             WHERE thread_id = 140
               AND event_id = 7\G
*************************** 1. row ***************************
sql_text: start transaction
1 row in set (0.0434 sec)
```

This shows that the transaction executed by thread_id = 140 was started using a START TRANSACTION statement. Since the events_statements_history table only includes the last ten statements for the connection, it is not guaranteed that the statement that started the transaction is still in the history table. If you are looking at a single-statement transaction or the first statement (while it is still executing) when autocommit is disabled, you will need to query the events_statements_current table instead.

The relationship between transactions and statements also goes the other way.

Given a transaction event id and the thread id, you can query the last ten statements executed for that transaction using the statement event history and current tables. Listing 4-3 shows an example for thread_id = 140 and transaction EVENT_ID = 8 (from row 1 of Listing 4-2) where both the statement starting the transaction and subsequent statements are included.

Listing 4-3. Finding the last ten statements executed in a transaction

```
-- Investigation #4
Connection 3> SET @thread_id = 140,
                 @event_id = 8,
                 @nesting_event_id = 7;
Query OK, 0 rows affected (0.0007 sec)

-- Investigation #6
Connection 3> SELECT event_id, sql_text,
                 FORMAT_PICO_TIME(timer_wait) AS latency,
                 IF(end_event_id IS NULL, 'YES', 'NO') AS current
          FROM ((SELECT event_id, end_event_id,
                        timer_wait,
                        sql_text, nesting_event_id,
                        nesting_event_type
                 FROM performance_schema.events_statements_current
                 WHERE thread_id = @thread_id
                ) UNION (
                  SELECT event_id, end_event_id,
                         timer_wait,
                         sql_text, nesting_event_id,
                         nesting_event_type
```

```
                       FROM performance_schema.events_statements_history
                       WHERE thread_id = @thread_id
                   )
                ) events
          WHERE (nesting_event_type = 'TRANSACTION'
                 AND nesting_event_id = @event_id)
                OR event_id = @nesting_event_id
          ORDER BY event_id DESC\G
*************************** 1. row ***************************
event_id: 12
sql_text: UPDATE world.city SET Population = 2000000 WHERE ID = 133
 latency: 384.00 us
 current: NO
*************************** 2. row ***************************
event_id: 11
sql_text: UPDATE world.city SET Population = 2400000 WHERE ID = 132
 latency: 316.20 us
 current: NO
*************************** 3. row ***************************
event_id: 10
sql_text: UPDATE world.city SET Population = 4900000 WHERE ID = 131
 latency: 299.30 us
 current: NO
*************************** 4. row ***************************
event_id: 9
sql_text: UPDATE world.city SET Population = 5200000 WHERE ID = 130
 latency: 176.95 ms
 current: NO
*************************** 5. row ***************************
event_id: 7
sql_text: start transaction
 latency: 223.20 us
 current: NO
5 rows in set (0.0016 sec)
```

The subquery (a derived table) finds all statement events for the thread from the
events_statements_current and events_statements_history tables. It is necessary
to include the current events as there may be an ongoing statement for the transaction.
The statements are filtered by either being a child of the transaction or the nesting event
for the transaction (event_id = 7). This will include all statements beginning with the
one starting the transactions. There will be up to 11 statements if there is an ongoing
statement and otherwise up to ten.

The end_event_id is used to determine whether the statement is currently
executing, and the statements are ordered in reverse using the event_id, so the most
recent statement is in row 1 and the oldest (the START TRANSACTION statement) in row 5.

This type of query is not only useful to investigate transactions still executing
queries. It can also be very useful when you encounter an idle transaction and you want
to know what the transaction did before it was left abandoned. Another related way
to look for active transactions is to use the sys.session view which uses the events_
transactions_current table to include information about the transactional state for
each connection. Listing 4-4 shows an example of querying for active transactions
excluding the row for the connection executing the query.

Listing 4-4. Finding active transactions with sys.session

```
-- Investigation #7
Connection 3> SELECT *
                FROM sys.session
               WHERE trx_state = 'ACTIVE'
                 AND conn_id <> CONNECTION_ID()\G
*************************** 1. row ***************************
              thd_id: 140
             conn_id: 57
                user: mysqlx/worker
                  db: NULL
             command: Sleep
               state: NULL
                time: 449
   current_statement: UPDATE world.city SET Population = 2000000
WHERE ID = 133
   statement_latency: NULL
```

```
             progress: NULL
          lock_latency: 111.00 us
         rows_examined: 1
             rows_sent: 0
         rows_affected: 1
            tmp_tables: 0
       tmp_disk_tables: 0
             full_scan: NO
        last_statement: UPDATE world.city SET Population = 2000000
WHERE ID = 133
last_statement_latency: 384.00 us
        current_memory: 228.31 KiB
             last_wait: NULL
     last_wait_latency: NULL
                source: NULL
           trx_latency: 7.48 min
             trx_state: ACTIVE
        trx_autocommit: NO
                   pid: 30936
          program_name: mysqlsh
*************************** 2. row ***************************
                thd_id: 141
               conn_id: 58
                  user: mysqlx/worker
                    db: NULL
               command: Sleep
                 state: NULL
                  time: 449
     current_statement: UPDATE world.city SET Population = 900000
WHERE ID = 3805
     statement_latency: NULL
              progress: NULL
          lock_latency: 387.00 us
         rows_examined: 1
             rows_sent: 0
```

```
          rows_affected: 1
             tmp_tables: 0
        tmp_disk_tables: 0
              full_scan: NO
         last_statement: UPDATE world.city SET Population = 900000
WHERE ID = 3805
 last_statement_latency: 49.39 ms
         current_memory: 70.14 KiB
              last_wait: NULL
      last_wait_latency: NULL
                 source: NULL
            trx_latency: 7.48 min
              trx_state: ACTIVE
         trx_autocommit: NO
                    pid: 30936
           program_name: mysqlsh
2 rows in set (0.0422 sec)
```

This shows that the transaction in the first row has been active for more than 7 minutes and it is 449 seconds (7.5 minutes) since the last query was executed (your values will differ). The last_statement can be used to determine the last query executed by the connection. This is an example of an abandoned transaction which prevents InnoDB from purging its undo logs. The most common causes of abandoned transactions are a database administrator starting a transaction interactively and getting distracted or that autocommit is disabled and it is not realized a transaction was started.

Caution   If you disable autocommit, be careful always to commit or roll back at the end of the work. Some connectors disable autocommit by default, so be aware that your application may not be using the server default.

You can roll the transactions back to avoid changing any data (if you use the MySQL Shell script to reproduce the example, this is done automatically when hitting enter without an answer for the next investigation). For the first (normal) transaction

```
-- Connection 1
Connection 1> ROLLBACK;
Query OK, 0 rows affected (0.0303 sec)
```

And for the XA transaction:

```
-- Connection 2
Connection 2> XA END 'abc', 'def', 1;
Query OK, 0 rows affected (0.0002 sec)

Connection 2> XA ROLLBACK 'abc', 'def', 1;
Query OK, 0 rows affected (0.0308 sec)
```

Another way the Performance Schema tables are useful for analyzing transactions is to use the summary tables to obtain aggregate data.

Transaction Summary Tables

In the same way as there are statement summary tables that can be used to get reports of the statements that are executed, there are transaction summary tables that can be used to analyze the use of transactions. While they are not quite as useful as their statement counterparts, they do offer insight into which connections and accounts that use transactions in different ways.

There are five transaction summary tables grouping the data globally or by account, host, thread, or user. All of the summaries also group by the event name, but as currently there is only one transaction event (transaction), it is a nil operation. The tables are

- **events_transactions_summary_global_by_event_name**: All transactions aggregated. There is only a single row in this table.

- **events_transactions_summary_by_account_by_event_name**: The transactions grouped by username and hostname.

- **events_transactions_summary_by_host_by_event_name**: The transactions grouped by hostname of the account.

- **events_transactions_summary_by_thread_by_event_name**: The transactions grouped by thread. Only currently existing threads are included.

- **events_transactions_summary_by_user_by_event_name:** The
  events grouped by the username part of the account.

Each table includes the columns that the transaction statistics are grouped by
and three groups of columns: total, for read-write transactions, and for read-only
transactions. For each of these three groups of columns, there is the total number of
transactions as well as the total, minimum, average, and maximum latencies. Listing 4-5
shows an example of the data from the events_transactions_summary_global_by_
event_name table.

Listing 4-5. The events_transactions_summary_global_by_event_name table

```
-- Connection    Processlist ID    Thread ID    Event ID
-- --------------------------------------------------------
--          1                60          143           6

-- Connection 1
Connection 1> SELECT *
        FROM performance_schema.events_transactions_summary_global_by_
        event_name\G
*************************** 1. row ***************************
          EVENT_NAME: transaction
          COUNT_STAR: 40485
      SUM_TIMER_WAIT: 90259064465300000
      MIN_TIMER_WAIT: 4800000
      AVG_TIMER_WAIT: 2229444500000
      MAX_TIMER_WAIT: 62122342944500000
    COUNT_READ_WRITE: 40483
SUM_TIMER_READ_WRITE: 90230783742700000
MIN_TIMER_READ_WRITE: 4800000
AVG_TIMER_READ_WRITE: 2228856100000
MAX_TIMER_READ_WRITE: 62122342944500000
     COUNT_READ_ONLY: 2
 SUM_TIMER_READ_ONLY: 28280722600000
 MIN_TIMER_READ_ONLY: 9561820600000
 AVG_TIMER_READ_ONLY: 14140361300000
 MAX_TIMER_READ_ONLY: 18718902000000
1 row in set (0.0007 sec)
```

It may surprise you when you study the output how many transactions there are, particularly read-write transactions. Remember that when querying an InnoDB table, everything is a transaction even if you have not explicitly specified one. So even a simple SELECT statement querying a single row counts as a transaction. Regarding the distribution between read-write and read-only transactions, then the Performance Schema only considers a transaction read-only if you explicitly started it as such

```
START TRANSACTION READ ONLY;
```

When InnoDB determines that an autocommitting single-statement transaction can be treated as a read-only transaction, that is still counting toward the read-write statistics in the Performance Schema.

Summary

In this chapter, the transaction-related tables in the Performance Schema have been introduced, and it has been shown how you can join to other tables. First the three tables with one row per transaction event, events_transactions_current, events_transactions_history, and events_transactions_history_long, were discussed, and then they were used to join on the statement event tables to obtain the most recent statements executed in a transaction. Finally, the transaction summary tables were covered.

You have now covered the most important resources for monitoring locks and transactions, and it is time to go into detail about locks. First, you will learn about the lock access levels.

CHAPTER 5

Lock Access Levels

In the first chapter where locks were introduced, there was no mention of how locks work. It would be possible to implement locking in the database by just allowing one query access at a time irrespective of what kind of work will be done. However, this would be woefully inefficient.

Keeping to the analogy of a traffic light, another approach is grant access based on what work will be done. A traffic light grants access to the intersection not just to one car at a time but to all driving in the same direction. Similarly, in a database, you distinguish between shared (read) and exclusive (write) access. The access levels do what their names suggest. A shared lock allows other connections to also get a shared lock. This is the most permissive lock access level. An exclusive lock only allows that one connection to get the lock. A shared lock is also known as a read lock, and an exclusive lock is also known as a write lock.

Note The lock access level is also sometimes called the lock type, but since that can be confused with the lock granularity, which is also sometimes called a type, the term lock access level is used here.

MySQL also has a concept called intention locks which specify the intention of a transaction. An intention lock can be either shared or exclusive.

The rest of this chapter goes into more detail about shared and exclusive locks as well as intention locks.

Shared Locks

When a thread needs to protect a resource, but it is not going to change the resource, it can use a shared lock to prevent other threads from changing the resource while still allowing them to access the same resource. This is the most commonly used access level.

© Jesper Wisborg Krogh 2021
J. W. Krogh, *MySQL Concurrency*, https://doi.org/10.1007/978-1-4842-6652-6_5

Whenever a statement selects from a table, MySQL will take a shared lock on the tables involved in the query. For the data locks, it works differently as InnoDB does not in general acquire a shared lock when reading a row. That only happens when a shared lock is explicitly requested, in the SERIALIZABLE transaction isolation level, or it is required by the workflow such as when foreign keys are involved.

You can explicitly request a shared lock on the rows accessed by a query by adding the FOR SHARE or its synonym LOCK IN SHARE MODE as shown in Listing 5-1.

Listing 5-1. Example of obtaining a shared lock

```
-- Connection   Processlist ID   Thread ID   Event ID
-- ------------------------------------------------------
--          1              36          80          6

-- Connection 1
Connection 1> START TRANSACTION;
Query OK, 0 rows affected (0.0003 sec)

Connection 1> SELECT * FROM world.city WHERE ID = 130 FOR SHARE;
+-----+--------+-------------+-----------------+------------+
| ID  | Name   | CountryCode | District        | Population |
+-----+--------+-------------+-----------------+------------+
| 130 | Sydney | AUS         | New South Wales |    3276207 |
+-----+--------+-------------+-----------------+------------+
1 row in set (0.0047 sec)

Connection 1> SELECT object_type, object_schema, object_name,
                     lock_type, lock_duration, lock_status
                FROM performance_schema.metadata_locks
               WHERE OWNER_THREAD_ID = PS_CURRENT_THREAD_ID()
                 AND OBJECT_SCHEMA <> 'performance_schema'\G
*************************** 1. row ***************************
  object_type: TABLE
object_schema: world
  object_name: city
    lock_type: SHARED_READ
lock_duration: TRANSACTION
```

```
       lock_status: GRANTED
1 row in set (0.0005 sec)

Connection 1> SELECT engine, object_schema, object_name,
                     lock_type, lock_mode, lock_status
                FROM performance_schema.data_locks
               WHERE THREAD_ID = PS_CURRENT_THREAD_ID()\G
*************************** 1. row ***************************
        engine: INNODB
 object_schema: world
   object_name: city
     lock_type: TABLE
     lock_mode: IS
   lock_status: GRANTED
*************************** 2. row ***************************
        engine: INNODB
 object_schema: world
   object_name: city
     lock_type: RECORD
     lock_mode: S,REC_NOT_GAP
   lock_status: GRANTED
2 rows in set (0.0005 sec)

mysql> ROLLBACK;
Query OK, 0 rows affected (0.0004 sec)
```

When querying the metadata_locks table, locks on the Performance Schema tables are excluded as they are for the investigation query itself rather than for the previous query. Here a shared lock is taken on world.city table as well as the record with the primary key (the ID column) equals to 130. That they are shared locks can be seen from the lock_type column in the metadata_locks table which has a value of SHARED_READ and from the S in the lock_mode column of data_locks in the second row. The value of IS for the first row from data_locks means it is a shared intention lock which will be discussed in more detail shortly.

While shared locks do allow other queries also using shared locks to proceed, they do block attempts to get an exclusive lock

Exclusive Locks

Exclusive locks are the counterpart to shared lock. They ensure that only the thread granted the exclusive lock can access the resource for the duration of the lock. As exclusive locks are used to ensure only one thread is modifying a resource at a time, they are also known as write locks.

Exclusive locks are mostly obtained by data definition language (DDL) statements such as ALTER TABLE and when modifying data using data modification language (DML) statements such as UPDATE and DELETE. As example of obtaining an exclusive lock and the data in the lock tables can be found in Listing 5-2.

Listing 5-2. Example of obtaining exclusive locks

```
-- Connection   Processlist ID   Thread ID   Event ID
-- -------------------------------------------------
--           1              38          84          6

-- Connection 1
Connection 1> START TRANSACTION;
Query OK, 0 rows affected (0.0003 sec)

Connection 1> UPDATE world.city
                 SET Population = Population + 1
              WHERE ID = 130;
Query OK, 1 row affected (0.0028 sec)

Rows matched: 1  Changed: 1  Warnings: 0


Connection 1> SELECT object_type, object_schema, object_name,
                 lock_type, lock_duration, lock_status
              FROM performance_schema.metadata_locks
              WHERE OWNER_THREAD_ID = PS_CURRENT_THREAD_ID()
                 AND OBJECT_SCHEMA <> 'performance_schema'\G
*************************** 1. row ***************************
  object_type: TABLE
object_schema: world
  object_name: city
    lock_type: SHARED_WRITE
```

```
   lock_duration: TRANSACTION
     lock_status: GRANTED
*************************** 2. row ***************************
      object_type: TABLE
    object_schema: world
      object_name: country
        lock_type: SHARED_READ
   lock_duration: TRANSACTION
     lock_status: GRANTED
2 rows in set (0.0008 sec)

Connection 1> SELECT engine, object_schema, object_name,
                     lock_type, lock_mode, lock_status
                FROM performance_schema.data_locks
               WHERE THREAD_ID = PS_CURRENT_THREAD_ID()\G
*************************** 1. row ***************************
          engine: INNODB
   object_schema: world
     object_name: city
       lock_type: TABLE
       lock_mode: IX
     lock_status: GRANTED
*************************** 2. row ***************************
          engine: INNODB
   object_schema: world
     object_name: city
       lock_type: RECORD
       lock_mode: X,REC_NOT_GAP
     lock_status: GRANTED
2 rows in set (0.0005 sec)

mysql> ROLLBACK;
Query OK, 0 rows affected (0.3218 sec)
```

Most of the example reflects the example of obtaining shared locks, but there are also some surprises. To start with the data_locks table, it shows an exclusive insert intention (IX) lock on the table and an exclusive (X) record lock. This is as expected.

It becomes more complicated with the `metadata_locks` table where there are now two table locks, a `SHARED_WRITE` lock on the `city` table and a `SHARED_READ` lock on the `country` table. How can a lock both be shared and write at the same time, why is the lock on the `city` table shared when it was modified, and why is there a lock on the `country` table?

A `SHARED_WRITE` lock tells that the data is locked for updates but that the metadata lock itself is a shared lock. The reason for this is that the metadata for the table is not modified, so it is safe to allow other concurrent shared access to the table metadata. Remember that the `metadata_locks` table does not care about the locks held on individual records, so from a metadata perspective, the access to the `city` table is shared.

The metadata lock on the `country` table comes from the foreign key on the `city` table to the `country` table. The shared lock prevents modifications to the `country` metadata, such as dropping the column involved in the foreign key, while the transaction is still ongoing. Chapter 10 will go into more detail about the effect of foreign keys on locking.

Intention Locks

In the two examples this far in this chapter, there have been intention locks. What are those? It is a lock that signals the intention of an InnoDB transaction and can be either shared or exclusive. It can at first seem an unnecessary complication, but the intention locks allow InnoDB to resolve the lock requests in order without blocking compatible operations. The details are beyond the scope of this discussion. The important thing is that you know that the intention locks exist, so when you see them you know where they come from.

Intention locks from a more functional perspective are covered in Chapter 6, and a related concept, insert intention locks are covered with the InnoDB locks in Chapter 7.

Lock Compatibility

The lock compatibility matrix defines whether two lock requests conflict with each other. The introduction of intention locks makes this a little more complex than saying that shared locks are compatible with each other and exclusive locks are not compatible with any other locks.

Two intention locks are always compatible with each other. This means that even if a transaction has an intention exclusive lock, it will not prevent another transaction to take an intention lock. It will however stop the other transaction from upgrading its intention lock to a full lock. Table 5-1 shows the compatibility between the lock types. Shared locks are denoted S and exclusive locks X. Intention locks are prefixed I, so IS is an intention shared lock and IX is an intention exclusive lock.

Table 5-1. *InnoDB lock compatibility*

	Exclusive (X)	Intention Exclusive (IX)	Shared (S)	Intention Shared (IS)
Exclusive (X)	✗	✗	✗	✗
Intention Exclusive (IX)	✗	✔	✗	✔
Shared (S)	✗	✗	✔	✔
Intention Shared (IS)	✗	✔	✔	✔

In the table, a checkmark indicates that the two locks are compatible, whereas a cross mark indicates the two locks are conflicting with each other. The only conflicts of intention locks are with the exclusive and shared locks. An exclusive lock conflicts with all other locks including both intention lock types. A shared lock conflicts only with an exclusive lock and an intention exclusive lock.

This does sound fairly simple; however, this only applies to two of the same kind of locks. When you start to include different locks at the InnoDB level, it becomes more complex as will be discussed in Chapter 8 when lock contention is discussed.

This is all handled automatically by MySQL and InnoDB; however, you need to understand these rules when investigating lock issues.

Summary

This chapter has discussed the MySQL lock access levels. A lock can either be a shared lock, an exclusive lock, an intention shared lock, or an intention exclusive lock.

A shared lock is for read access to a resource and allows multiple threads to access the same resource concurrently. An exclusive lock on the other hand only allows a single thread to access the resource at a time which makes it safe to update the resource.

Intention locks are an InnoDB concept that allows InnoDB to resolve lock requests with less blocked requests as a result. All intention locks are compatible with each other, even intention exclusive locks, but intention exclusive locks block shared locks.

In this as well as the previous chapters, you have also encountered examples of how locks guard different resources such as tables and records. In the next chapter, it is time to learn more about the high-level lock access types such as table and metadata locks.

CHAPTER 6

High-Level Lock Types

In the previous chapter, you learned about the shared and exclusive access levels. In principle, you can make a locking system that does not consist of anything but one type of lock that can either be shared or exclusive. It would however mean that it would have to work at the instance level and thus be very poorly at allowing concurrent read-write access to the data. In this and the next chapter, you will learn how there are many kinds of locks depending on the resource they protect. While this does make locking much more complex, it does also allow for a much fine grainer locks that leads to support for a higher concurrency.

This chapter discusses the high-level locks in MySQL starting with the user-level locks and going through the various types of locks that are handled at the MySQL level (i.e., above the storage engine). Included are flush locks, metadata locks, explicit and implicit table locks (which are an exception as they are handled by InnoDB), backup locks, and log locks.

User-Level Locks

User-level locks are an explicit lock type the application can use to protect, for example, a workflow. They are not often used, but they can be useful for some complex tasks where you want to serialize access. All user locks are exclusive locks and are obtained using a name which can be up to 64 characters long.

You manipulate user-level locks with a set of functions:

- **`GET_LOCK(name, timeout)`:** Obtains a lock by specifying the name of the lock. The second argument is a timeout in seconds; if the lock is not obtained within that time, the function returns 0. If the lock is obtained, the return value is 1. If the timeout is negative, the function will wait indefinitely for the lock to become available.

© Jesper Wisborg Krogh 2021
J. W. Krogh, *MySQL Concurrency*, https://doi.org/10.1007/978-1-4842-6652-6_6

- **IS_FREE_LOCK(name):** Checks whether the named lock is available or not. The function returns 1 if the lock is available and 0 if it is not available.

- **IS_USED_LOCK(name):** This is the opposite of the IS_FREE_LOCK() function. The function returns the connection id of the connection holding the lock if the lock is in use (not available) and NULL if it is not in use (available).

- **RELEASE_ALL_LOCKS():** Releases all user-level locks held by the connection. The return value is the number of locks released.

- **RELEASE_LOCK(name):** Releases the lock with the provided name. The return value is 1 if the lock is released, 0 if the lock exists but is not owned by the connection, or NULL if the lock does not exist.

It is possible to obtain multiple locks by invoking GET_LOCK() multiple times. If you do that, be careful to ensure locks are obtained in the same order by all users as otherwise a deadlock can occur. If a deadlock occurs, an ER_USER_LOCK_DEADLOCK error (error code 3058) is returned. An example of this is shown in Listing 6-1.

Listing 6-1. A deadlock for user-level locks

```
-- Connection    Processlist ID    Thread ID    Event ID
-- ------------------------------------------------------
--          1               322          617           6
--          2               323          618           6

-- Connection 1
Connection 1> SELECT GET_LOCK('my_lock_1', -1);
+---------------------------+
| GET_LOCK('my_lock_1', -1) |
+---------------------------+
|                         1 |
+---------------------------+
1 row in set (0.0003 sec)

-- Connection 2
Connection 2> SELECT GET_LOCK('my_lock_2', -1);
```

```
+---------------------------+
| GET_LOCK('my_lock_2', -1) |
+---------------------------+
|                         1 |
+---------------------------+
1 row in set (0.0003 sec)

Connection 2> SELECT GET_LOCK('my_lock_1', -1);

-- Connection 1
Connection 1> SELECT GET_LOCK('my_lock_2', -1);
```
ERROR: 3058: Deadlock found when trying to get user-level lock; try rolling back transaction/releasing locks and restarting lock acquisition.

When Connection 2 attempts to get the my_lock_1 lock, the statement will block until Connection 1 attempts to get the my_lock_2 lock triggering the deadlock. If you obtain multiple locks, you should be prepared to handle deadlocks. Note that for user-level locks, a deadlock does not trigger a rollback of the transaction.

The granted and pending user-level locks can be found in the performance_schema. metadata_locks table with the OBJECT_TYPE column set to USER LEVEL LOCK as shown in Listing 6-2. The locks listed assume you left the system as it was at the time the deadlock in Listing 6-1 was triggered. Note that some values such as OBJECT_INSTANCE_BEGIN will be different for you and you will have to change the ids for owner_thread_id in the WHERE clause to match yours from Listing 6-1.

Listing 6-2. Listing user-level locks

```
-- Investigation #1
-- Connection 3
Connection 3> SELECT *
              FROM performance_schema.metadata_locks
              WHERE object_type = 'USER LEVEL LOCK'
                AND owner_thread_id IN (617, 618)\G
*************************** 1. row ***************************
        OBJECT_TYPE: USER LEVEL LOCK
      OBJECT_SCHEMA: NULL
        OBJECT_NAME: my_lock_1
        COLUMN_NAME: NULL
```

```
OBJECT_INSTANCE_BEGIN: 2124404669104
            LOCK_TYPE: EXCLUSIVE
        LOCK_DURATION: EXPLICIT
          LOCK_STATUS: GRANTED
               SOURCE: item_func.cc:5067
      OWNER_THREAD_ID: 617
       OWNER_EVENT_ID: 8
*************************** 2. row ***************************
          OBJECT_TYPE: USER LEVEL LOCK
        OBJECT_SCHEMA: NULL
          OBJECT_NAME: my_lock_2
          COLUMN_NAME: NULL
OBJECT_INSTANCE_BEGIN: 2124463901664
            LOCK_TYPE: EXCLUSIVE
        LOCK_DURATION: EXPLICIT
          LOCK_STATUS: GRANTED
               SOURCE: item_func.cc:5067
      OWNER_THREAD_ID: 618
       OWNER_EVENT_ID: 8
*************************** 3. row ***************************
          OBJECT_TYPE: USER LEVEL LOCK
        OBJECT_SCHEMA: NULL
          OBJECT_NAME: my_lock_1
          COLUMN_NAME: NULL
OBJECT_INSTANCE_BEGIN: 2124463901088
            LOCK_TYPE: EXCLUSIVE
        LOCK_DURATION: EXPLICIT
          LOCK_STATUS: PENDING
               SOURCE: item_func.cc:5067
      OWNER_THREAD_ID: 618
       OWNER_EVENT_ID: 9
3 rows in set (0.0015 sec)
```

The OBJECT_TYPE for user-level locks is USER LEVEL LOCK, and the lock duration is EXPLICIT as it is up to the user or application to release the lock again. In row 1, the connection with Performance Schema thread id 617 has been granted the my_lock_1 lock, and in row 3 thread id 618 is waiting (pending) for it to be granted. Thread id 618 also has a granted lock which is included in row 2. Once you are done with the investigation, remember to release the locks, for example, executing SELECT RELEASE_ ALL_LOCKS() first in connection 1 and then in connection 2 (this happens automatically when exiting the workload using the MySQL Shell concurrency_book module).

The next level of locks involves non-data table-level locks. The first of these that will be discussed is the flush lock.

Flush Locks

A flush lock will be familiar to most who have been involved in taking backups. It is taken when you use the FLUSH TABLES statement and last for the duration of the statement unless you add WITH READ LOCK in which case a shared (read) lock is held until the lock is explicitly released. An implicit table flush is also triggered at the end of the ANALYZE TABLE statement. The flush lock is a table-level lock. The read lock taken with FLUSH TABLES WITH READ LOCK is discussed later under explicit table locks.

A common cause of lock issues for the flush lock is long-running queries. A FLUSH TABLES statement cannot flush a table as long as there is a query that has the table open. This means that if you execute a FLUSH TABLES statement while there is a long-running query using one or more of the tables being flushed, then the FLUSH TABLES statement will block all other statements needing any of those tables until the lock situation has been resolved.

Flush locks are subject to the lock_wait_timeout setting. If it takes more than lock_wait_timeout seconds to obtain the lock, MySQL will abandon the lock. The same applies if the FLUSH TABLES statement is killed. However, due to the internals of MySQL, a lower-level lock called the table definition cache (TDC) version lock cannot always be released until the long-running query completes.[1] That means that the only way to be sure the lock problem is resolved is to kill the long-running query, but be aware that if the query has changed many rows, it may take a long time to roll back the query.

When there is lock contention around the flush lock, both the FLUSH TABLES statement and the queries started subsequently will have the state set to "Waiting for table flush." Listing 6-3 shows an example of this involving three queries. If you are reproducing the scenario yourself (as opposed to using the MySQL Shell concurrency_book module),

---

[1]https://bugs.mysql.com/bug.php?id=44884

then you can change the argument to SLEEP() in connection 1 to give yourself more time to complete the example.

Listing 6-3. Example of waiting for a flush lock

```
-- Connection   Processlist ID   Thread ID   Event ID
-- ------------------------------------------------------
--          1              375         691          6
--          2              376         692          6
--          3              377         693          6
--          4              378         694          6

-- Connection 1
Connection 1> SELECT city.*, SLEEP(3) FROM world.city WHERE ID = 130;

-- Connection 2
Connection 2> FLUSH TABLES world.city;

-- Connection 3
Connection 3> SELECT * FROM world.city WHERE ID = 201;

-- Connection 4
-- Query sys.session for the three threads involved in the lock situation
Connection 4> SELECT thd_id, conn_id, state,
                     current_statement
                FROM sys.session
               WHERE current_statement IS NOT NULL
                 AND thd_id IN (691, 692, 693)
               ORDER BY thd_id\G
*************************** 1. row ***************************
         thd_id: 691
        conn_id: 375
          state: User sleep
current_statement: SELECT city.*, SLEEP(3) FROM world.city WHERE ID = 130
*************************** 2. row ***************************
         thd_id: 692
        conn_id: 376
```

```
           state: Waiting for table flush
current_statement: FLUSH TABLES world.city
*************************** 3. row ***************************
          thd_id: 693
         conn_id: 377
           state: Waiting for table flush
current_statement: SELECT * FROM world.city WHERE ID = 201
3 rows in set (0.0586 sec)
```

The example uses the sys.session view; similar results can be obtained using performance_schema.threads and SHOW PROCESSLIST. In order to reduce the output to only include the queries of relevance for the flush lock discussion, the WHERE clause is set to only include the threads ids of the first three connections.

The connection with conn_id = 375 is executing a slow query that uses the world.city table (a SLEEP(3) was used to ensure it took enough time to execute the statements for the other connections). In the meantime, conn_id = 376 executed a FLUSH TABLES statement for the world.city table. Because the first query still has the table open (it is released once the query completes), the FLUSH TABLES statement ends up waiting for the table flush lock. Finally, conn_id = 377 attempts to query the table and thus must wait for the FLUSH TABLES statement.

Another non-data table lock is a metadata lock.

Metadata Locks

Metadata locks are one of the newer lock types in MySQL. They were introduced in MySQL 5.5, and their purpose is to protect the schema, so it does not get changed while queries or transactions rely on the schema to be unchanged. Metadata locks work at the table level, but they should be considered as an independent lock type to table locks as they do not protect the data in the tables.

SELECT statements and DML queries take a shared metadata lock, whereas DDL statements take an exclusive lock. A connection takes a metadata lock on a table when the table is first used and keeps the lock until the end of the transaction. While the metadata lock is held, no other connection is allowed to change the schema definition of the table. However, other connections that execute SELECT statements and DML statements are not restricted. Usually the biggest gotcha with respect to metadata locks is long-running transactions, possibly being idle, preventing DDL statements from starting their work.

If you encounter a conflict around a metadata lock, you will see the query state in the process list set to "Waiting for table metadata lock." An example of this including queries to setup is shown in Listing 6-4.

Listing 6-4. Example of waiting for table metadata lock

```
-- Connection    Processlist ID    Thread ID    Event ID
-- -------------------------------------------------------
--          1               428          768           6
--          2               429          769           6

-- Connection 1
Connection 1> START TRANSACTION;
Query OK, 0 rows affected (0.0003 sec)

Connection 1> SELECT * FROM world.city WHERE ID = 130\G
*************************** 1. row ***************************
         ID: 130
       Name: Sydney
CountryCode: AUS
   District: New South Wales
 Population: 3276207
1 row in set (0.0006 sec)

-- Connection 2
Connection 2> OPTIMIZE TABLE world.city;
```

Connection 2 blocks, and while you are in this situation, you can query `sys.session` or similar as shown in Listing 6-5.

Listing 6-5. `sys.session` for the connections involved in the metadata lock

```
-- Investigation #1
-- Connection 3
Connection 3> SELECT thd_id, conn_id, state,
                     current_statement, statement_latency,
                     last_statement, trx_state
```

```
              FROM sys.session
              WHERE conn_id IN (428, 429)
              ORDER BY conn_id\G
*************************** 1. row ***************************
            thd_id: 768
           conn_id: 428
             state: NULL
 current_statement: SELECT * FROM world.city WHERE ID = 130
 statement_latency: NULL
    last_statement: SELECT * FROM world.city WHERE ID = 130
         trx_state: ACTIVE
*************************** 2. row ***************************
            thd_id: 769
           conn_id: 429
             state: Waiting for table metadata lock
 current_statement: OPTIMIZE TABLE world.city
 statement_latency: 26.62 s
    last_statement: NULL
         trx_state: COMMITTED
2 rows in set (0.0607 sec)
```

In this example, the connection with conn_id = 428 has an ongoing transaction and in the previous statement queried the world.city table (the current statement in this case is the same as it is not cleared until the next statement is executed). While the transaction is still active, conn_id = 429 has executed an OPTIMIZE TABLE statement which is now waiting for the metadata lock. (Yes, OPTIMIZE TABLE does not change the schema definition, but as a DDL statement, it is still affected by the metadata lock.) Since MySQL does not have transactional DDL statements, the transaction state for conn_id = 429 shows up as committed.

It is convenient when it is the current or last statement that is the cause of the metadata lock. In more general cases, you can use the performance_schema.metadata_locks table with the OBJECT_TYPE column set to TABLE to find granted and pending metadata locks. Listing 6-6 shows an example of granted and pending metadata locks using the same setup as in the previous example. Chapter 14 goes into more detail about investigating metadata locks.

Listing 6-6. Example of metadata locks

```
-- Investigation #2
Connection 3> SELECT object_type, object_schema, object_name,
                     lock_type, lock_duration, lock_status,
                     owner_thread_id
                FROM performance_schema.metadata_locks
               WHERE owner_thread_id IN (768, 769)
                 AND object_type = 'TABLE'\G
*************************** 1. row ***************************
    object_type: TABLE
  object_schema: world
    object_name: city
      lock_type: SHARED_READ
  lock_duration: TRANSACTION
    lock_status: GRANTED
owner_thread_id: 768
*************************** 2. row ***************************
    object_type: TABLE
  object_schema: world
    object_name: city
      lock_type: SHARED_NO_READ_WRITE
  lock_duration: TRANSACTION
    lock_status: PENDING
owner_thread_id: 769
2 rows in set (0.0010 sec)
```

In the example, thread id 768 (the same as conn_id = 428 from the sys.session output) owns a shared read lock on the world.city table due to an ongoing transaction, and thread id 769 is waiting for a lock as it is trying to execute a DDL statement on the table.

When you are done, make sure you roll back or commit the transaction in Connection 1, so the OPTIMIZE TABLE can complete:

```
-- Connection 1
Connection 1> ROLLBACK;
Query OK, 0 rows affected (0.0004 sec)
```

A special case of metadata locks are locks taken explicitly with the LOCK TABLES statement.

Explicit Table Locks

Explicit table locks are taken with the LOCK TABLES and the FLUSH TABLES WITH READ LOCK statements. With the LOCK TABLES statement, it is possible to take shared or exclusive locks; FLUSH TABLES WITH READ LOCK always takes a shared lock. The tables are locked, until they are explicitly released with the UNLOCK TABLES statement. When FLUSH TABLES WITH READ LOCK is executed without listing any tables, the global read lock (i.e., affecting all tables) is taken. While these locks also protect the data, they are considered as metadata locks in MySQL.

Explicit table locks, other than FLUSH TABLES WITH READ LOCK in connection with backups, are not often used with InnoDB as InnoDB's sophisticated lock features are in most cases superior to handling locks yourself. However, if you really need to lock the entire tables, explicit locks can be useful as they are very cheap for MySQL to check.

An example of a connection taking an explicit read lock on the world.country and world.countrylanguage tables and a write lock on the world.city table is shown in Listing 6-7.

Listing 6-7. Using explicit table locks

```
-- Connection   Processlist ID   Thread ID   Event ID
-- -----------------------------------------------------
--          1              432         772          6

-- Connection 1
Connection 1> LOCK TABLES world.country READ,
                          world.countrylanguage READ,
                          world.city WRITE;
Query OK, 0 rows affected (0.0029 sec)
```

When you take explicit locks, you are only allowed to use the tables you have locked and in accordance with the requested locks. This means you will get an error if you take a read lock and attempt to write to the table (ER_TABLE_NOT_LOCKED_FOR_WRITE) or if you try to use a table you did not take a lock for (ER_TABLE_NOT_LOCKED), for example (continuation of Listing 6-7)

```
Connection 1> UPDATE world.country
              SET Population = Population + 1
            WHERE Code = 'AUS';
```
ERROR: 1099: Table 'country' was locked with a READ lock and can't be updated

```
Connection 1> SELECT *
                FROM sakila.film
              WHERE film_id = 1;
```
ERROR: 1100: Table 'film' was not locked with LOCK TABLES

Since explicit locks are considered metadata locks, the symptoms and information in the performance_schema.metadata_locks table are the same as for implicit metadata locks, and you also unlock the tables using the UNLOCK TABLES statement:

```
Connection 1> UNLOCK TABLES;
Query OK, 0 rows affected (0.0006 sec)
```

Another table-level lock but handled implicitly is plainly called a table lock.

Implicit Table Locks

MySQL takes implicit table locks when a table is queried. Table locks do not play a large role for InnoDB tables except for flush, metadata, and explicit locks as InnoDB uses record locks to allow concurrent access to a table as long as the transactions do not modify the same rows (roughly speaking – as the next chapter shows – there is more to it than that).

InnoDB does however work with the concept of intention locks at the table level. Since you are likely to encounter those when investigating lock issues, it is worth familiarizing yourself with them. As mentioned in the discussion of lock access levels, intention locks mark what the intention of the transaction is.

For locks taken by transactions, first, an intention lock is taken, and then it may if needed be upgraded. This is unlike an explicit LOCK TABLES that does not change. To get a shared lock, the transaction first takes an intention shared lock and then the shared lock. Similarly, for an exclusive lock, an intention exclusive lock is first taken. Some examples of intention locks are as follows:

- A SELECT ... FOR SHARE statement takes an intention shared lock on the tables queried. The SELECT ... LOCK IN SHARE MODE syntax is a synonym.

- A SELECT ... FOR UPDATE statement takes an intention exclusive lock on the tables queried.

- A DML statement (not including SELECT) takes an intention exclusive lock on the modified tables. If a foreign key column is modified, an intention shared lock is taken on the parent table.

The table-level locks can be found in the performance_schema.data_locks table with the LOCK_TYPE column set to TABLE. Listing 6-8 shows an example of an intention shared lock.

Listing 6-8. Example of an InnoDB intention shared lock

```
-- Connection    Processlist ID   Thread ID   Event ID
-- --------------------------------------------------
--          1              446        796          6
--          2              447        797          6

-- Connection 1
Connection 1> START TRANSACTION;
Query OK, 0 rows affected (0.0003 sec)

Connection 1> SELECT *
                FROM world.city
               WHERE ID = 130
                 FOR SHARE\G
*************************** 1. row ***************************
        ID: 130
      Name: Sydney
CountryCode: AUS
  District: New South Wales
 Population: 3276207
1 row in set (0.0010 sec)

-- Connection 2
```

```
Connection 2> SELECT engine, thread_id, object_schema,
                     object_name, lock_type, lock_mode,
                     lock_status, lock_data
                FROM performance_schema.data_locks
               WHERE lock_type = 'TABLE'
                 AND thread_id = 796\G
*************************** 1. row ***************************
        engine: INNODB
     thread_id: 796
 object_schema: world
   object_name: city
     lock_type: TABLE
     lock_mode: IS
   lock_status: GRANTED
     lock_data: NULL
1 row in set (0.0011 sec)

-- Connection 1
Connection 1> ROLLBACK;
Query OK, 0 rows affected (0.0004 sec)
```

This shows an intention shared lock on the world.city table. Notice that the engine is set to INNODB and that lock_data is NULL.

Backup Locks

The backup lock is an instance-level lock; that is, it affects the system as a whole. It is a new lock introduced in MySQL 8. The backup lock prevents statements that can make a backup inconsistent while still allowing other statements to be executed concurrently with the backup. Currently the primary user of the backup lock is MySQL Enterprise Backup which uses it together with the log lock to avoid executing FLUSH TABLES WITH READ LOCK for InnoDB tables. The statements that are blocked include

- Statements that create, rename, or remove files. These include CREATE TABLE, CREATE TABLESPACE, RENAME TABLE, and DROP TABLE statements.

- Account management statements such as CREATE USER, ALTER USER, DROP USER, and GRANT.

- DDL statements that do not log their changes to the redo log. These, for example, include adding an index.

A backup lock is created with the LOCK INSTANCE FOR BACKUP statement, and the lock is released with the UNLOCK INSTANCE statement. It requires the BACKUP_ADMIN privileges to execute LOCK INSTANCE FOR BACKUP. An example of obtaining the backup lock and releasing it again is

```
mysql> LOCK INSTANCE FOR BACKUP;
Query OK, 0 rows affected (0.0002 sec)

mysql> UNLOCK INSTANCE;
Query OK, 0 rows affected (0.0003 sec)
```

Note   At the time of writing, taking a backup lock and releasing it is not allowed when using the X Protocol (connecting through the port specified with mysqlx_port or the socket specified with mysqlx_socket). Attempting to do so returns an ER_PLUGGABLE_PROTOCOL_COMMAND_NOT_SUPPORTED error: ERROR: 3130: Command not supported by pluggable protocols.

Additionally, statements that conflict with the backup lock also take the backup lock. Since DDL statements sometimes consist of several steps, for example, rebuilding a table in a new file and renaming the file, the backup lock can be released between the steps to avoid blocking LOCK INSTANCE FOR BACKUP for longer than necessary.

Backup locks can be found in the performance_schema.metadata_locks table with the OBJECT_TYPE column set to BACKUP LOCK. Listing 6-9 shows an example of a query waiting for a backup lock held by LOCK INSTANCE FOR BACKUP.

Listing 6-9. Example of a conflict for the backup lock

```
-- Connection   Processlist ID   Thread ID   Event ID
-- ----------------------------------------------------
--          1              484         851           1
--          2              485         852           1
--          3              486         853           1
```

```
-- Connection 1
Connection 1> LOCK INSTANCE FOR BACKUP;
Query OK, 0 rows affected (0.0004 sec)

-- Connection 2
Connection 2> OPTIMIZE TABLE world.city;

-- Connection 3
Connection 3> SELECT object_type, object_schema, object_name,
                     lock_type, lock_duration, lock_status,
                     owner_thread_id
                FROM performance_schema.metadata_locks
               WHERE object_type = 'BACKUP LOCK'
                 AND owner_thread_id IN (851, 852)\G
*************************** 1. row ***************************
    object_type: BACKUP LOCK
  object_schema: NULL
    object_name: NULL
      lock_type: SHARED
  lock_duration: EXPLICIT
    lock_status: GRANTED
owner_thread_id: 851
*************************** 2. row ***************************
    object_type: BACKUP LOCK
  object_schema: NULL
    object_name: NULL
      lock_type: INTENTION_EXCLUSIVE
  lock_duration: TRANSACTION
    lock_status: PENDING
owner_thread_id: 852
2 rows in set (0.0007 sec)

-- Connection 1
Connection 1> UNLOCK INSTANCE;
Query OK, 0 rows affected (0.0003 sec)
```

In the example, the connection with thread id 851 owns the backup lock, whereas the connection with thread id 852 is waiting for it. Notice that LOCK INSTANCE FOR BACKUP holds a shared lock, whereas the DDL statement requests an intention exclusive lock.

Related to the backup lock is the log lock which has also been introduced to reduce locking during backups.

Log Locks

When you create a backup, you typically want to include information about the log positions and GTID set the backup is consistent with. In MySQL 5.7 and earlier, you needed the global read lock while obtaining this information. In MySQL 8, the log lock was introduced to allow you to read information such as the executed global transaction identifiers (GTIDs), the binary log position, and the log sequence number (LSN) for InnoDB without taking a global read lock.

The log lock prevents operations that make changes to log-related information. In practice this means commits, FLUSH LOGS, and similar. The log lock is taken implicitly by querying the performance_schema.log_status table. It requires the BACKUP_ADMIN privilege to access the table. Listing 6-10 shows an example output of the log_status table.

Listing 6-10. Example output of the log_status table

```
-- Connection   Processlist ID   Thread ID   Event ID
-- -----------------------------------------------------
--          1              490         857          6

-- Connection 1
Connection 1 > SELECT *
              FROM performance_schema.log_status\G
*************************** 1. row ***************************
    SERVER_UUID: fcbb7afc-bdde-11ea-b95f-ace2d35785be
          LOCAL: {"gtid_executed": "d2549c41-86ca-11ea-9dc7-
          ace2d35785be:1-351", "binary_log_file": "binlog.000002",
          "binary_log_position": 39348}
    REPLICATION: {"channels": [{"channel_name": "", "relay_log_file":
    "relay-bin.000002", "relay_log_position": 39588}]}
```

```
STORAGE_ENGINES: {"InnoDB": {"LSN": 2073604726, "LSN_checkpoint":
2073604726}}
1 row in set (0.0012 sec)
```

The information available depends on the configuration of the instance, and the values depend on the usage.

That concludes the review of the main high-lock types in MySQL.

Summary

In this chapter the high-level lock types have been discussed. These are mostly independent of the storage engine used and include a range of locks from user-level and instance-level locks to table and metadata locks.

The user-level locks can be used to protect workflows in the application and are the most generic lock type. The flush locks are experienced when tables are flushed and can cause hard to diagnose issues due to the low-level table definition cache (TDC) version lock. The metadata locks protect the metadata of schema objects such as the column definitions for a table.

There are both explicit table locks and implicit table locks of which the implicit locks are the most common when working with InnoDB tables. The implicit locks also include the intention locks.

At the instance level, there are two lock types that were developed with backups in mind. The backup locks protect against changes that will make a backup inconsistent such as changes to users and privileges and certain schema changes. The log lock is an implicit lock taken when querying the performance_schema.log_status to ensure log-related status values can be obtained in a consistent way with minimal locking.

In addition to the high-level locks, InnoDB has its own set of locks working at the record level that will be discussed in the next chapter.

CHAPTER 7

InnoDB Locks

The locks studied in the previous chapter were all, apart from the InnoDB intention locks, general for MySQL. InnoDB has its own sophisticated locking system that allows for a highly concurrent access to the data. In online transaction processing (OLTP) workloads, benchmarks show that depending on the workload, InnoDB handles up to over 100 concurrent queries well.[1] This is not only related to the record-level locks but also low-level semaphores, and the latter is an area of ongoing improvement which is the main reason that newer versions of MySQL handle concurrency better than old versions.

Tip   Newer versions of MySQL support higher degrees of concurrent query execution than older versions. Latest in 8.0.21, the lock system mutex was sharded to reduce contention on high-concurrency systems.

In this chapter, first, the InnoDB record locks and next-key locks will be discussed followed by gap locks and predicate locks. The last of the data-level locks that are covered is auto-increment locks which are also important to maintain a good performance at high concurrency inserts. The final topic of the chapter is semaphores.

Record Locks and Next-Key Locks

Record locks are often called row locks; however, it is more than just locks on rows as it also includes index and gap locks. Related are next-key locks. A next-key lock is the combination of a record lock and a gap lock on the gap before the record. A next-key lock is actually the default lock type in InnoDB, and thus you will just see it as S (shared) and X (exclusive) in the lock outputs.

---

[1]http://dimitrik.free.fr/blog/posts/mysql-performance-80-ga-and-tpcc-workloads.html

Record and next-key locks are typically the locks that are meant when talking about InnoDB locks. They are fine-grained locks that aim at just locking the least amount of data while still ensuring the data integrity.

A record or next-key lock can be shared or exclusive and affect just the rows and indexes accessed by the transaction. The duration of exclusive locks is usually the transaction with exceptions, for example, delete-marked records used for uniqueness checks in INSERT INTO ... ON DUPLICATE KEY and REPLACE statements. For shared locks, the duration can depend on the transaction isolation level as discussed in Chapters 9 and 12.

Record and next-key locks can be found using the performance_schema.data_locks table. Listing 7-1 shows an example of the locks from updating rows in the world.city table using the secondary index CountryCode.

Listing 7-1. Example of InnoDB record locks

```
-- Connection    Processlist ID    Thread ID    Event ID
-- -------------------------------------------------------
--            1               544          919           6
--            2               545          920           6

-- Connection 1
Connection 1> START TRANSACTION;
Query OK, 0 rows affected (0.0002 sec)

Connection 1> UPDATE world.city
                 SET Population = Population + 1
               WHERE CountryCode = 'LUX';
Query OK, 1 row affected (0.0008 sec)

Rows matched: 1  Changed: 1  Warnings: 0


-- Connection 2
Connection 2> SELECT thread_id, event_id,
                 object_schema, object_name, index_name,
                 lock_type, lock_mode, lock_status, lock_data
              FROM performance_schema.data_locks
              WHERE thread_id = 919\G
```

```
*************************** 1. row ***************************
     thread_id: 919
      event_id: 10
 object_schema: world
   object_name: city
    index_name: NULL
     lock_type: TABLE
     lock_mode: IX
   lock_status: GRANTED
     lock_data: NULL
*************************** 2. row ***************************
     thread_id: 919
      event_id: 10
 object_schema: world
   object_name: city
    index_name: CountryCode
     lock_type: RECORD
     lock_mode: X
   lock_status: GRANTED
     lock_data: 'LUX', 2452
*************************** 3. row ***************************
     thread_id: 919
      event_id: 10
 object_schema: world
   object_name: city
    index_name: PRIMARY
     lock_type: RECORD
     lock_mode: X,REC_NOT_GAP
   lock_status: GRANTED
     lock_data: 2452
*************************** 4. row ***************************
     thread_id: 919
      event_id: 10
 object_schema: world
   object_name: city
```

```
   index_name: CountryCode
    lock_type: RECORD
    lock_mode: X,GAP
  lock_status: GRANTED
    lock_data: 'LVA', 2434
4 rows in set (0.0014 sec)

-- Connection 1
Connection 1> ROLLBACK;
Query OK, 0 rows affected (0.1702 sec)
```

The first row is the intention exclusive table lock that has already been discussed. The second row is a next-key lock on the CountryCode index for the value ('LUX', 2452) where 'LUX' is the country code used in the WHERE clause and 2452 is the primary key id added to the nonunique secondary index. The city with ID = 2452 is the only city matching the WHERE clause, and the primary key record (the row itself) is shown in the third row of the output. The lock mode is X,REC_NOT_GAP which means it is an exclusive lock on the record but not on the gap.

What is a gap? An example is shown in the fourth row of the output. Gap locks are so important that the discussion of the gap lock is split out into its own.

Gap Locks

A gap lock protects the space between two records. This can be in the row through the clustered index or in a secondary index. Before the first record in an index page and after the last in the page, there are pseudo-records called the *infimum record* and *supremum record*, respectively. Gap locks are often the lock type causing the most confusion. Experience from studying lock issues is the best way to become familiar with them.

Consider the query from the previous example:

```
UPDATE world.city
   SET Population = Population + 1
 WHERE CountryCode = 'LUX';
```

This query changes the population of all cities with CountryCode = 'LUX'. What happens if a new city is inserted between the update and the commit of the transaction? If the UPDATE and INSERT statements commit in the same order they are executed, all is as such fine. However, if you commit the changes in the opposite order, then the result is inconsistent as it would be expected the inserted row would also have been updated.

This is where the gap lock comes into play. It guards the space where new records (including records moved from a different position) would be inserted, so it is not changed until the transaction holding the gap lock is completed. If you look at the fourth row in the output from the example in Listing 7-1, you can see an example of a gap lock:

```
*************************** 4. row ***************************
    thread_id: 919
     event_id: 10
object_schema: world
  object_name: city
   index_name: CountryCode
    lock_type: RECORD
    lock_mode: X,GAP
  lock_status: GRANTED
    lock_data: 'LVA', 2434
4 rows in set (0.0014 sec)
```

This is an exclusive gap lock on the CountryCode index for the value ('LVA', 2434). Since the query requested to update all rows with the CountryCode set to "LUX," the gap lock ensures that no new rows are inserted for the "LUX" country code. The country code "LVA" is the next value in the CountryCode index, so the gap between "LUX" and "LVA" is protected with an exclusive lock. On the other hand, it is still possible to insert new cities with CountryCode = 'LVA'. In some places, this is referred to as a "gap before record" which makes it easier to understand how the gap lock works.

One peculiarity of gap locks is that gap locks do not conflict with another gap lock even if both are exclusive. The purpose of gap locks is not to prevent access to the gap but exclusively to prevent inserting data into the gap. When discussing insert intention locks, you will see how a gap lock blocks the insert.

Gap locks are taken to a much less degree when you use the READ COMMITTED transaction isolation level rather than REPEATABLE READ or SERIALIZABLE.

Related to gap locks are predicate locks.

Predicate and Page Locks

A predicate lock is similar to a gap lock but applies to spatial indexes where an absolute ordering cannot be made and thus a gap lock does not make sense. Instead of a gap lock, for spatial indexes in the REPEATABLE READ and SERIALIZABLE transaction isolation levels, InnoDB creates a predicate lock on the minimum bounding rectangle (MBR) used for the query or for entire pages. This will allow consistent reads by preventing changes to the data within the minimum bounding rectangle or pages.

When querying the performance_schema.data_locks table, predicate locks will have either PREDICATE or PRDT_PAGE with the latter being a page lock.

As an example of predicate locks, consider the address table in the sakila database. This has the column location which is of the geometry data type with the Spatial Reference System Identifier (SRID) set to 0. (An SRID is required in MySQL 8 to have a spatial index.) The index on the location column is named idx_location. Listing 7-2 shows how a predicate lock is taken when updating one of the addresses.

Listing 7-2. Example of predicate/page locks

```
-- Connection   Processlist ID   Thread ID   Event ID
-- --------------------------------------------------
--          1             562          954          6
--          2             563          955          6

-- Connection 1
Connection 1> START TRANSACTION;
Query OK, 0 rows affected (0.0002 sec)

Connection 1> UPDATE sakila.address
                SET address = '42 Concurrency Boulevard',
                    district = 'Punjab',
                    city_id = 208,
                    postal_code = 40509,
                    location = ST_GeomFromText('POINT(75.91 31.53)', 0)
              WHERE address_id = 372;
Query OK, 1 row affected (0.0008 sec)
```

Rows matched: 1 Changed: 1 Warnings: 0

```
-- Connection 2
Connection 2> SELECT engine_lock_id, thread_id, event_id,
                     object_schema, object_name, index_name,
                     lock_type, lock_mode, lock_status, lock_data
                FROM performance_schema.data_locks
               WHERE thread_id = 954
                 AND index_name = 'idx_location'\G
*************************** 1. row ***************************
engine_lock_id: 2123429833312:1074:12:0:2123393008216
     thread_id: 954
      event_id: 10
 object_schema: sakila
   object_name: address
    index_name: idx_location
     lock_type: RECORD
     lock_mode: S,PRDT_PAGE
   lock_status: GRANTED
     lock_data: infimum pseudo-record
*************************** 2. row ***************************
engine_lock_id: 2123429833312:1074:13:0:2123393008560
     thread_id: 954
      event_id: 10
 object_schema: sakila
   object_name: address
    index_name: idx_location
     lock_type: RECORD
     lock_mode: S,PRDT_PAGE
   lock_status: GRANTED
     lock_data: infimum pseudo-record
2 rows in set (0.0006 sec)

-- Connection 1
Connection 1> ROLLBACK;
Query OK, 0 rows affected (0.0435 sec)
```

The important part of the update is that the `location` column is changed. In the output from the `data_locks` table, it can be seen a predicate page lock was taken.

One final lock type related to records that you should know is insert intention locks.

Insert Intention Locks

Remember that for table locks, InnoDB has intention locks for whether the transaction will use the table in a shared or exclusive manner. Similarly, InnoDB has insert intention locks at the record level. InnoDB uses these locks – as the name suggests – with `INSERT` statements to signal the intention to other transactions. As such, the lock is on a yet to be created record (so it is a gap lock) rather than on an existing record. The use of insert intention locks can help increase the concurrency that inserts can be performed at.

You are not very likely to see insert intention locks in lock outputs unless an `INSERT` statement is waiting for a lock to be granted. You can force a situation where this happens by creating a gap lock in another transaction that will prevent the `INSERT` statement from completing. The example in Listing 7-3 creates a gap lock in Connection 1 and then in Connection 2 attempts to insert a row which conflicts with the gap lock. Finally, in a third connection, the lock information is retrieved.

Listing 7-3. Example of an insert intention lock

```
-- Connection    Processlist ID    Thread ID    Event ID
-- -------------------------------------------------------
--             1              577          972           6
--             2              578          973           6
--             3              579          974           6

-- Connection 1
Connection 1> START TRANSACTION;
Query OK, 0 rows affected (0.0003 sec)

Connection 1> SELECT *
                FROM world.city
               WHERE ID > 4079
                 FOR UPDATE\G
0 rows in set (0.0007 sec)
```

```
-- Connection 2
Connection 2> START TRANSACTION;
Query OK, 0 rows affected (0.0002 sec)

Connection 2> INSERT INTO world.city
              VALUES (4080, 'Darwin', 'AUS',
                     'Northern Territory', 146000);

-- Connection 3
Connection 3> SELECT thread_id, event_id,
                    object_schema, object_name, index_name,
                    lock_type, lock_mode, lock_status, lock_data
               FROM performance_schema.data_locks
              WHERE thread_id IN (972, 973)
                    AND object_name = 'city'
                    AND index_name = 'PRIMARY'\G
*************************** 1. row ***************************
    thread_id: 972
     event_id: 10
object_schema: world
  object_name: city
   index_name: PRIMARY
    lock_type: RECORD
    lock_mode: X
  lock_status: GRANTED
    lock_data: supremum pseudo-record
*************************** 2. row ***************************
    thread_id: 973
     event_id: 10
object_schema: world
  object_name: city
   index_name: PRIMARY
    lock_mode: X,INSERT_INTENTION
  lock_status: WAITING
    lock_data: supremum pseudo-record
2 rows in set (0.0007 sec)
```

```
-- Connection 1
Connection 1> ROLLBACK;
Query OK, 0 rows affected (0.0003 sec)

-- Connection 2
Connection 2> ROLLBACK;
Query OK, 0 rows affected (0.3035 sec)
```

Notice that for the RECORD lock, the lock mode includes INSERT_INTENTION – the insert intention lock. In this case, the data locked is the supremum pseudo-record, but that can also be the value of the primary key depending on the situation. If you recall the next-key lock discussion, then X means a next-key lock, but this is a special case as the lock is on the supremum pseudo-record, and it is not possible to lock that, so effectively it is just a gap lock on the gap before the supremum pseudo-record.

Another lock that you need to be aware of when inserting data is the auto-increment lock.

Auto-Increment Locks

When you insert data into a table that has an auto-increment counter, it is necessary to protect the counter so two transactions are guaranteed to get unique values. If you use statement-based logging to the binary log, there are further restrictions as the auto-increment value is recreated for all rows except the first when the statement is replayed.

InnoDB supports three lock modes, so you can adjust the amount of locking according to your needs. You choose the lock mode with the innodb_autoinc_lock_mode option which takes the values 0, 1, and 2 with 2 being the default in MySQL 8. It requires a restart of MySQL to change the value. The meaning of the values is summarized in Table 7-1.

Table 7-1. *Supported values for the* `innodb_autoinc_lock_mode` *option*

Value	Mode	Description
0	Traditional	The locking behavior of MySQL 5.0 and earlier. The lock is held until the end of the statement, so values are assigned in repeatable and consecutive order.
1	Consecutive	For the `INSERT` statement where the number of rows is known at the start of the query, the required number of auto-increment values is assigned under a lightweight mutex, and the auto-increment lock is avoided. For statements where the number of rows is not known, the auto-increment lock is taken and held to the end of the statement. This was the default in MySQL 5.7 and earlier.
2	Interleaved	The auto-increment lock is never taken, and the auto-increment values for concurrent inserts may be interleaved. This mode is only safe when binary logging is disabled or `binlog_format` is set to ROW. It is the default value in MySQL 8.

The higher the value of `innodb_autoinc_lock_mode`, the less locking. The price to pay for that is increased number of gaps in the sequence of auto-increment values and for `innodb_autoinc_lock_mode = 2` the possibility of interleaved values. Unless you cannot use row-based binary logging or have special needs for consecutive auto-increment values, it is recommended to use the value of 2.

That concludes the discussion of data-level locks, but when discussing MySQL concurrency, there is one important topic left: mutexes and rw-lock semaphores.

Mutexes and RW-Lock Semaphores

Inside the MySQL source code, it is necessary to protect code paths. An example is to protect the code that modifies the content of the buffer pool to avoid two threads modifying the buffer pool content at the same time and thus potentially causing conflicting changes. In some way, you can compare mutexes to the user-level locks, except the former is for the MySQL code paths and the latter for the application code paths using MySQL.

> **Note**   InnoDB uses the terms mutex and semaphore somewhat interchangeably. For example, the SEMAPHORES section in the InnoDB monitor also includes information of mutex waits and SHOW ENGINE INNODB MUTEX includes semaphores.

It is not only InnoDB that uses synchronization objects in MySQL; for example, the table open cache is also guarded by a mutex. However, in most cases, when you encounter problems with contention on the synchronization objects, it is related to InnoDB as that is where the pressure of high concurrency operations is usually the largest, and for InnoDB there are readily available monitoring tools for investigating the contention. For this reason, only the InnoDB will be discussed here.

The mutexes and semaphores are much more difficult to study than the data locks as it is not possible to pause the code execution while the locks are in place and study them directly. (Well it is, but that requires using a debugger such as gdb and the use of breakpoints.) Even with the synchronization waits enabled in the Performance Schema, you will usually fall short as there will be some many waits that even the long history table with a default of 10000 rows will quickly get exhausted even by a single connection as it can be seen from Listing 7-4.

Listing 7-4. Example of synchronization waits

```
-- Connection    Processlist ID    Thread ID    Event ID
-- -------------------------------------------------------
--           1              638          1057           6
--           2              639          1058           6

-- Connection 1
Connection 1> UPDATE performance_schema.setup_instruments
                SET ENABLED = 'YES',
                    TIMED = 'YES'
              WHERE NAME LIKE 'wait/synch/%';
Query OK, 323 rows affected (0.0230 sec)

Rows matched: 323  Changed: 323  Warnings: 0
```

```
Connection 1> UPDATE performance_schema.setup_consumers
              SET ENABLED = 'YES'
             WHERE NAME IN ('events_waits_current', 'events_waits_
             history_long');
Query OK, 2 rows affected (0.0004 sec)

Rows matched: 2  Changed: 2  Warnings: 0

-- Connection 2
Connection 2> UPDATE world.city
              SET Population = Population + 1
             WHERE CountryCode = 'USA';
Query OK, 274 rows affected (0.1522 sec)

Rows matched: 274  Changed: 274  Warnings: 0

-- Connection 1
Connection 1> SELECT REPLACE(event_name, 'wait/synch/', '') AS event,
COUNT(*)
              FROM performance_schema.events_waits_history_long
             WHERE thread_id = 1058
                 AND event_name LIKE 'wait/synch/%'
             GROUP BY event_name
              WITH ROLLUP
             ORDER BY COUNT(*);
+-------------------------------------------------+----------+
| event                                           | COUNT(*) |
+-------------------------------------------------+----------+
| mutex/sql/MYSQL_BIN_LOG::LOCK_done              |        1 |
| mutex/innodb/purge_sys_pq_mutex                 |        1 |
| mutex/sql/MYSQL_BIN_LOG::LOCK_sync              |        1 |
| mutex/sql/MYSQL_BIN_LOG::LOCK_log               |        1 |
| mutex/mysqlx/vio_shutdown                       |        1 |
| mutex/sql/LOCK_plugin                           |        1 |
| mutex/sql/LOCK_slave_trans_dep_tracker          |        1 |
| mutex/sql/MYSQL_BIN_LOG::LOCK_binlog_end_pos    |        1 |
| mutex/sql/MYSQL_BIN_LOG::LOCK_commit            |        1 |
```

```
| mutex/sql/MYSQL_BIN_LOG::LOCK_xids          |      1 |
| sxlock/innodb/rsegs_lock                    |      1 |
| sxlock/innodb/undo_spaces_lock              |      1 |
| mutex/sql/MYSQL_BIN_LOG::LOCK_sync_queue    |      2 |
| mutex/innodb/lock_sys_table_mutex           |      2 |
| mutex/sql/MYSQL_BIN_LOG::LOCK_flush_queue   |      2 |
| mutex/sql/Gtid_state                        |      2 |
| mutex/sql/LOCK_table_cache                  |      2 |
| mutex/sql/MYSQL_BIN_LOG::LOCK_commit_queue  |      2 |
| mutex/sql/THD::LOCK_thd_query               |      2 |
| mutex/innodb/undo_space_rseg_mutex          |      3 |
| mutex/sql/THD::LOCK_thd_data                |      3 |
| rwlock/sql/gtid_commit_rollback             |      3 |
| mutex/mysys/THR_LOCK_open                   |      4 |
| mutex/sql/THD::LOCK_query_plan              |      4 |
| mutex/innodb/flush_list_mutex               |      5 |
| sxlock/innodb/index_tree_rw_lock            |      5 |
| mutex/innodb/trx_undo_mutex                 |    274 |
| mutex/innodb/trx_sys_mutex                  |    279 |
| sxlock/innodb/hash_table_locks              |    288 |
| sxlock/innodb/btr_search_latch              |    550 |
| sxlock/innodb/lock_sys_global_rw_lock       |    551 |
| sxlock/innodb/log_sn_lock                   |    551 |
| mutex/innodb/lock_sys_page_mutex            |    554 |
| mutex/innodb/trx_mutex                      |    850 |
| NULL                                        |   3950 |
+---------------------------------------------+--------+
35 rows in set (0.0173 sec)

Connection 1> UPDATE performance_schema.setup_instruments
                 SET ENABLED = 'NO',
                     TIMED = 'NO'
               WHERE NAME LIKE 'wait/synch/%';
Query OK, 323 rows affected (0.0096 sec)
```

```
Rows matched: 323  Changed: 323  Warnings: 0

Connection 1> UPDATE performance_schema.setup_consumers
              SET ENABLED = 'NO'
              WHERE NAME IN ('events_waits_current', 'events_waits_
              history_long');
Query OK, 2 rows affected (0.0004 sec)

Rows matched: 2  Changed: 2  Warnings: 0
```

In this simple example, almost 4000 (the NULL row at the bottom of the result of querying events_waits_history_long) synchronization objects were requested. The exact list of waits and the number of them will vary from execution to execution and system to system depending on the state of the system (like whether the data is already in the buffer pool) and the configuration. If there is enough other activity, the number may also be much lower as some of the waits may have been pushed out of the events_ waits_history_long table by newer events. To complicate matters, background threads also generate wait events, so even if the system has no connections, wait events are created.

While it is hard to set up test cases that demonstrate the use of individual synchronization objects, the good news is that you as an end user mostly need to worry about contention, and the SHOW ENGINE INNODB STATUS and SHOW ENGINE INNODB MUTEX statements will provide you information about the contention of InnoDB mutexes and semaphores.

In general, you will need to study the source code to understand what the wait is for; however, alone considering the file can often provide a good indication of the functional area where the contention happens. Table 7-2 shows a few examples of how to map the file name provided by the mutex and semaphore information to the functional area. The source code path is relative to storage/innobase which contains the implementation of the InnoDB storage engine.

Table 7-2. *Mutex and semaphore file names and their functional area*

File Name	Source Code Path	Functional Area
btr0sea.cc	btr/btr0sea.cc	The adaptive hash index.
buf0buf.cc	buf/buf0buf.cc	The buffer pool.
buf0flu.cc	buf/buf0flu.cc	The buffer pool flushing algorithm.
dict0dict.cc	dict/dict0dict.cc	The InnoDB data dictionary.
sync0sharded_rw.h	include/sync0sharded_rw.h	The sharded read-write lock for threads.
hash0hash.cc	ha/hash0hash.cc	For protecting hash tables.
fil0fil.cc	fil/fil0fil.cc	The tablespace memory cache.

Other than for mutexes and semaphores implemented in header files, in general, you get to the source code file by using the name before the 0 in the file name (e.g., btr in btr0sea.cc) as the name of the directory and then the file name itself. If you open the file in an editor, then just after the license and copyright header, you will see a brief comment describing what the file is for, for example, from storage/innobase/btr/btr0sea.cc:

```
/** @file btr/btr0sea.cc
 The index tree adaptive search

 Created 2/17/1996 Heikki Tuuri
 *******************************************************************/
```

So, the btr0sea.cc file implements the adaptive search on the index tree of which the adaptive hash index is part of (and where the contention most commonly occurs).

WHY INNOBASE? A BRIEF HISTORY OF INNODB

It may have puzzled you why the path to the InnoDB source code is storage/innobase/ using "innobase" rather than "innodb." To understand that, you need to dive into the history of InnoDB – which turns out to be quite interesting.

Innobase was a company founded by Heikki Tuuri (yep, the same that is listed in the comment for the file `storage/innobase/btr/btr0sea.cc`) in 1995, the same year as the initial release of MySQL, but at that time the two had nothing to do with each other. Innobase was used to develop InnoDB which at the time meant to be an independent product. It was not until later when MySQL added support for third-party storage engines that Heikki released InnoDB as open source and it was integrated with MySQL.

In 2005, Oracle acquired Innobase and thus InnoDB which made for an interesting situation with MySQL's main transactional storage engine (another much less used engine was Berkley DB, BDB, which also was acquired by Oracle) being maintained by a competitor. This was one reason for the effort to develop the Falcon storage engine for MySQL 6. However, before that work was completed, Sun Microsystems acquired MySQL, and Oracle in turn acquired Sun Microsystems, so in 2010, MySQL and InnoDB were finally part of the same company, and today InnoDB and MySQL are developed by the same unit within Oracle. This also meant that the Falcon storage engine was abandoned and never released with a general availability (GA) status.

While Innobase as a company has disappeared a long time ago, its name still lives on in the MySQL source code both in the path to the InnoDB source code and as names within the source code.

Summary

In this chapter the InnoDB data-level locks as well as mutexes and rw-lock semaphores have been covered. These locks are all important to support concurrent access to the InnoDB data which is one of InnoDB's strengths.

First, the record locks and next-key locks were discussed. These are usually what are meant when discussing InnoDB record locks. The next-key locks are the default locks in InnoDB and protect the record as well as the gab before the record. Second, the concept of gap locks was discussed. When mentioning gap locks, it refers to protecting the space between two records without protecting the record itself. Third, the related concepts of predicate and page locks that are used with spatial indexed were covered.

Fourth and fifth were two lock types that you will not encounter to the same degree as the first three lock types. The insert intention locks are as the name suggest used in connection with inserting data, and the auto-increment lock is used to ensure that auto-increment values are assigned correctly.

## CHAPTER 8

Working with Lock Conflicts

The whole idea of locks is to restrict access to objects or records to avoid conflicting operations to concurrently access the object or records in a safe way. That means that, sometimes, a lock cannot be granted. What happens in that case? It depends on the locks requested and the circumstances. Metadata (including explicitly requested table locks) and InnoDB locks operate with a timeout, and for some lock cases explicit deadlock detection exist.

It is important to understand that failures to obtain locks are a fact of life when working with databases. In principle you can use very coarse-grained locks and avoid failed locks except for timeouts – this is what the MyISAM storage engine does with very poor write concurrency as a result. However, in practice, to allow for high concurrency of write workloads, fine-grained locks are preferred which also introduce the possibility of deadlocks.

The conclusion is that you should always make your application prepared to retry getting a lock or fail gracefully. This applies whether it is an explicit or implicit lock.

Tip Always be prepared to handle failures to obtain locks. Failing to get a lock is not a catastrophic error and should not normally be considered a bug. That said, as discussed in Chapter 9, "Reducing Locking Issues," there are techniques to reduce lock contention that are worth having in mind when developing an application.

The rest of this chapter will discuss how InnoDB chooses which transaction should first be granted a lock request when there are multiple requests for the same data lock, the compatibility of InnoDB data locks, as well as the specifics of table-level timeouts, record-level timeouts, InnoDB deadlocks, and InnoDB mutex and semaphore waits.

© Jesper Wisborg Krogh 2021
J. W. Krogh, *MySQL Concurrency*, https://doi.org/10.1007/978-1-4842-6652-6_8

Contention-Aware Transaction Scheduling (CATS)

An important decision when there are multiple requests for the same lock is to decide in which order locks should be granted. The simplest solution, and the most commonly used in databases, is to maintain a queue and serve the requests on a first-in-first-out (FIFO) principle. This is also how locks were granted in MySQL 5.7 and earlier; however in MySQL 8, a new scheduling algorithm was implemented.

The new implementation is based on the contention-aware transaction scheduling (CATS) algorithm developed by Professor Barzan Mozafari's team at the University of Michigan and implemented in MySQL by Sunny Bains in collaboration with Professor Mozafari's team, particularly Jiamin Huang.

Tip   If you want to learn more about the CATS algorithm, then `https://mysqlserverteam.com/contention-aware-transaction-scheduling-arriving-in-innodb-to-boost-performance/` is a good starting point, and there are links to two of the research papers in the comments – the main paper being `http://web.eecs.umich.edu/~mozafari/php/data/uploads/pvldb_2018_sched.pdf`. Another source is `https://dev.mysql.com/doc/refman/en/innodb-transaction-scheduling.html` in the reference manual.

The CATS algorithm works on the principle that transactions that already hold a large number of locks are most important to drive to completion, so their locks can be released as quickly as possible to the benefit of all transactions. One potential downside of this approach is that if there continuously are transactions with many existing locks waiting for a given lock, then they can potentially starve transactions with few locks from ever getting the lock. To prevent that, the algorithm has safeguards to prevent starvation. The safeguard works by adding a barrier at the end of the current queue of lock requests, and all requests that are ahead of the barrier are handled before later arriving requests will be considered.

The primary benefit of the CATS algorithm is under high concurrency workloads, and until MySQL 8.0.20, it was only used when InnoDB detected heavy lock contention. The algorithm was improved in 8.0.20 to improve the scalability, and the `trx_schedule_weight` column was added to `information_schema.INNODB_TRX`, so it is possible to query the current weight a transaction in the LOCK WAIT state has according to the CATS algorithm. At the same time, it was changed so the CATS algorithm is always used, and the FIFO algorithm has been retired.

InnoDB Data Lock Compatibility

Remember when discussing lock access level compatibility, the rules were relatively simple. However, whether two InnoDB data locks are compatible with each other is very complex to determine. It becomes particularly interesting as the relationship is not symmetric, that is, a lock may be allowed in the presence of another lock, but not vice versa. For example, an insert intention lock must wait for a gap lock, but a gap lock does not have to wait for an insert intention lock. Another example (of lack of transitivity) is that a gap plus record lock must wait for a record-only lock, and an insert intention lock must wait for a gap plus record lock, but an insert intention lock does not need to wait for a record-only lock.

What does that mean to you? It means that when you investigate lock contention issues, you need to be aware that the lock order is significant, so when reproducing the issue, all locks must be obtained in the same order.

Enough about the theory behind InnoDB algorithm for handling lock contention and what may cause a lock not to be granted. What happens when a lock cannot be granted is the next topic to be discussed.

Metadata and Backup Lock Wait Timeouts

When you request a flush, metadata, or backup lock, the attempt to get the lock will time out after lock_wait_timeout seconds. The default timeout is 31,536,000 seconds (365 days). You can set the lock_wait_timeout option dynamically and both at the global and session scopes, which allows you to adjust the timeout to the specific needs for a given process.

When a timeout occurs, the statement fails with an ER_LOCK_WAIT_TIMEOUT (error number 1205) error as shown in Listing 8-1.

Listing 8-1. Lock wait timeout for table lock request

```
-- Connection   Processlist ID   Thread ID   Event ID
-- ------------------------------------------------------
--           1              647        1075          6
--           2              648        1076          6

-- Connection 1
Connection 1> LOCK TABLES world.city WRITE;
Query OK, 0 rows affected (0.0015 sec)

-- Connection 2
Connection 2> SET SESSION lock_wait_timeout = 5;
Query OK, 0 rows affected (0.0003 sec)

Connection 2> LOCK TABLES world.city WRITE;
ERROR: 1205: Lock wait timeout exceeded; try restarting transaction

-- Connection 1
Connection 1> UNLOCK TABLES;
Query OK, 0 rows affected (0.0003 sec)
```

The session value of lock_wait_timeout is set to 5 seconds to reduce how long a time Connection 2 will block for when it attempts to get the write lock on the world.city table. After waiting for 5 seconds, the error is returned with the error number set to 1205.

The recommended setting for the lock_wait_timeout option depends on the requirements of the application. It can be an advantage to use a small value to prevent the lock request to block other queries for a long time. This will typically require you to implement handling of a lock request failure, for example, by retrying the statement. A large value can on the other hand be useful to avoid having to retry the statement.

For the FLUSH TABLES statement, also remember that it interacts with the lower-level table definition cache (TDC) version lock which may mean that abandoning the statement does not allow subsequent queries to progress. In that case, it can be better to have a high value for lock_wait_timeout to make it clearer what the lock relationship is.

InnoDB Lock Wait Timeouts

When a query requests a record-level lock in InnoDB, it is subject to a timeout similarly to the timeout for flush, metadata, and backup locks. Since record-level lock contention is more common than table-level lock contention, and record-level locks increase the potential for deadlocks, the timeout defaults to 50 seconds. It can be set using the innodb_lock_wait_timeout option which can be set both for the global and session scopes.

When a timeout occurs, the query fails with the ER_LOCK_WAIT_TIMEOUT error (error number 1205) just like for a table-level lock timeout. Listing 8-2 shows an example where an InnoDB lock wait timeout occurs.

Listing 8-2. Example of an InnoDB lock wait timeout

```
-- Connection    Processlist ID    Thread ID    Event ID
-- -----------------------------------------------------
--          1              656         1087            6
--          2              657         1088            6

-- Connection 1
Connection 1> START TRANSACTION;
Query OK, 0 rows affected (0.0002 sec)

Connection 1> UPDATE world.city
              SET Population = Population + 1
            WHERE ID = 130;
Query OK, 1 row affected (0.0006 sec)

Rows matched: 1  Changed: 1  Warnings: 0


-- Connection 2
Connection 2> SET SESSION innodb_lock_wait_timeout = 3;
Query OK, 0 rows affected (0.2621 sec)

Connection 2> UPDATE world.city
              SET Population = Population + 1
            WHERE ID = 130;
ERROR: 1205: Lock wait timeout exceeded; try restarting transaction
```

```
-- Connection 1
Connection 1> ROLLBACK;
Query OK, 0 rows affected (0.0751 sec)
```

In this example, the lock wait timeout for Connection 2 is set to 3 seconds, so it is not necessary to wait the usual 50 seconds for the timeout to occur.

When the timeout occurs, the `innodb_rollback_on_timeout` option defines how much of the work done by the transaction is rolled back. When `innodb_rollback_on_timeout` is disabled (the default), only the statement that triggered the timeout is rolled back. When the option is enabled, the whole transaction is rolled back. The `innodb_rollback_on_timeout` option can only be configured at the global level, and it requires a restart to change the value.

Caution   It is very important that a lock wait timeout is handled as otherwise it may leave the transaction with locks that are not released. If that happens, other transactions may not be able to acquire the locks they require. So, you need ensure that you either retry the remaining part of the transaction, explicitly roll back the transaction, or enable `innodb_rollback_on_timeout` to automatically roll back the transaction on a lock wait timeout.

It is in general recommended to keep the timeout for InnoDB record-level locks low. Often it is best to lower the value from the default 50 seconds. The longer a query is allowed to wait for a lock, the larger the potential for other lock requests to be affected which can lead to other queries stalling as well. It also makes deadlocks more likely to occur. If you disable deadlock detection (discussed next), you should use a very small value for `innodb_lock_wait_timeout` such as 1 or 2 seconds as you will be using the timeout to detect deadlocks. Without deadlock detection, it is also recommended to enable the `innodb_rollback_on_timeout` option.

Deadlocks

Deadlocks sound like a very scary concept, but you should not let the name deter you. Just like lock wait timeout, deadlocks are a fact of life in the world of high-concurrency databases. What it really means is that there is a circular relationship between the lock requests as illustrated by a traffic gridlock in Figure 8-1. The only way to resolve the gridlock is to force one of the requests to abandon. In that sense, a deadlock is no different from a lock wait timeout. In fact, you can disable deadlock detection in which case, one of the locks will end up with a lock wait timeout instead.

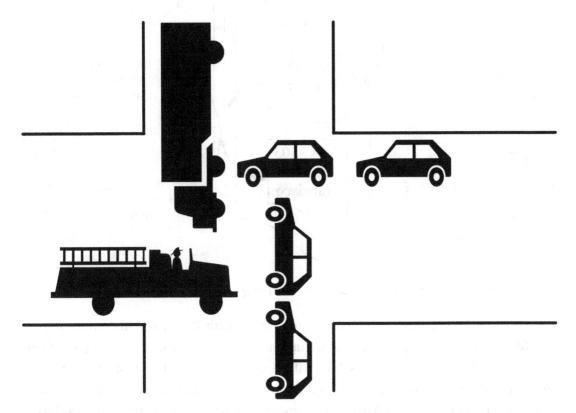

Figure 8-1. *A traffic gridlock*

So why are there deadlocks at all if they are not really needed? Since deadlocks occur when there is a circular relationship between the lock requests, it is possible for InnoDB to detect them as soon as the circle is completed. This allows InnoDB to tell the user immediately that a deadlock has occurred without having to wait for the lock wait timeout to happen. It is also useful to be told that a deadlock has occurred as it often provides opportunities to improve data access in the application. You should thus consider deadlocks a friend rather than a foe. Figure 8-2 shows an example of two transactions querying a table which causes a deadlock.

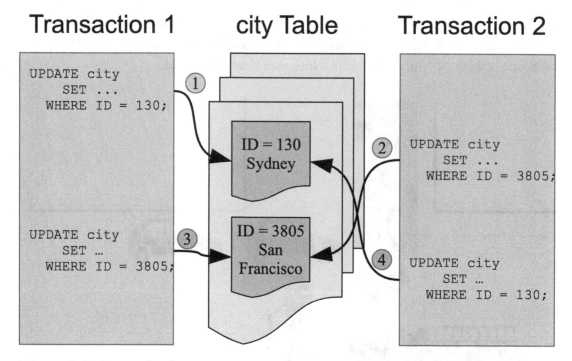

Figure 8-2. *Example of two transactions causing a deadlock*

In the example, transaction 1 first updates the row with ID = 130 and then the row with ID = 3805. In between, transaction 2 updates first the row with ID = 3805 and then the row with ID = 130. This means that by the time transaction 1 tries to update ID = 3805, transaction 2 already has a lock on the row. Transaction 2 can also not proceed as it cannot get a lock on ID = 130 because transaction 1 already holds that. This is a classic example of a simple deadlock. The circular lock relationship is also shown in Figure 8-3.

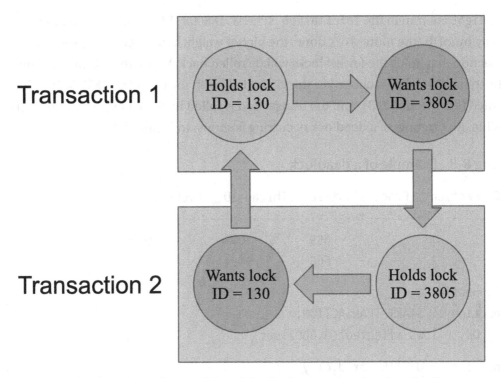

Figure 8-3. *The circular relationship of the locks causing the deadlock*

In this figure, it is clear which lock is held by transactions 1 and 2 and which locks are requested and how the conflict can never be resolved without intervention. That makes it qualify as a deadlock.

In the real world, deadlocks are often more complicated. In the example that has been discussed here, only primary key record locks have been involved. In general, often secondary keys, gap locks, and possible other lock types are also involved. There may also be more than two transactions involved. The principle, however, remains the same.

Note   A deadlock may even occur with as little as one query for each of two transactions. If one query reads the records in ascending order and the other on descending order, it is possible to get a deadlock.

When a deadlock occurs, InnoDB chooses the transaction that has "done the least work" to become a victim. This is similar to the "Shoot The Other Node In The Head" (STONITH) approach used in some high availability solutions such as MySQL NDB Cluster except here it is a transaction that is being "shot in the head." You can check the trx_weight column in the information_schema.INNODB_TRX view to see the weight used by InnoDB (the more work done, the higher weight). In practice this means that the transaction that holds the fewest locks will be rolled back. When this occurs, the query in the transaction that is chosen as the victim fails with the error ER_LOCK_DEADLOCK returned (error code 1213), and the transaction is rolled back to release as many locks as possible. An example of a deadlock occurring is shown in Listing 8-3.

Listing 8-3. Example of a deadlock

```
-- Connection    Processlist ID    Thread ID    Event ID
-- -----------------------------------------------------
--            1              659         1093           6
--            2              660         1094           6
-- Connection 1
Connection 1> START TRANSACTION;
Query OK, 0 rows affected (0.0002 sec)

Connection 1> UPDATE world.city
              SET Population = Population + 1
            WHERE ID = 130;
Query OK, 1 row affected (0.0098 sec)

Rows matched: 1  Changed: 1  Warnings: 0

-- Connection 2
Connection 2> START TRANSACTION;
Query OK, 0 rows affected (0.0003 sec)

Connection 2> UPDATE world.city
              SET Population = Population + 1
            WHERE ID = 3805;
Query OK, 1 row affected (0.0009 sec)

Rows matched: 1  Changed: 1  Warnings: 0

Connection 2> UPDATE world.city
              SET Population = Population + 1
            WHERE ID = 130;
```

```
-- Connection 1
Connection 1> UPDATE world.city
              SET Population = Population + 1
            WHERE ID = 3805;
```
ERROR: 1213: Deadlock found when trying to get lock; try restarting transaction

```
-- Connection 2
Query OK, 1 row affected (0.1019 sec)

Rows matched: 1  Changed: 1  Warnings: 0

-- Connection 1
Connection 1> ROLLBACK;
Query OK, 0 rows affected (0.0002 sec)

-- Connection 2
Connection 2> ROLLBACK;
Query OK, 0 rows affected (0.0293 sec)
```

A deadlock can be even simpler than in this example (though it is rare unless you use locking SELECT statements either explicitly or using the SERIALIZABLE transaction isolation level). Listing 8-4 shows a deadlock that occurs using just a single row.

Listing 8-4. A single row deadlock

```
-- Connection    Processlist ID   Thread ID   Event ID
-- -----------------------------------------------------
--        1             663          1097         6
--        2             664          1098         6

-- Connection 1
Connection 1> START TRANSACTION;
Query OK, 0 rows affected (0.0004 sec)
```

```
Connection 1> SELECT * FROM world.city WHERE ID = 130 FOR SHARE;
+-----+--------+-------------+-----------------+------------+
| ID  | Name   | CountryCode | District        | Population |
+-----+--------+-------------+-----------------+------------+
| 130 | Sydney | AUS         | New South Wales |    3276207 |
+-----+--------+-------------+-----------------+------------+
1 row in set (0.0005 sec)

-- Connection 2
Connection 2> START TRANSACTION;
Query OK, 0 rows affected (0.0002 sec)

Connection 2> UPDATE world.city
              SET Population = Population + 1
            WHERE ID = 130;

-- Connection 1
Connection 1> UPDATE world.city
              SET Population = Population + 1
            WHERE ID = 130;
Query OK, 1 row affected (0.0447 sec)

Rows matched: 1  Changed: 1  Warnings: 0
```

-- Connection 2
ERROR: 1213: Deadlock found when trying to get lock; try restarting
transaction

```
-- Connection 1
Connection 1> ROLLBACK;
Query OK, 0 rows affected (0.0280 sec)

-- Connection 2
Connection 2> ROLLBACK;
Query OK, 0 rows affected (0.0003 sec)
```

In this case, Connection 2 becomes a victim of a deadlock without having ever being granted a record lock. This deadlock happens because InnoDB currently does not allow the request to upgrade the shared lock to an exclusive lock in Connection 1 to jump ahead of Connection 2's lock request. It is something that can potentially be implemented, but because these scenarios are relatively rare, it has not been done yet. That said, if you have foreign keys, a DML statement may take a shared lock on the other table in the foreign key relationship (see also Chapter 10), so if a subsequent statement in the same transaction tried to upgrade that shared lock, then you can see the same kind of deadlocks as in this example.

In most cases, the automatic deadlock detection is great to avoid queries stalling for longer than necessary. Deadlock detection is not for free though. For MySQL instances with a very high query concurrency, the cost of looking for deadlocks can become significant, and you are better off disabling the deadlock detection which is done by setting the innodb_deadlock_detect option to OFF. That said, in MySQL 8.0.18 and later, the deadlock detection has been moved to a dedicated background thread which improves the performance.

If you do disable deadlock detection, it is recommended to set innodb_lock_wait_timeout to a very low value such as 1 second to quickly detect lock contention. Additionally, enable the innodb_rollback_on_timeout option to ensure the locks are released.

The last kind of lock conflict handling occurs with InnoDB mutexes and semaphores.

InnoDB Mutex and Semaphore Waits

When InnoDB requests a mutex or rw-lock semaphore and it cannot be immediately obtained, it will have to wait. Because the waits happen at a lower level than data locks, InnoDB will resort to one of two approaches while waiting. It can enter a loop and poll for the lock to become available, or it can suspend the thread and make it available for other tasks.

Polling allows the lock to be obtained more quickly but it keeps the CPU thread busy, and polling can cause CPU cache invalidation for other threads. There are three configuration options that can be used to control the behavior:

- **innodb_spin_wait_delay:** When polling, InnoDB will calculate a random number between zero and innodb_spin_wait_delay. This is multiplied with innodb_spin_wait_pause_multiplier to determine the number of PAUSE instructions that occur in the poll loop. The random number of PAUSE events is used to reduce the impact of cache invalidation. Smaller values – or even 0 – can potentially help on systems with a single shared fast CPU cache. Larger values can reduce the impact of cache invalidation particularly on multi-CPU systems.

- **innodb_spin_wait_pause_multiplier:** The multiplier used with the spin wait delay. This option is new from MySQL 8.0.16 and was introduced to accommodate for the change in the duration of the PAUSE instructions introduced with the Skylake generation of processors. The primary use of changing the value is using MySQL on architectures that have a different duration of the PAUSE instructions than x86/x86-64 before the Skylake generation. In earlier releases, the multiplier is hardcoded to 50 which is also the default value for innodb_spin_wait_pause_multiplier.

- **innodb_sync_spin_loops:** The number of spin loops to perform before suspending the thread. The lower the value, the quicker the CPU thread is made available for other tasks at the expense of more context switches. When the spin loops are exceeded, the OS waits counter for the rw-lock increments. The higher the value, the quicker the lock can be obtained at the cost of higher CPU usage. The default is 30.

You will rarely have to adjust these settings; however, in rare cases, they can improve performance to some degree. That said, if you are not using the latest MySQL version, you may benefit in terms of reducing mutex/semaphore contention more from upgrading than tuning these options. In all cases, if you decide to change these settings, make sure you test the performance thoroughly on the same architecture and hardware configuration as your production system and with a workload that is a very good representation of your production workload.

If an InnoDB mutex or rw-lock semaphore wait cannot be obtained immediately, InnoDB will also register this internally. The relevant counter exposed through SHOW ENGINE INNODB MUTEX will increment (though only mutexes and rw-locks with at least one OS wait are displayed), and if you generate the InnoDB monitor report while the wait is ongoing, it will be included in the SEMAPHORES wait section of the rapport. If a wait continues without progress being detected for more than 240 seconds, InnoDB will automatically enable the InnoDB monitor and write the output to the error log, so you can investigate the issue. If no progress is detected for another 600 seconds, then InnoDB will shut down MySQL as a preventive measure as it assumes an unresolvable situation has occurred. In that case, you will see an error explaining the reason for the shutdown, for example (yes, the duration printed is somewhat misleading as it is the time since the "long semaphore wait" condition triggered at 240 seconds)

```
2020-07-05T09:30:24.151782Z 0 [ERROR] [MY-012872] [InnoDB] Semaphore wait
has lasted > 600 seconds. We intentionally crash the server because it
appears to be hung.
```

By crashing the server, InnoDB ensures that if a bug internally in InnoDB has been encountered, the situation is resolved, but at the cost that MySQL will have to restart and go through a crash recovery. For this reason, it is considered a last resort, and at present, the timeout is not configurable.

Note   When executing CHECK TABLE, the timeout threshold is increased to 7200 seconds (2 hours).

A shutdown like this typically happens for one of two reasons:

- There is a hardware or operating system issue that prevents InnoDB progressing.
- There is a bug in InnoDB, for example, that progress for a slow operation is not detected or a deadlock has occurred for the acquisition of a mutex or semaphore.

If you encounter a shutdown like this, verify from the InnoDB monitor outputs in the error log where the wait occurred. In some cases, you can use the thread ids to determine which query is causing the wait. You should also check your system logs to verify the health of your hardware and whether there are any indications of problems at the operating system level.

Summary

This chapter has provided an overview of what happens when a lock cannot immediately be obtained. First, the contention-aware transaction scheduling (CATS) algorithm was described. That is used in MySQL 8 to allow transactions that already hold many locks to have their lock requests granted quicker, so their locks also can be more quickly released again.

Second, it was discussed how the compatibility of InnoDB data locks is a very a complex issue which means that the lock order must be taken into account when trying to reproduce issues.

The rest of the chapter went through metadata, backup, and InnoDB lock wait timeouts, deadlocks, and InnoDB mutex and rw-lock semaphore waits. Lock waits and deadlocks are naturally occurring in high concurrency systems and should not on their own be a cause for alarm. The main issue is when they become frequent. The default lock wait timeouts may also be too long, so reducing them and handling the timeout can be an option.

Now that you have an understanding of how locks work and how lock requests can fail, you need to consider how you can reduce the impact of locking which is the topic of the next chapter.

CHAPTER 9

Reducing Locking Issues

Remember that the locking in MySQL and InnoDB is a means to provide concurrent access, and in general the fine-grained locking of InnoDB allows for a highly concurrent workload. Yet, if you have excessive locking, it will cause reduced concurrency and query pileups, and in the worst case, it can cause an application to come to a grinding halt and cause a poor user experience.

Thus, it is important to have locks in mind when you write an application and design the schema for its data and access. The strategies to reduce locking include adding indexes, changing the transaction isolation level, changing the configuration, and preemptive locking. This chapter covers each of these strategies.

Tip Do not be carried away in optimizing locks. If you only occasionally encounter lock wait timeouts and deadlocks, it is usually better to retry the query or transaction rather than spend time avoiding the issue. How frequent is too frequent depends on your workload, but several retries every hour will not be an issue for many applications.

Transaction Size and Age

An important strategy to reduce lock issues is to keep your transactions small and to avoid delays that keep the transactions open for longer than necessary. Among the most common causes of lock issues are transactions that modify a large number of rows or that are active for longer than necessary.

The size of the transaction is the amount of work the transaction does, particularly the number of locks it takes, but the time the transaction takes to execute is also important. As some of the other topics in this discussion will address, you can partly reduce the impact through indexes and the transaction isolation level. However, it is

157

© Jesper Wisborg Krogh 2021
J. W. Krogh, *MySQL Concurrency*, https://doi.org/10.1007/978-1-4842-6652-6_9

also important to have the overall result in mind. If you need to modify many rows, ask yourself if you can split the work into smaller batches or whether it is required that everything is done in the same transaction. It may also be possible to split out some preparation work and do it outside the main transaction.

The duration of the transaction is also important. One common problem is connections using `autocommit = 0`. This starts a new transaction every time a query (including `SELECT`) is executed without an active transaction, and the transaction is not completed until an explicit `COMMIT` or `ROLLBACK` is executed, a DDL statement is executed, or the connection is closed. Some connectors disable autocommit by default, so you may be using this mode without realizing it which can leave transactions open for hours by mistake.

Tip   Enable the `autocommit` option unless you have a specific reason to disable it. When you have autocommitting enabled, InnoDB can also for many `SELECT` queries detect it is a read-only transaction and reduce the overhead of the query.

Another pitfall is to start a transaction and perform slow operations in the application while the transaction is active. This can be data that is sent back to the user, interactive prompts, or file I/O. Make sure that you do these kinds of slow operations when you do not have an active transaction open in MySQL.

Indexes

Indexes reduce the amount of work performed to access a given row. That way indexes are a great tool to reduce locking as only records accessed while executing the query will be locked.

Consider a simple example where you query cities with the name Sydney in the `world.city` table:

```
START TRANSACTION;

SELECT *
  FROM world.city
 WHERE Name = 'Sydney'
   FOR SHARE;
```

The FOR SHARE option is used to force the query to take a shared lock on the records read. By default, there is no index on the Name column, so the query will perform a full table scan to find the rows needed in the result. Without an index, there are 4103 record locks (24 of the locks are on the supremum pseudo-record of the primary key) as shown in Listing 9-1.

Listing 9-1. Record locks without an index on the Name column

```
-- Connection    Processlist ID    Thread ID    Event ID
-- ---------------------------------------------------------
--         1              697          1143           6
--         2              698          1144           6

-- Connection 1
Connection 1> START TRANSACTION;
Query OK, 0 rows affected (0.0002 sec)

Connection 1> SELECT ID, Name, CountryCode, District
                FROM world.city
                WHERE Name = 'Sydney'
                FOR SHARE;
+-----+--------+-------------+-----------------+
| ID  | Name   | CountryCode | District        |
+-----+--------+-------------+-----------------+
| 130 | Sydney | AUS         | New South Wales |
+-----+--------+-------------+-----------------+
1 row in set (0.0034 sec)

-- Connection 2
Connection 2> SELECT index_name, lock_type,
                lock_mode, COUNT(*)
              FROM performance_schema.data_locks
              WHERE object_schema = 'world'
                AND object_name = 'city'
                AND thread_id = 1143
              GROUP BY index_name, lock_type, lock_mode;
```

```
+------------+-----------+-----------+----------+
| index_name | lock_type | lock_mode | COUNT(*) |
+------------+-----------+-----------+----------+
| NULL       | TABLE     | IS        |        1 |
| PRIMARY    | RECORD    | S         |     4103 |
+------------+-----------+-----------+----------+
2 rows in set (0.0323 sec)

-- Connection 1
Connection 1> ROLLBACK;
Query OK, 0 rows affected (0.0005 sec)
```

If you add an index on the Name column, the lock count decreases to a total of three record locks as shown in Listing 9-2.

Listing 9-2. Record locks with an index on the Name column

```
-- Connection   Processlist ID   Thread ID   Event ID
-- ----------------------------------------------------
--           1            699        1145           6
--           2            700        1146           6

-- Connection 1
Connection 1> ALTER TABLE world.city
                 ADD INDEX (Name);
Query OK, 0 rows affected (1.5063 sec)

Records: 0  Duplicates: 0  Warnings: 0

Connection 1> START TRANSACTION;
Query OK, 0 rows affected (0.0003 sec)

Connection 1> SELECT ID, Name, CountryCode, District
                 FROM world.city
                WHERE Name = 'Sydney'
                  FOR SHARE;
```

```
+-----+--------+-------------+-----------------+
| ID  | Name   | CountryCode | District        |
+-----+--------+-------------+-----------------+
| 130 | Sydney | AUS         | New South Wales |
+-----+--------+-------------+-----------------+
1 row in set (0.0004 sec)

-- Connection 2
Connection 2> SELECT index_name, lock_type,
                     lock_mode, COUNT(*)
                FROM performance_schema.data_locks
               WHERE object_schema = 'world'
                 AND object_name = 'city'
                 AND thread_id = 1145
            GROUP BY index_name, lock_type, lock_mode;
+------------+-----------+----------------+----------+
| index_name | lock_type | lock_mode      | COUNT(*) |
+------------+-----------+----------------+----------+
| NULL       | TABLE     | IS             |        1 |
| Name       | RECORD    | S              |        1 |
| PRIMARY    | RECORD    | S,REC_NOT_GAP  |        1 |
| Name       | RECORD    | S,GAP          |        1 |
+------------+-----------+----------------+----------+
4 rows in set (0.0011 sec)

-- Connection 1
Connection 1> ROLLBACK;
Query OK, 0 rows affected (0.0004 sec)

Connection 1> ALTER TABLE world.city
              DROP INDEX Name;
Query OK, 0 rows affected (0.3288 sec)

Records: 0  Duplicates: 0  Warnings: 0
```

On the flip side, more indexes provide more ways to access the same rows which potentially can increase the number of deadlocks.

Record Access order

Ensure that you to as large degree as possible access the records in the same order for different transactions. In the deadlock example discussed in Chapter 8, what led to the deadlock was that the two transactions accessed the rows in opposite order. If they had accessed the rows in the same order, there would have been no deadlock. This also applies when you access records in different tables.

Ensuring the same access order is by no means a trivial task. Different access orders may even happen when you perform joins and the optimizer decides on different join orders for two queries. If different join orders lead to excessive lock issues, you can consider using optimizer hints to tell the optimizer to change the join order[1], but you should of course also have the query performance in mind in such cases.

Transaction Isolation Levels

InnoDB supports several transaction isolation levels. Different isolation levels have different lock requirements: particularly REPEATABLE READ and SERIALIZABLE require more locks than READ COMMITTED.

The READ COMMITTED transaction isolation level can help on locking issues in two ways. Far less gap locks are taken, and rows that are accessed during a DML statement but not modified have their locks released again after the statement has completed. For REPEATABLE READ and SERIALIZABLE, locks are only released at the end of the transaction.

Note   It is often said that the READ COMMITTED transaction isolation level does not take gap locks. That is a myth and not correct. While far fewer gap locks are taken, there are still some that are required. This, for example, includes when InnoDB with checking foreign keys and unique key constraints as well as when a page split occurs.

---

[1]https://dev.mysql.com/doc/refman/en/optimizer-hints.html#optimizer-hints-join-order

Consider an example where the population of the city named Sydney is changed using the CountryCode column to limit the query to one country. This can be done with the following query:

```
START TRANSACTION;

UPDATE world.city
   SET Population = 5000000
 WHERE Name = 'Sydney'
       AND CountryCode = 'AUS';
```

There is no index on the Name column, but there is one on CountryCode. So, the update requires a scan of part of the CountryCode index. Listing 9-3 shows an example of executing the query in the REPEATABLE READ transaction isolation level.

Listing 9-3. The locks held in the REPEATABLE READ transaction isolation level

```
-- Connection    Processlist ID    Thread ID    Event ID
-- -----------------------------------------------------
--            1              701         1149           6
--            2              702         1150           6

-- Connection 1
Connection 1> SET SESSION transaction_isolation = 'REPEATABLE-READ';
Query OK, 0 rows affected (0.2697 sec)

Connection 1> START TRANSACTION;
Query OK, 0 rows affected (0.0007 sec)

Connection 1> UPDATE world.city
                 SET Population = 5000000
               WHERE Name = 'Sydney'
                     AND CountryCode = 'AUS';
Query OK, 1 row affected (0.0024 sec)

Rows matched: 1  Changed: 1  Warnings: 0

-- Connection 2
Connection 2> SELECT index_name, lock_type,
                     lock_mode, COUNT(*)
                FROM performance_schema.data_locks
```

```
              WHERE object_schema = 'world'
                AND object_name = 'city'
                AND thread_id = 1149
              GROUP BY index_name, lock_type, lock_mode;
+-------------+-----------+---------------+----------+
| index_name  | lock_type | lock_mode     | COUNT(*) |
+-------------+-----------+---------------+----------+
| NULL        | TABLE     | IX            |        1 |
| CountryCode | RECORD    | X             |       14 |
| PRIMARY     | RECORD    | X,REC_NOT_GAP |       14 |
| CountryCode | RECORD    | X,GAP         |        1 |
+-------------+-----------+---------------+----------+
4 rows in set (0.0102 sec)

-- Connection 1
Connection 1> ROLLBACK;
Query OK, 0 rows affected (0.0730 sec)

Connection 1> SET SESSION transaction_isolation = @@global.transaction_
isolation;
Query OK, 0 rows affected (0.0004 sec)
```

Fourteen record locks are taken on each of the CountryCode index and the primary key, and one gap lock is taken on the CountryCode index. Compare this to the locks held after executing the query in the READ COMMITTED transaction isolation level as shown in Listing 9-4.

Listing 9-4. The locks held in the READ-COMMITTED transaction isolation level

```
-- Connection   Processlist ID   Thread ID   Event ID
-- -------------------------------------------------
--          1            703         1153           6
--          2            704         1154           6

-- Connection 1
Connection 1> SET SESSION transaction_isolation = 'READ-COMMITTED';
Query OK, 0 rows affected (0.0003 sec)
```

```
Connection 1> START TRANSACTION;
Query OK, 0 rows affected (0.0002 sec)

Connection 1> UPDATE world.city
                 SET Population = 5000000
               WHERE Name = 'Sydney'
                 AND CountryCode = 'AUS';
Query OK, 1 row affected (0.0014 sec)

Rows matched: 1  Changed: 1  Warnings: 0

-- Connection 2
Connection 2> SELECT index_name, lock_type,
                 lock_mode, COUNT(*)
               FROM performance_schema.data_locks
             WHERE object_schema = 'world'
               AND object_name = 'city'
               AND thread_id = 1153
             GROUP BY index_name, lock_type, lock_mode;
+-------------+-----------+----------------+----------+
| index_name  | lock_type | lock_mode      | COUNT(*) |
+-------------+-----------+----------------+----------+
| NULL        | TABLE     | IX             |        1 |
| CountryCode | RECORD    | X,REC_NOT_GAP  |        1 |
| PRIMARY     | RECORD    | X,REC_NOT_GAP  |        1 |
+-------------+-----------+----------------+----------+
3 rows in set (0.0035 sec)

-- Connection 1
Connection 1> ROLLBACK;
Query OK, 0 rows affected (0.0780 sec)

Connection 1> SET SESSION transaction_isolation = @@global.transaction_
isolation;
Query OK, 0 rows affected (0.0003 sec)
```

Here the record locks are reduced to one lock on each of the CountryCode index and primary key. There are no gap locks.

It is not all workloads that can use the READ COMMITTED transaction isolation level. If you must have SELECT statements return the same result when executed multiple times in the same transaction or have different queries correspond to the same point in time, you must use REPEATABLE READ or SERIALIZABLE. However, in many cases, it is an option to reduce the isolation level, and you can choose different isolation levels for different transactions. If you are migrating an application from Oracle DB, you are already using READ COMMITTED, and you can also use it in MySQL.

Configuration

There are not many configuration options that directly affect locking, but it is good to be familiar with those that do exist particularly as some can affect the level of mutex and semaphore contention. This section covers splitting resources into multiple partitions, disabling the InnoDB adaptive hash index, and limiting the number of write locks.

Resource Partitioning

Mutex and semaphore contention arises from many threads using the same resource concurrently. A simple but powerful way to reduce the contention is to split a single resource into multiple parts which is exactly what has been done for the InnoDB buffer pool, the InnoDB adaptive hash index, and the table open cache. Table 9-1 shows the configuration options that control how many instances a resource is split into.

Table 9-1. *Configuration options controlling number of instances for resources*

Option	Default Value	Description
innodb_adaptive_ hash_index_parts	8	The number of partitions for the adaptive hash index. The partitioning is over the indexes.
innodb_buffer_ pool_instances	1 or 8	How many parts the buffer pool is split into. The default is 1 if the total size of the buffer pool is less than 1 GiB, otherwise 8 unless on a 32-bit Windows system.
table_open_cache_ instances	16	The number of parts for the table open cache.

Note   For all three options, they require a restart of MySQL to change the value.

For the InnoDB buffer pool, the default number of instances depends on the platform and the size of the buffer pool. The default is 1 if the total size is less than 1 GiB and otherwise 8. For 32-bit Windows, the default is 1 below 1.3 GiB; otherwise, each instance is made to be 128 MiB. The maximum number of instances is 64.

Note   You may also have heard of the `metadata_locks_hash_instances` option. This was deprecated in MySQL 5.7 and removed in MySQL 8.0.13. The reason for this was a change to the implementation of metadata locks rendering the option unnecessary.

If multiple partitions of a resource help reduce the contention, it may seem like a no brainer to increase the number of partitions. However, it is more complex than this as more partitions also introduce an overhead, so it is a matter of balancing this overhead over the reduced contention on the resource latches. In the extreme of a database that never executes more than a single concurrent query, you are usually better off with just one partition of each resource. "Usually" because for large table open caches, multiple partitions help making the least recently used (LRU) algorithm more efficient when it is necessary to evict a table from the cache.

In general, you should not have the number of partitions larger than the number of CPU cores. That said, the default values are a good starting point, and, in the end, you will need to test with your combination of system and workload to verify the optimal settings. In case of the adaptive hash index, you may even need to disable it altogether.

Disabling the InnoDB Adaptive Hash Index

The adaptive hash index feature works automatically within InnoDB. If InnoDB detects that you are using a secondary index frequently and adaptive hash indexes are enabled, it will build a hash index on the fly of the most frequently used values. The hash index is exclusively stored in the buffer pool and thus is not persisted when you restart MySQL. If InnoDB detects that the memory can be used better for loading more pages into the buffer pool, it will discard part of the hash index. This is what is meant when it is said that it is an adaptive index: InnoDB will try to adapt it to be optimal for your queries.

167

In theory, the adaptive hash index is a win-win situation. You get the advantages of having a hash index without the need to consider which columns you need to add it for, and the memory usage is all automatically handled. However, there is an overhead of having it enabled, and not all workloads benefit from it. In fact, for some workloads, the overhead can become so large that there are severe performance issues, and in those cases, it does not help to change the number of hash partitions.

The larger the part of the working data set that does not fit into the buffer pool, the more changes you have to the secondary indexes, and the less the secondary indexes are used for filtering, the more likely you will benefit from disabling the adaptive hash index. Cases where the adaptive hash index is a problem typically manifest themselves through a high number of waits on mutexes and rw-lock semaphores in the btr0sea.cc file which is where the adaptive hash index search is implemented.

If you experience that the adaptive hash index becomes a bottleneck, you can enable or disable the feature using the innodb_adaptive_hash_index option. Do be aware that while you can enable and disable the feature dynamically, disabling the adaptive hash index evicts all hash indexes from the buffer pool, and a warmup period is required upon re-enabling the index. For this reason, in replication setups, it is worth disabling the adaptive hash index in one replica first, and monitor whether your application benefits from the change before disabling it system-wide. If you need to re-enable the adaptive hash index on the read-write replica, consider failing over to another replica where the feature is still enabled, so the application is less affected while the re-enabled replica goes through its warmup period.

Tip   If you want to disable the adaptive hash index, do it first on a single replica, so you avoid having all replicas going through a warmup period if you need to re-enable the feature.

The last configuration option that will be discussed allows you to reduce the priority of metadata write locks.

Reducing Priority of Metadata Write Locks

By default, if there are two metadata lock requests for a table and one is a read request and the other a write request, then the write request is given priority. This is usually fine as writes are more intrusive than reads, so in most cases, it is best to give them priority, so they can complete as quickly as possible.

However, in case of foreign keys, you may run into problems with this approach. When you perform DDL against a table with a foreign key, the statement requests a shared metadata lock on the parent table. If you have continued transactions holding write locks against the parent table, the DDL statement on the child table will never be able to proceed even if the child table is never used. So, you need some way to make MySQL stop up and allow the read metadata lock request to move ahead.

You can do that with the `max_write_lock_count` option which takes a value between 1 and the maximum supported integer for your system. The default is the maximum supported value. Every time `max_write_lock_count` locks have been granted, MySQL will give priority to some read locks. This helps ensuring that read lock requests are not starved.

You need to be careful in changing the value of `max_write_lock_count` as a too low value can cause transactions with write locks – remember they are exclusive locks – to take too long to complete. While the write transactions are outstanding, their locks can prevent other transactions to proceed. As you can change `max_write_lock_count` dynamically, keep a close eye with the system, and be prepared to revert the change, if it causes side effects that are worse than the cure.

Preemptive Locking

The last strategy that will be discussed is preemptive locking. If you have a complex transaction executing several queries, it can in some cases be an advantage to execute a `SELECT ... FOR UPDATE` or `SELECT ... FOR SHARE` query to take locks on the records you know you will need later in the transaction. Another case where it can be useful is to ensure you access the rows in the same order for different tasks.

Preemptive locking is particularly effective to reduce the frequency of deadlocks. One drawback is that you will end up holding the locks for longer. Overall, preemptive locking is a strategy that should be used sparingly, but when used for the right cases, it can be powerful to prevent deadlocks.

Summary

This chapter has looked into strategies to reduce the impact of locks with the strategies ranging from reducing the number of locks and for how long they are held to change the configuration to reduce the impact of locking.

Most importantly, you should not hold more locks than necessary and not hold them for longer than required. Reducing the size of your transactions and the time it takes to complete the transaction are two of the most powerful ways to reduce lock contention. Furthermore, by choosing indexes appropriately, you can reduce the number of locks required by a given statement. Similarly, the transaction isolation level impacts the number of locks and duration of them with the READ COMMITTED transaction isolation level being a common choice to reduce the lock impact.

With respect to deadlocks, then it is important to access records in the same order as much as possible throughout your application. One option to ensure this is preemptive locking, though that should be used sparingly as it increases the duration the locks are held.

Finally, change the configuration to reduce the impact of locks. If you have mutex contention on the buffer pool, adaptive hash index, or the table open cache, you can partition the resource, or for the adaptive hash index, you can disable the feature altogether. For DDL statements requesting metadata read locks due to foreign keys, it can also be useful to limit the number of write locks that will be granted before a read lock is given priority.

This chapter has touched on the impact of indexes and foreign keys on locking. The next chapter will go into more detail on those topics.

CHAPTER 10

Indexes and Foreign Keys

In the previous chapter, you learned how indexes and foreign keys can influence locking. This is a topic that is worth diving further into as it is important to understand the effects.

The first part of this chapter investigates how primary, secondary, ascending, descending, and unique indexes affect locking. The second part covers foreign keys and how they affect locking for DML and DDL statements.

Indexes

In short indexes provide a shortcut to access a given record, so that the number of records examined is reduced. This has a positive effect on the number of locks as only rows accessed are subject to locking. This was what you saw in the previous chapter when an index was added to the Name column of the world.city table for a query that filtered on the Name column. Indexes become particularly important when you join tables as without indexes, the number of accessed rows is the product of the number of rows in the joined tables.

Note   You may consider indexes less important with the support for hash joins in MySQL 8. While this is to some degree true for non-locking statement, it is much less the case for statements taking locks as excessive locking can cause lock waits and deadlocks. As discussed in Chapter 11, locks also consume memory in the buffer pool, so more locks mean less memory for caching data. Similarly, reducing the number of rows accessed also reduces the turnover of pages in the buffer pool which improves buffer pool hit rate.

This section first discusses the use of primary versus secondary indexes, then ascending versus descending indexes, and finally unique indexes.

Primary vs. Secondary Indexes

The most effective way to access a row is by its primary key as that ensures just the rows that are affected by the statement are accessed. As an example, consider Listing 10-1 which adds a secondary index on the Name column of world.city and updates the population of the city names Sydney.

Listing 10-1. Updating row by non-unique secondary index

```
-- Connection    Processlist ID    Thread ID    Event ID
-- ---------------------------------------------------
--            1              713         1171           6
--            2              714         1172           6
-- Connection 1
Connection 1> ALTER TABLE world.city
              ADD INDEX (Name);
Query OK, 0 rows affected (1.3916 sec)

Records: 0  Duplicates: 0  Warnings: 0

Connection 1> START TRANSACTION;
Query OK, 0 rows affected (0.0002 sec)

Connection 1> UPDATE world.city
              SET Population = 5000000
              WHERE Name = 'Sydney';
Query OK, 1 row affected (0.0007 sec)

Rows matched: 1  Changed: 1  Warnings: 0


-- Connection 2
Connection 2> SELECT index_name, lock_type,
                 lock_mode, lock_data
              FROM performance_schema.data_locks
              WHERE object_schema = 'world'
                 AND object_name = 'city'
                 AND thread_id = 1171\G
```

```
*************************** 1. row ***************************
index_name: NULL
 lock_type: TABLE
 lock_mode: IX
 lock_data: NULL
*************************** 2. row ***************************
index_name: Name
 lock_type: RECORD
 lock_mode: X
 lock_data: 'Sydney                           ', 130
*************************** 3. row ***************************
index_name: PRIMARY
 lock_type: RECORD
 lock_mode: X,REC_NOT_GAP
 lock_data: 130
*************************** 4. row ***************************
index_name: Name
 lock_type: RECORD
 lock_mode: X,GAP
 lock_data: 'Syktyvkar                        ', 3660
4 rows in set (0.0006 sec)

-- Connection 1
Connection 1> ROLLBACK;
Query OK, 0 rows affected (0.0625 sec)

Connection 1> ALTER TABLE world.city
              DROP INDEX Name;
Query OK, 0 rows affected (0.4090 sec)

Records: 0  Duplicates: 0  Warnings: 0)
```

Despite that the update only affects one row, there are three exclusive record level locks with a record as well as gap lock on the Name index and lock on the row record using the primary key.

If you on the other hand perform the same update but access the row using the primary key, only the record lock on the primary key will be required as shown in Listing 10-2.

Listing 10-2. Updating row by the primary index

```
-- Connection    Processlist ID    Thread ID    Event ID
-- ---------------------------------------------------
--          1              719         1180           6
--          2              720         1181           6

-- Connection 1
Connection 1> ALTER TABLE world.city
              ADD INDEX (Name);
Query OK, 0 rows affected (1.1499 sec)

Records: 0  Duplicates: 0  Warnings: 0


Connection 1> SELECT ID
                FROM world.city
               WHERE Name = 'Sydney';
+-----+
| ID  |
+-----+
| 130 |
+-----+
1 row in set (0.0004 sec)

Connection 1> START TRANSACTION;
Query OK, 0 rows affected (0.0002 sec)

Connection 1> UPDATE world.city
                 SET Population = 5000000
               WHERE ID = 130;
Query OK, 1 row affected (0.0027 sec)

Rows matched: 1  Changed: 1  Warnings: 0
```

```
-- Connection 2
Connection 2> SELECT index_name, lock_type,
                     lock_mode, lock_data
                FROM performance_schema.data_locks
               WHERE object_schema = 'world'
                 AND object_name = 'city'
                 AND thread_id = 1180\G
*************************** 1. row ***************************
index_name: NULL
 lock_type: TABLE
 lock_mode: IX
 lock_data: NULL
*************************** 2. row ***************************
index_name: PRIMARY
 lock_type: RECORD
 lock_mode: X,REC_NOT_GAP
 lock_data: 130
2 rows in set (0.0007 sec)

-- Connection 1
Connection 1> ROLLBACK;
Query OK, 0 rows affected (0.0410 sec)

Connection 1> ALTER TABLE world.city
                  DROP INDEX Name;
Query OK, 0 rows affected (0.3257 sec)

Records: 0  Duplicates: 0  Warnings: 0
```

In this case, the value of the primary key (the ID column) is first obtained outside the transaction that updates the row, and then the primary key value is used in the WHERE clause of the UPDATE statement. The result is that the only record level lock held is an exclusive lock on the primary key with a value of 130.

Caution   Determining the primary key outside the transaction does open for the possibility of the data changing between obtaining the primary key value and performing the update. So, you should take this as an example only.

Except when you need to change all rows in a table, you should aim at using an index to access the rows. Even for full table updates, if it is not a requirement for the changes to be applied atomically, then for large tables it is an advantage to apply the changes in relatively small batches defined by ranges on the primary key.

Tip   If you filter by functions, a great way to reduce the number of rows examined is to add a functional index (available in MySQL 8.0.13 and later). Alternatively, in MySQL 5.7 and later, you can add a generated column with an index.

There is more to indexes and locking though than the number of rows accessed. Both descending indexes as you will read about next and unique indexes that follow can also reduce the amount of locks.

Ascending vs. Descending Indexes

MySQL 8 has support for descending indexes which can improve the performance when accessing rows in descending order. You can use an ascending index to access rows in descending order, so the main benefit from a descending index in such a case is that there is no jumping forth and back in the page. Does that mean there is no benefit of choosing the order of your index when it comes to locking?

When you use an index in the opposite order of how it stores the index records, you will pay a small price as you will need to lock the gap at the beginning of the search. Listing 10-3 shows the locks held when using an ascending index when increasing the population with 10% of the three most populous cities with an existing population between one and two million.

Listing 10-3. Updating rows in descending order by ascending index

```
-- Connection    Processlist ID    Thread ID    Event ID
-- -------------------------------------------------------
--          1               836         1363           6

-- Connection 1
Connection 1> ALTER TABLE world.city
              ADD INDEX (Population);
Query OK, 0 rows affected (1.1838 sec)
```

Records: 0 Duplicates: 0 Warnings: 0

Connection 1> START TRANSACTION;
Query OK, 0 rows affected (0.0005 sec)

Connection 1> UPDATE world.city
              SET Population = Population * 1.10
           WHERE Population BETWEEN 1000000 AND 2000000
           ORDER BY Population DESC
           LIMIT 3;
Query OK, 3 rows affected (0.0014 sec)

Rows matched: 3 Changed: 3 Warnings: 0

-- Investigation #1
-- Connection 2
Connection 2> SELECT index_name, lock_type,
                 lock_mode, lock_data
              FROM performance_schema.data_locks
           WHERE object_schema = 'world'
               AND object_name = 'city'
               AND lock_type = 'RECORD'
               AND thread_id = 1363
           ORDER BY index_name, lock_data DESC;

index_name	lock_type	lock_mode	lock_data
Population	RECORD	X,GAP	2016131, 3018
Population	RECORD	X	1987996, 936
Population	RECORD	X	1977246, 2824
Population	RECORD	X	1975294, 3539
PRIMARY	RECORD	X,REC_NOT_GAP	936
PRIMARY	RECORD	X,REC_NOT_GAP	3539
PRIMARY	RECORD	X,REC_NOT_GAP	2824

7 rows in set (0.0008 sec)

There are, as expected, three locks on the primary key and the `Population` index with one lock per updated row. This is as optimal as it can be. The price in terms of locks of using an ascending index is that there is also a gap lock on the index record with a population of 2016131 and the primary key set to 3018.

Tip   InnoDB always appends the primary key to the end of non-unique secondary indexes, so it is easy to go to the row from the index record. The reason for this is that InnoDB organizes the rows according to the clustered index and when there is an explicit primary key that is used for the clustered index.

There are two more things to note about the locks in this example. First, if you update from the end of the index (the cities with the highest population), then you will see a record lock on the supremum pseudo-record rather than a gap lock and the high population end of the interval. This is because the supremum pseudo-record is not a real record, so a record lock on it is effectively just a lock on the gap before it. Second, the exact lock types involved depends on the `WHERE` clause, so if you change or remove the `WHERE` clause, you may see additional gap locks on the secondary index. These additional gap locks will also be present in the same example using a descending index.

If you use a descending index, the list of locks is the same except for the gap lock. Listing 10-4 shows an example of this.

Listing 10-4. Updating rows in descending order by descending index

```
-- Connection   Processlist ID   Thread ID   Event ID
-- ----------------------------------------------------
--          1              843        1374          6

-- Connection 1
Connection 1> ALTER TABLE world.city
              ADD INDEX (Population DESC);
Query OK, 0 rows affected (0.8885 sec)

Records: 0  Duplicates: 0  Warnings: 0

Connection 1> START TRANSACTION;
Query OK, 0 rows affected (0.0006 sec)
```

```
Connection 1> UPDATE world.city
                 SET Population = Population * 1.10
              WHERE Population BETWEEN 1000000 AND 2000000
              ORDER BY Population DESC
              LIMIT 3;
Query OK, 3 rows affected (0.0021 sec)

Rows matched: 3  Changed: 3  Warnings: 0

-- Investigation #1
-- Connection 2
Connection 2> SELECT index_name, lock_type,
                 lock_mode, lock_data
                FROM performance_schema.data_locks
              WHERE object_schema = 'world'
                AND object_name = 'city'
                AND lock_type = 'RECORD'
                AND thread_id = 1374
              ORDER BY index_name, lock_data DESC;
+------------+-----------+---------------+---------------+
| index_name | lock_type | lock_mode     | lock_data     |
+------------+-----------+---------------+---------------+
| Population | RECORD    | X             | 1987996, 936  |
| Population | RECORD    | X             | 1977246, 2824 |
| Population | RECORD    | X             | 1975294, 3539 |
| PRIMARY    | RECORD    | X,REC_NOT_GAP | 936           |
| PRIMARY    | RECORD    | X,REC_NOT_GAP | 3539          |
| PRIMARY    | RECORD    | X,REC_NOT_GAP | 2824          |
+------------+-----------+---------------+---------------+
6 rows in set (0.0008 sec)
```

The conclusion is that the main benefit from descending indexes for descending access to the data is the performance gain for a more sequential data access rather than from reduced locking. However, that said, if you have many descending range scans when updating or deleting data, you will also benefit from fewer gap locks.

Another index type that will reduce locking is unique indexes.

Unique Indexes

The primary purpose of a unique index compared to an equivalent non-unique index is to add the constraint that each value is only allowed once. So, at the surface, unique indexes seem to have little relevance for the discussion of locks beyond what has already been mentioned. However, InnoDB can take advantage of knowing that at most one record (except where the value is NULL) can exist for a given equity condition and use this to reduce the amount of locking required.

As an example, consider two tables, _tmp_city1 and _tmp_city2, containing the same subset of rows from the world.city table. The _tmp_city1 table has a non-unique index on the Name column, whereas the _tmp_city2 table has a unique index on the column. Then a single row is updated using a condition on the Name column. Listing 10-5 shows this.

Listing 10-5. The difference between non-unique and unique secondary indexes

```
-- Connection    Processlist ID    Thread ID    Event ID
-- -------------------------------------------------------
--            1             736          1209           6
--            2             737          1210           6

-- Connection 1
Connection 1> DROP TABLE IF EXISTS world._tmp_city1;
Query OK, 0 rows affected (0.0643 sec)
Note (code 1051): Unknown table 'world._tmp_city1'

Connection 1> CREATE TABLE world._tmp_city1
              SELECT *
                FROM world.city
               WHERE CountryCode = 'AUS';
Query OK, 14 rows affected (1.3112 sec)

Records: 14  Duplicates: 0  Warnings: 0

Connection 1> ALTER TABLE world._tmp_city1
                ADD PRIMARY KEY (ID),
                ADD INDEX (Name);
Query OK, 0 rows affected (2.5572 sec)
```

Records: 0 Duplicates: 0 Warnings: 0

Connection 1> START TRANSACTION;
Query OK, 0 rows affected (0.0002 sec)

Connection 1> UPDATE world._tmp_city1
              SET Population = 5000000
              WHERE Name = 'Sydney';
Query OK, 1 row affected (0.0007 sec)

Rows matched: 1 Changed: 1 Warnings: 0

-- Connection 2
Connection 2> DROP TABLE IF EXISTS world._tmp_city2;
Query OK, 0 rows affected (0.1361 sec)
Note (code 1051): Unknown table 'world._tmp_city2'

Connection 2> CREATE TABLE world._tmp_city2
              SELECT *
                FROM world.city
               WHERE CountryCode = 'AUS';
Query OK, 14 rows affected (0.8276 sec)

Records: 14 Duplicates: 0 Warnings: 0

Connection 2> ALTER TABLE world._tmp_city2
              ADD PRIMARY KEY (ID),
              ADD UNIQUE INDEX (Name);
Query OK, 0 rows affected (2.4895 sec)

Records: 0 Duplicates: 0 Warnings: 0

Connection 2> START TRANSACTION;
Query OK, 0 rows affected (0.0003 sec)

Connection 2> UPDATE world._tmp_city2
              SET Population = 5000000
              WHERE Name = 'Sydney';
Query OK, 1 row affected (0.0005 sec)

Rows matched: 1 Changed: 1 Warnings: 0

While the transactions are still ongoing, you can check the locks held by each connection. For Connection 1, the record locks are shown in Listing 10-6 which is investigation number 1 for the workload executed in Listing 10-5.

Listing 10-6. The record locks for Connection 1 (investigation number 1)

```
-- Investigation #1
-- Connection 3
Connection 3> SELECT index_name, lock_mode, lock_data
    b             FROM performance_schema.data_locks
              WHERE object_schema = 'world'
                    AND lock_type = 'RECORD'
                    AND thread_id = 1209\G
*************************** 1. row ***************************
index_name: Name
 lock_mode: X
 lock_data: 'Sydney                             ', 130
*************************** 2. row ***************************
index_name: PRIMARY
 lock_mode: X,REC_NOT_GAP
 lock_data: 130
*************************** 3. row ***************************
index_name: Name
 lock_mode: X,GAP
 lock_data: 'Townsville                         ', 142
3 rows in set (0.0094 sec)
```

This is what is expected based on the experience of the previous examples, a record lock on the primary key as well as a record and gap lock on the index. For Connection 2, only two of these locks exist as the output in Listing 10-7 of investigation number 2 from Listing 10-5 shows.

Listing 10-7. The record locks for Connection 2 (investigation number 2)

```
-- Investigation #2
Connection 3> SELECT index_name, lock_mode, lock_data
              FROM performance_schema.data_locks
            WHERE object_schema = 'world'
```

```
                    AND lock_type = 'RECORD'
                    AND thread_id = 1210\G
*************************** 1. row ***************************
index_name: Name
 lock_mode: X,REC_NOT_GAP
 lock_data: 'Sydney                              ', 130
*************************** 2. row ***************************
index_name: PRIMARY
 lock_mode: X,REC_NOT_GAP
 lock_data: 130
2 rows in set (0.0006 sec)
```

Here only the two record locks on the secondary index and primary key are needed.

Tip   For a comprehensive list of the locks taken by various statements with and without unique indexes in InnoDB, see `https://dev.mysql.com/doc/refman/en/innodb-locks-set.html`.

Finally, roll back and drop the test tables:

```
-- Connection 1
Connection 1> ROLLBACK;
Query OK, 0 rows affected (0.0714 sec)

Connection 1> DROP TABLE world._tmp_city1;
Query OK, 0 rows affected (0.7642 sec)

-- Connection 2
Connection 2> ROLLBACK;
Query OK, 0 rows affected (0.1038 sec)

Connection 2> DROP TABLE world._tmp_city2;
Query OK, 0 rows affected (1.4438 sec)
```

Unlike unique keys that can be used to reduce locking, foreign keys will add locks as it is discussed next.

Foreign Keys

Foreign keys are a powerful tool to ensure data consistency between tables in a database. However, they have a drawback as to provide this safety, additional locks on the parent and child tables are required.

The additional locks required depends on whether it is the parent or child table of the foreign key relationship that is changed and which columns are changed. For metadata locks, a shared lock is in most cases taken on the tables involved in the foreign key relationship. An exception is when inserting into the parent table of a foreign key relationship; in which case, a shared metadata lock is not taken on the child table.

At the InnoDB level, if a column included in a foreign key is modified, a shared record-level lock is set on the table at the other end of the relationship for the row with the new value of the foreign key column, and an intention shared lock is set for the table. This happens whether the foreign key is violated or not. If no foreign key columns are changed, InnoDB does not take any extra locks even if the column is used for filtering.

To understand how this affects you, it is worth considering a couple of examples. They both use the sakila.inventory table which has two foreign keys to the film and store tables. At the same time, it is the parent table for a foreign key from the film_ rental table. This is shown in Figure 10-1.

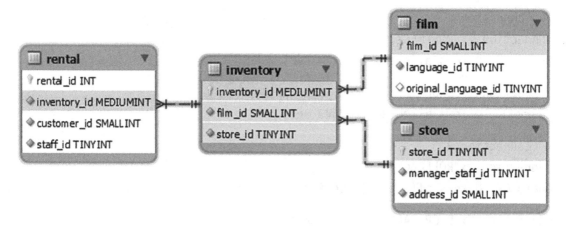

Figure 10-1. *The* sakila.inventory *table and its foreign key relationships*

In the figure only the columns involved in the primary keys and foreign keys are included. First an example of updating a row in the inventory table will be discussed and then a DDL statement.

DML Statement

As an example of the locks caused by foreign keys for DML statements, consider an UPDATE statement moving a film from one store to the other. The update is by the primary key with an example of this shown in Listing 10-8.

Listing 10-8. Updating a row in a table with foreign keys relationships

```
-- Connection    Processlist ID    Thread ID   Event ID
-- -----------------------------------------------------
--          1                814         1329          6

-- Connection 1
Connection 1> START TRANSACTION;
Query OK, 0 rows affected (0.0002 sec)

Connection 1> UPDATE sakila.inventory
              SET store_id = 1
            WHERE inventory_id = 4090;
Query OK, 1 row affected (0.0008 sec)

Rows matched: 1  Changed: 1  Warnings: 0
```

Because of the foreign keys, this simple single table and row update takes a number of locks across a large number of tables in the sakila database. Listing 10-9 shows the InnoDB locks caused by the statement (this is investigation number 1).

Listing 10-9. The InnoDB data locks caused by the UPDATE statement

```
-- Investigation #1
-- Connection 2
Connection 2> SELECT object_schema, object_name, lock_type,
                     index_name, lock_mode, lock_data
                FROM performance_schema.data_locks
               WHERE thread_id = 1329\G
```

```
*************************** 1. row ***************************
object_schema: sakila
  object_name: inventory
    lock_type: TABLE
   index_name: NULL
    lock_mode: IX
    lock_data: NULL
*************************** 2. row ***************************
object_schema: sakila
  object_name: inventory
    lock_type: RECORD
   index_name: PRIMARY
    lock_mode: X,REC_NOT_GAP
    lock_data: 4090
*************************** 3. row ***************************
object_schema: sakila
  object_name: store
    lock_type: TABLE
   index_name: NULL
    lock_mode: IS
    lock_data: NULL
*************************** 4. row ***************************
object_schema: sakila
  object_name: store
    lock_type: RECORD
   index_name: PRIMARY
    lock_mode: S,REC_NOT_GAP
    lock_data: 1
4 rows in set (0.0102 sec)
```

In this case, InnoDB takes an intention shared lock on the store tables as well as a shared lock on the record with the primary keys set 1. There are no locks on the film table as the UPDATE statement does not change the value of the film_id column.

For the metadata locks, it is more complicated as can be seen from Listing 10-10 (investigation number 2).

Listing 10-10. The metadata locks caused by the UPDATE statement

```
-- Investigation #2
Connection 2> SELECT object_type, object_schema, object_name,
                     column_name, lock_type, lock_duration
                FROM performance_schema.metadata_locks
               WHERE owner_thread_id = 1329
               ORDER BY object_type, object_schema, object_name,
                        column_name, lock_type\G
*************************** 1. row ***************************
  object_type: SCHEMA
object_schema: sakila
  object_name: NULL
  column_name: NULL
    lock_type: INTENTION_EXCLUSIVE
lock_duration: TRANSACTION
*************************** 2. row ***************************
  object_type: TABLE
object_schema: sakila
  object_name: customer
  column_name: NULL
    lock_type: SHARED_READ
lock_duration: TRANSACTION
*************************** 3. row ***************************
  object_type: TABLE
object_schema: sakila
  object_name: film
  column_name: NULL
    lock_type: SHARED_READ
lock_duration: TRANSACTION
*************************** 4. row ***************************
  object_type: TABLE
object_schema: sakila
  object_name: inventory
```

```
  column_name: NULL
    lock_type: SHARED_WRITE
lock_duration: TRANSACTION
*************************** 5. row ***************************
  object_type: TABLE
object_schema: sakila
  object_name: payment
  column_name: NULL
    lock_type: SHARED_WRITE
lock_duration: TRANSACTION
*************************** 6. row ***************************
  object_type: TABLE
object_schema: sakila
  object_name: rental
  column_name: NULL
    lock_type: SHARED_WRITE
lock_duration: TRANSACTION
*************************** 7. row ***************************
  object_type: TABLE
object_schema: sakila
  object_name: staff
  column_name: NULL
    lock_type: SHARED_READ
lock_duration: TRANSACTION
*************************** 8. row ***************************
  object_type: TABLE
object_schema: sakila
  object_name: store
  column_name: NULL
    lock_type: SHARED_READ
lock_duration: TRANSACTION
8 rows in set (0.0007 sec)
```

You will not always see the INTENTION_EXCLUSIVE lock on the sakila schema, so your result may only include the seven table level metadata locks.

This shows that there is a SHARED_READ lock on the film and store tables, and a SHARED_WRITE on the rental table which is expected from the discussion this far. However, there are several more metadata locks. The extra locks are because the rental table's foreign key to inventory is ON UPDATE CASCADE. That makes the metadata locks cascade as well to the foreign key relations for the rental table. The lesson of the example is that with foreign keys, particularly cascading relations, you need to be aware that the number of metadata locks quickly increases.

Finally, roll back the transaction:

```
-- Connection 1
Connection 1> ROLLBACK;
Query OK, 0 rows affected (0.1104 sec)
```

DDL Statement

When you execute DDL statements against a table with a foreign key, then a SHARED_UPGRADABLE metadata lock is taken for each of the parent and child tables of the modified table. An example of this is shown in Listing 10-11.

Listing 10-11. Performing DDL on a table with foreign key relations

```
-- Connection   Processlist ID   Thread ID   Event ID
-- ----------------------------------------------------
--           1              820        1340          6
--           2              821        1341          6

-- Connection 1
Connection 1> OPTIMIZE TABLE sakila.inventory;

-- Connection 2
Connection 2> SELECT object_name, lock_type, lock_duration
                FROM performance_schema.metadata_locks
               WHERE owner_thread_id = 1340
                 AND object_type = 'TABLE';
```

```
+---------------+--------------------+---------------+
| object_name   | lock_type          | lock_duration |
+---------------+--------------------+---------------+
| inventory     | SHARED_NO_WRITE    | TRANSACTION   |
| film          | SHARED_UPGRADABLE  | STATEMENT     |
| rental        | SHARED_UPGRADABLE  | STATEMENT     |
| store         | SHARED_UPGRADABLE  | STATEMENT     |
| #sql-8490_334 | EXCLUSIVE          | STATEMENT     |
+---------------+--------------------+---------------+
5 rows in set (0.0014 sec)
```

In this case the cascading foreign key on the rental table does not cause further metadata locks as there is no update to cascade. The #sql-8490_334 table is the build table for the OPTIMIZE TABLE statement, and the name depends on the id of the mysqld process and the process list id of the connection executing the statement.

The conclusion is that while foreign keys are very important to ensure data consistency, in high concurrency workloads, they can become a bottleneck due to the additional locking (and time spend on constraint validation). However, do not by default dismiss foreign keys as you will risk the integrity of your data, and they are also useful for documenting the relationship between tables; the figure earlier in this chapter was automatically generated by MySQL Workbench based on the foreign keys.

Caution   Do not dismiss foreign keys because of the additional locking as they are necessary to ensure data consistency. If they become prohibitively expensive for your workload, you will need to ensure the data consistency in your application which is far from a trivial task. If you do not have good enough data integrity constraints, then you may end up returning invalid data to the users.

Summary

This chapter has taken a deep dive into the effects of indexes and foreign keys on locking. Indexes can help reduce locking, while foreign keys add locking.

The more selective an index you use, the fewer rows are accessed which translates into less locking. Thus, primary key access is the most optimal followed by unique indexes. Accessing using an index that is stored in the same order as you access the rows also helps.

For foreign keys, they do require additional locks to maintain data integrity. InnoDB adds a shared lock on the rows in the other end of the foreign key when modifying columns included in the foreign key, and an intention shared lock is set for the table. Additionally, a shared metadata lock is taken in most cases on the tables involved in the foreign key relationship. For cascading foreign keys, the metadata locks also cascade.

That concludes the discussion with the primary focus being on locks. There is another side to the coin though, transactions. Transactions are relevant both in the direct context of concurrency and with respect to locks. The next chapter starts out looking at transactions in general.

## CHAPTER 11

Transactions

Transactions are the big brother of statements. They group multiple changes together whether in a single statement or several statements, so they are applied or abandoned as a single unit. Mostly transactions are not much more than an afterthought and just considered when it is necessary to apply several statements together. That is a bad way to consider transactions. They are very important to ensure data integrity, and when used wrong, they can cause severe performance issues.

This chapter starts out discussing what transactions and the ACID concept are and then moves on to discussing why you need to take transactions seriously from a performance point of view by reviewing the impacts of transactions on locks and performance. Finally, it is discussed how the group commit feature can improve the performance of high concurrency systems.

Transactions and ACID

At the simplest point of view, a transaction is a container that includes one or more statements. However, that is a too simplistic view as a transaction also has properties of its own. Most importantly, it is the main tool to accomplishing *atomicity, consistency, isolation, and durability* (*ACID*). This section takes a closer look at each of these four properties.

Atomicity

The concept of atomicity means that all changes in a transaction are either committed or rolled back. This is where the idea of a container comes into play, so that all statements are treated as a unit of work – or in other words, a transaction is atomic.

© Jesper Wisborg Krogh 2021
J. W. Krogh, *MySQL Concurrency*, https://doi.org/10.1007/978-1-4842-6652-6_11

The classic example of why atomicity is important is a financial transaction between two bank accounts. An amount is withdrawn from the payer's account and inserted into the receiver's account. Without atomicity, you can end up with the money withdrawn but never inserted leaving one of the two parties out of pocket. That a transaction is atomic guarantees that if the money is withdrawn, the receiver also receives the money on their account.

Consistency

That the database fulfills the consistency property means that there are checks in place to ensure that if a transaction commits successfully, then the data is consistent. What consistency means is largely defined by the business logic. An example is that you cannot create a bank account for a nonexisting entity. Inside the database, it is the job of the constraints, including foreign keys, to ensure data consistency. By using a transaction, due to its atomic behavior, even if a constraint fails in the second or later step, then the whole transaction can be reverted (rolled back) and the database is left in its original and consistent state.

In some databases, the constraint checks can be deferred until the time the transaction is committed. If you consider the example where you are not allowed to have a bank account for a nonexisting entity, deferred constraints allows you to first create the account and then later - but within the same transaction - register the entity owning the account. Deferred constraints are primarily useful in connection with circular relations such as adding a group that must have a default group member, but since the member must belong to a group, it is necessary to temporarily relax the constraints while adding the group and its initial members.

Note   The use of deferred constraints is a debated topic, and it can be argued that it violates the principles of relational database theory. For example, C.J. Date argues that constraints must be satisfied at statement boundaries; see `https://www.brcommunity.com/articles.php?id=b065b`.

InnoDB does not support deferred constraints but does support disabling foreign key checks by explicitly disabling the `foreign_key_checks` variable which can be changed both at the global and session scope.

Tip   Disabling the foreign key checks can be useful when performing bulk load where you already have ensured that the data is consistent.

Unique key constraint checks cannot be disabled for InnoDB as the unique_checks option only dictates that a check is not required; InnoDB will still do it in some cases. (As an aside, the NDBCluster does defer some constraint checks till the time of commit.)

Isolation

The isolation property is what links transactions and locking. That two transactions are isolated means that they do not interfere with each other's view of the data. The isolation is at the data content level; two concurrent transactions may still interfere with each other in terms of performance and locking. MySQL, as most database systems, implements isolation using locks, and InnoDB has the concept of transaction isolation levels to define what isolation means. The transaction isolation levels are discussed in more detail in the next chapter.

Durability

That the data is durable means that data changes are not lost. In MySQL this only applies to committed data or for XA transactions for transactions in the prepared stage. InnoDB implements durability at the local level through the redo log and the binary log (if enabled which is the default in MySQL 8) with an internal XA transaction being used to ensure consistency between the two logs.

Note   XA transactions is a feature that allows distributed transactions, for example, spanning two systems or in case of the MySQL internals to make changes to InnoDB and the binary log commit or roll back together. It works by having a transaction manager and one or more resource managers (e.g., a database). For more information about MySQL and XA transactions, see https://dev.mysql.com/doc/refman/en/xa.html.

The commits are only guaranteed to be durable if both `innodb_flush_log_at_trx_commit` and `sync_binlog` are set to 1 (the default). To ensure durability if the local system crashes, you must also ensure that the binary log events have replicated to at least one replica. MySQL Group Replication or MySQL InnoDB Cluster is the best way to achieve this.

Tip   Replication is beyond the scope of this book. For an introduction to MySQL Group Replication and InnoDB Cluster, see, for example, *Introducing InnoDB Cluster* by Charles Bell (Apress) (`https://www.apress.com/gp/book/9781484238844`).

Impact of Transactions

Transactions may seem as an innocent concept if you think of them as containers used to group queries. However, it is important to understand that since transactions provide atomicity for groups of queries, the longer a transaction is active, the longer resources associated with the queries are held, and the more work done in a transaction, the more resources are required. What resources are used by queries that remain in use until the transaction has been committed? The main two are locks and undo logs.

Tip   InnoDB supports read-only transactions which have a lower overhead than read-write transactions. For auto-committing single-statement transactions, InnoDB will try to determine if the statement is read-only automatically. For multi-statement transactions, you can specify explicitly that it is a read-only transaction, when you start it: `START TRANSACTION READ ONLY;`

Locks

When the query executes, it takes locks, and when you use the default transaction isolation level – REPEATABLE READ – all locks are kept until the transaction is committed or rolled back. When you use the READ COMMITTED transaction isolation level, some locks may be released, but at least those involving the changed records are kept. Locks themselves are a resource, but it also requires memory to store the information about the locks. You may not think much of this for a normal workload, but huge transactions can end up using so much memory that the transaction fails with the `ER_LOCK_TABLE_FULL` error:

```
ERROR: 1206: The total number of locks exceeds the lock table size
```

As it can be seen from the warning message logged to the error log (more shortly), the memory required for the locks is taken from the buffer pool. Thus, the more locks you hold and the longer they are held, the less memory is available for caching data and indexes.

Caution   Having a transaction aborted because it has used all the lock memory is a quadruple whammy. First, it would have taken a while to update enough rows to use enough lock memory to trigger the error. That work has been wasted. Second, because of the number of changes required, it is likely going to take a very long time to roll back the transaction. Third, while the lock memory is used, InnoDB is effectively in read-only mode (some small transactions may be possible), and the lock memory is not released until the rollback has completed. Fourth, there is very little space left in the buffer pool to cache data and indexes.

The error is preceded by a warning in the error log saying that more than 67% of the buffer pool is used for locks or the adaptive hash index:

```
2020-06-08T10:47:11.415127Z 10 [Warning] [MY-011958] [InnoDB] Over 67
percent of the buffer pool is occupied by lock heaps or the adaptive hash
index! Check that your transactions do not set too many row locks. Your
buffer pool size is 7 MB. Maybe you should make the buffer pool bigger?
Starting the InnoDB Monitor to print diagnostics, including lock heap and
hash index sizes.
```

The warning is followed by regular repeating outputs of the InnoDB monitor, so you can determine which transactions are the culprits.

One lock type that is often neglected when it comes to transactions is the metadata lock. When a statement queries a table, a shared metadata lock is taken, and that metadata lock is held until the end of the transaction. While there is a metadata lock on a table, no connections can execute any DDL statements – including `OPTIMIZE TABLE` – against the table. If a DDL statement is blocked by a long-running transaction, it will in turn block all new queries from using that table. Chapter 14 will show an example of investigating such an issue.

The locks are held while the transaction is active. The transaction can however still have an impact even after it has completed through the undo logs.

Undo Logs

The changes that have been made during the transaction must also be stored as they are required, if you choose to roll back the transaction. This is easy to understand. More surprising is that even a transaction that has made no changes also can make undo information from other transactions stay around. This happens when the transaction requires a read view (a consistent snapshot), which is the case for the duration of the transaction when using the REPEATABLE READ transaction isolation level. The read view means that the transaction will return the row data that corresponds to the time when the transaction was started no matter whether other transactions change the data. In order to be able to deliver that, it is necessary to keep the old values of the rows that change during the lifetime of the transaction. Long-running transactions with a read view are the most common reason for ending up with huge undo logs, which in MySQL 5.7 and earlier could mean the ibdata1 file ended up being large. (In MySQL 8, the undo logs are always stored in separate undo tablespaces that can be truncated.)

Tip   The READ COMMITTED transaction isolation level is much less prone to large undo logs as the read views are only maintained for the duration of a statement.

The size of the active part of the undo log is measured in the history list length. The history list length is the number of transactions committed where the undo log has not yet been purged. This means that you cannot use the history list length to get a measure of the total amount of row changes. What it does tell you is how many units of old rows (one unit per transaction) there is in the linked list of changes that must be taken into consideration when you execute a query. The longer this linked list is, the more expensive it becomes to find the correct version of each row. In the end, if you have a large history list, it can severely impact the performance of all queries.

Note   The issue with the history list length is one of the biggest issues creating backups of large databases using logical backup tools such as `mysqlpump` and `mysqldump` using a single transaction to get a consistent backup. The backup can cause the history list length to become very large if there are many transactions committed during the backup.

What constitutes a large history list length? There are no firm rules about that – just that the smaller, the better. Typically, performance issues start to show up when the list is some thousand to a million transactions long, but the point where it becomes a bottleneck depends on the transactions committed in the undo logs and the workload while the history list length is large.

InnoDB automatically purges the history list in the background when the oldest parts are no longer needed. There are two options to control the purge as well as two to influence what happens, when the purge cannot be done. The options are

- **innodb_purge_batch_size:** The number of undo log pages that are purged per batch. The batch is divided among the purge threads. This option is not intended to be changed on production systems. The default is 300 with valid values between 1 and 5000.

- **innodb_purge_threads:** The number of purge threads to use in parallel. A higher parallelism can be useful if the data changes span many tables. On the other hand, if all changes are concentrated on few tables, a low value is preferred. Changing the number of purge threads requires a restart of MySQL. The default is 4 with valid values between 1 and 32.

- **innodb_max_purge_lag:** When the history list length is longer than the value of innodb_max_purge_lag, a delay is added to operations changing data to reduce the rate the history list is growing at the expense of higher statement latencies. The default value is 0 which means that a delay will never be added. Valid values are 0–4294967295.

- **innodb_max_purge_lag_delay:** The maximum delay that can be added to DML queries when the history list length is larger than innodb_max_purge_lag.

It is usually not necessary to change any of these settings; however, in special circumstances, it can be useful. If the purge threads cannot keep up, you can try to change the number of purge threads based on the number of tables that get modified; the more tables that are modified, the more purge threads are useful. When you change the number of purge threads, it is important to monitor the effect starting with a baseline before the change, so you can see whether the change makes an improvement.

The maximum purge lag options can be used to slow down DML statements modifying data. It is mostly useful when writes are limited to specific connections and delays do not cause additional write threads to be created in order to maintain the same throughput.

Group Commit

Remember that for the D in ACID (durability) to be true for InnoDB, you need to keep the `innodb_flush_log_at_trx_commit` and `sync_binlog` settings at their default value of 1 so the changes made by a transaction are synced to disk as part of the commit. While this is great to ensure you do not lose changes that have been confirmed to be committed in case of a crash, it does come at a cost performance wise as often the flush performance of disks can become the bottleneck.

The group commit feature exists to reduce this performance impact by slightly delaying the commits and group all the commits (thus the name) occurring during the delay and flush them to disk at the same time. Essentially, the group commit sacrifices a little latency for a higher throughput. In systems with a high concurrency of data changes, the group commit can greatly improve the performance when `sync_binlog = 1` is used.

The group commit feature is controlled using two configuration options:

- **binlog_group_commit_sync_delay:** The delay in milliseconds for waiting for more transactions to commit. Allowed values are 0–1000000 with 0 being the default. The larger the value, the more transactions will be committed together and thus the fewer `fsync()` calls.

- **binlog_group_commit_sync_no_delay_count:** The maximum number of transactions to allow in the group commit queue before completing the group commit. If this option is set to a value larger than 0, the commits may occur more often than set by `binlog_group_commit_sync_delay`. A value of 0 means an unlimited number of commits may be queued. Allowed values are 0–1000000 with 0 being the default.

If you can accept a small delay when committing your transactions, it is recommended to increase `binlog_group_commit_sync_delay` to reduce the flush rate. In principle, the larger the value, the larger the throughput, but you should of course take into consideration the maximum acceptable increase in commit latency for your workload. You can use the `binlog_group_commit_sync_no_delay_count` to avoid the number of transactions becoming too large in each group commit.

If you have replication enabled, then increasing `binlog_group_commit_sync_delay` can also have a positive performance effect on the replicas as the more transactions that are committed together, the more effective the `LOGICAL_CLOCK` algorithm for parallel replication (the `slave_parallel_type` option) becomes. (If you have `binlog_transaction_dependency_tracking = WRITESET`, the effect is less as transactions can be parallelized across group commits.) You must set the `binlog_group_commit_sync_delay` on the replication source to improve the parallel replication performance on the replicas.

Summary

Transactions are an important concept in databases. They help ensure that you can apply changes to several rows as a unit and that you can choose whether to apply the changes or roll them back.

This chapter started out discussing what transactions and the ACID concept are. ACID stands for atomicity, consistency, isolation, and durability, and transactions are directly involved in ensuring the first three of these properties and partly for durability. Isolation is in the context of concurrency interesting as it is what ensures that you can safely execute multiple transactions concurrently. In MySQL, isolation is implemented through locking.

The next section discussed why it is important to be aware of how transactions are being used. While they as such can be considered a container for changes, locks are held until the transaction is committed or rolled back, and they can block the undo logs from being purged. Both locks and large undo logs can affect the performance of queries even if they are not executed in one of the transactions causing the high number of locks or large number of undo logs. Locks use memory, which is taken from the buffer pool, so there is less memory available for caching data and indexes. A large amount of undo logs as measured by the history list length means that more row versions must be considered when InnoDB executes statements.

Finally, the concept of group commits was discussed. When flushing changes to disk at each commit, the group commit feature can be used to reduce the number of `fsync()` calls by completing several commits together. A nice side effect of group replication is that it can improve the performance of the `LOGICAL_CLOCK` algorithm for parallel replication.

The concept of transaction isolation levels was mentioned a few times in this chapter. The next chapter goes into more detail how the four supported transaction isolation levels work and how each level affects locking.

CHAPTER 12

Transaction Isolation Levels

In the previous chapter, you learned that isolation is an important property of transactions. As it turns out, it is not so straightforward to answer whether two transactions are isolated as the answer depends on what degree of isolation is required. The degree of isolation is defined through the transaction isolation levels.

InnoDB supports the four transaction isolation levels defined by the SQL:1992 standard[1], and they are in descending degree of isolation: SERIALIZABLE, REPEATABLE READ, READ COMMITTED, and READ UNCOMMITTED. The repeatable read transaction isolation level is the default. This chapter goes through each of these isolation levels and discusses how they work and their impact on locking.

To compare the locks taken when updating rows in the different transaction isolation levels, an example of updating the cities in the district Bratislava in Slovakia will be used. There are three cities in the world.city table for Slovakia:

```
mysql> SELECT ID, Name, District
        FROM world.city
        WHERE CountryCode = 'SVK';
+------+------------+--------------------+
| ID   | Name       | District           |
+------+------------+--------------------+
| 3209 | Bratislava | Bratislava         |
| 3210 | Košice     | Východné Slovensko |
| 3211 | Prešov     | Východné Slovensko |
+------+------------+--------------------+
3 rows in set (0.0032 sec)
```

---

[1]http://www.contrib.andrew.cmu.edu/~shadow/sql/sql1992.txt – if you are interested in buying a copy, see, for example, https://modern-sql.com/standard for links.

© Jesper Wisborg Krogh 2021
J. W. Krogh, *MySQL Concurrency*, https://doi.org/10.1007/978-1-4842-6652-6_12

The UPDATE statement can use the index on CountryCode to narrow down the search to the three cities and then use a non-indexed filter on District to find the one city matching the district. This will help expose the different amounts of locks for the SERIALIZABLE, REPEATABLE READ, and READ COMMITTED transaction isolation levels. For SERIALIZABLE and REPEATBLE READ, additionally, a test using a SELECT statement will be used.

After each of the examples, you need to roll back the transaction to return the database to its original state:

```
-- Connection 1
Connection 1> ROLLBACK;
Query OK, 0 rows affected (0.3022 sec)
```

With that said, you are ready to explore the four transaction isolation levels.

Serializable

The SERIALIZABLE isolation level is the strictest available. Except for SELECT statements with autocommit enabled (and no explicit transaction has been started), all statements take locks. For SELECT statements that is equivalent to adding FOR SHARE. This ensures that all aspects of the transaction is repeatable but also means that it is the transaction isolation level that takes most locks. Listing 12-1 shows an example of the locks taken by a SELECT statement.

Listing 12-1. Read locking in the SERIALIZABLE transaction isolation level

```
-- Connection    Processlist ID   Thread ID   Event ID
-- ----------------------------------------------------
--          1              967        1560           6
--          2              968        1561           6

-- Connection 1
Connection 1> SET transaction_isolation = 'SERIALIZABLE';
Query OK, 0 rows affected (0.0007 sec)

Connection 1> START TRANSACTION;
Query OK, 0 rows affected (0.0003 sec)
```

```
Connection 1> SELECT ID, Name, Population
               FROM world.city
              WHERE CountryCode = 'SVK'
                AND District = 'Bratislava';
+------+------------+------------+
| ID   | Name       | Population |
+------+------------+------------+
| 3209 | Bratislava |     448292 |
+------+------------+------------+
1 row in set (0.0006 sec)

-- Connection 2
Connection 2> SELECT index_name, lock_type,
               lock_mode, lock_data
            FROM performance_schema.data_locks
           WHERE object_schema = 'world'
             AND object_name = 'city'
             AND lock_type = 'RECORD'
             AND thread_id = 1560
           ORDER BY index_name, lock_data DESC;
+-------------+-----------+----------------+-------------+
| index_name  | lock_type | lock_mode      | lock_data   |
+-------------+-----------+----------------+-------------+
| CountryCode | RECORD    | S,GAP          | 'SVN', 3212 |
| CountryCode | RECORD    | S              | 'SVK', 3211 |
| CountryCode | RECORD    | S              | 'SVK', 3210 |
| CountryCode | RECORD    | S              | 'SVK', 3209 |
| PRIMARY     | RECORD    | S,REC_NOT_GAP  | 3211        |
| PRIMARY     | RECORD    | S,REC_NOT_GAP  | 3210        |
| PRIMARY     | RECORD    | S,REC_NOT_GAP  | 3209        |
+-------------+-----------+----------------+-------------+
7 rows in set (0.0009 sec)

-- Connection 1
Connection 1> ROLLBACK;
Query OK, 0 rows affected (0.0003 sec)
```

The query uses a secondary index and ends up locking the primary key and CountryCode records of all records that are read. Additionally, there is a gap lock after the last index record for Slovakia. All the locks are shared locks.

Listing 12-2 instead considers an UPDATE statement that updates a subset of the rows that are examined.

Listing 12-2. Locking in the SERIALIZABLE transaction isolation level

```
-- Connection    Processlist ID    Thread ID    Event ID
-- -----------------------------------------------------
--          1            971          1567           6
--          2            972          1568           6

-- Connection 1
Connection 1> SET SESSION TRANSACTION ISOLATION LEVEL SERIALIZABLE;
Query OK, 0 rows affected (0.0004 sec)

Connection 1> START TRANSACTION;
Query OK, 0 rows affected (0.0002 sec)

Connection 1> UPDATE world.city
                 SET Population = Population * 1.10
               WHERE CountryCode = 'SVK'
                 AND District = 'Bratislava';
Query OK, 1 row affected (0.0006 sec)

Rows matched: 1  Changed: 1  Warnings: 0


-- Connection 2
Connection 2> SELECT index_name, lock_type,
                     lock_mode, lock_data
                FROM performance_schema.data_locks
               WHERE object_schema = 'world'
                 AND object_name = 'city'
                 AND lock_type = 'RECORD'
                 AND thread_id = 1567
            ORDER BY index_name, lock_data DESC;
```

```
+-------------+-----------+----------------+-------------+
| index_name  | lock_type | lock_mode      | lock_data   |
+-------------+-----------+----------------+-------------+
| CountryCode | RECORD    | X,GAP          | 'SVN', 3212 |
| CountryCode | RECORD    | X              | 'SVK', 3211 |
| CountryCode | RECORD    | X              | 'SVK', 3210 |
| CountryCode | RECORD    | X              | 'SVK', 3209 |
| PRIMARY     | RECORD    | X,REC_NOT_GAP  | 3211        |
| PRIMARY     | RECORD    | X,REC_NOT_GAP  | 3210        |
| PRIMARY     | RECORD    | X,REC_NOT_GAP  | 3209        |
+-------------+-----------+----------------+-------------+
7 rows in set (0.0007 sec)

-- Connection 1
Connection 1> ROLLBACK;
Query OK, 0 rows affected (0.0576 sec)
```

The statement updates a single city (with ID = 3209) but holds locks on all three Slovakian cities both on the primary key and the CountryCode index as well as a gap lock after the last index record.

Notice also how the SET TRANSACTION statement is used here to set the transaction isolation level instead of setting the transaction_isolation variable. The two methods are interchangeable though SET SESION TRANSACTION also supports setting whether it is a read-only or read-write transaction. If you use the SET TRANSACTION statement without neither the GLOBAL nor SESSION scope, then it only applies to the next transaction.

This transaction isolation level is not used very often, but it can be useful when investigating locking problems or when working with XA transactions. Other than SELECT statements taking locks, the isolation level is the same as REPEATABLE READ which is discussed next.

Repeatable Read

The REPETABLE READ isolation level is the default in InnoDB. As the name suggests, it ensures that if you repeat a read statement, then the same result is returned. This is also known as a consistent read, and it is implemented through read views called snapshots.

The snapshot is established when the first statement is executed within the transaction, or if the WITH CONSISTENT SNAPSHOT modifier is given with START TRANSACTION, then at the start of the transaction.

An important side effect of the consistent snapshots is that it is possible to have non-locking reads while still retrieving the same data repeatably. This extends to include all InnoDB tables, so executing multiple statements against different tables return data that corresponds to the same point in time. The REPEATABLE READ transaction isolation level with its consistent snapshots is also what allows for online consistent logical backups created with tools like mysqlpump and mysqldump.

While REPEATABLE READ has some nice isolation properties without being as intrusive as SERIALIZABLE, there is still a significant level of locking going on. Listing 12-3 shows a repeat of the example of selecting the cities in the district of Bratislava in Slovakia.

Listing 12-3. Read locking in the REPEATABLE READ transaction isolation level

```
-- Connection   Processlist ID   Thread ID   Event ID
-- -----------------------------------------------------
--            1             973        1571          6
--            2             974        1572          6

-- Connection 1
Connection 1> SET transaction_isolation = 'REPEATABLE-READ';
Query OK, 0 rows affected (0.0004 sec)

Connection 1> START TRANSACTION;
Query OK, 0 rows affected (0.0003 sec)

Connection 1> SELECT ID, Name, Population
                FROM world.city
               WHERE CountryCode = 'SVK'
                 AND District = 'Bratislava';
+------+------------+------------+
| ID   | Name       | Population |
+------+------------+------------+
| 3209 | Bratislava |     448292 |
+------+------------+------------+
1 row in set (0.0006 sec)
```

```
-- Connection 2
Connection 2> SELECT index_name, lock_type,
                     lock_mode, lock_data
                FROM performance_schema.data_locks
               WHERE object_schema = 'world'
                 AND object_name = 'city'
                 AND lock_type = 'RECORD'
                 AND thread_id = 1571
               ORDER BY index_name, lock_data DESC;
0 rows in set (0.0006 sec)

-- Connection 1
Connection 1> ROLLBACK;
Query OK, 0 rows affected (0.0004 sec)
```

In this case, no locks are held which is the important difference between the SERIALIZABLE and REPEATABLE READ transaction isolation levels. Listing 12-4 shows how it looks for the UPDATE statement.

Listing 12-4. Locking in the REPEATABLE READ transaction isolation level

```
-- Connection   Processlist ID   Thread ID   Event ID
-- --------------------------------------------------
--          1             975        1574           6
--          2             976        1575           6

-- Connection 1
Connection 1> SET transaction_isolation = 'REPEATABLE-READ';
Query OK, 0 rows affected (0.0004 sec)

Connection 1> START TRANSACTION;
Query OK, 0 rows affected (0.0002 sec)

Connection 1> UPDATE world.city
                 SET Population = Population * 1.10
               WHERE CountryCode = 'SVK'
                 AND District = 'Bratislava';
Query OK, 1 row affected (0.0007 sec)
```

```
Rows matched: 1  Changed: 1  Warnings: 0

-- Connection 2
Connection 2> SELECT index_name, lock_type,
                     lock_mode, lock_data
                FROM performance_schema.data_locks
               WHERE object_schema = 'world'
                 AND object_name = 'city'
                 AND lock_type = 'RECORD'
                 AND thread_id = 1574
               ORDER BY index_name, lock_data DESC;
+-------------+-----------+---------------+-------------+
| index_name  | lock_type | lock_mode     | lock_data   |
+-------------+-----------+---------------+-------------+
| CountryCode | RECORD    | X,GAP         | 'SVN', 3212 |
| CountryCode | RECORD    | X             | 'SVK', 3211 |
| CountryCode | RECORD    | X             | 'SVK', 3210 |
| CountryCode | RECORD    | X             | 'SVK', 3209 |
| PRIMARY     | RECORD    | X,REC_NOT_GAP | 3211        |
| PRIMARY     | RECORD    | X,REC_NOT_GAP | 3210        |
| PRIMARY     | RECORD    | X,REC_NOT_GAP | 3209        |
+-------------+-----------+---------------+-------------+
7 rows in set (0.0010 sec)

-- Connection 1
Connection 1> ROLLBACK;
Query OK, 0 rows affected (0.3036 sec)
```

These are the same seven locks as were held in SERIALIZABLE.

One important caveat of consistent snapshots that you need to be aware of is that they only apply for reads. This means that if you read from a table, then another transaction commits changes to rows so they match the filter used in the first transaction, then the first transaction will be able to modify these rows, and afterward, they will be included in snapshot. Listing 12-5 shows an example of this. There are two investigations available that you can explore if you want to take a look at the locks held.

Listing 12-5. Consistent reads mixed with DML

```
-- Connection   Processlist ID   Thread ID   Event ID
-- ------------------------------------------------------
--         1              977        1578          6
--         2              978        1579          6

-- Connection 1
Connection 1> SET transaction_isolation = 'REPEATABLE-READ';
Query OK, 0 rows affected (0.0005 sec)

Connection 1> START TRANSACTION;
Query OK, 0 rows affected (0.0004 sec)

Connection 1> SELECT ID, Name, Population
              FROM world.city
              WHERE CountryCOde = 'BHS';
+-----+--------+------------+
| ID  | Name   | Population |
+-----+--------+------------+
| 148 | Nassau |     172000 |
+-----+--------+------------+
1 row in set (0.0014 sec)

-- Connection 2
Connection 2> START TRANSACTION;
Query OK, 0 rows affected (0.0004 sec)

Connection 2> INSERT INTO world.city
              VALUES (4080, 'Freeport', 'BHS',
                      'Grand Bahama', 50000);
Query OK, 1 row affected (0.0022 sec)

Connection 2> COMMIT;
Query OK, 0 rows affected (0.0983 sec)

-- Connection 1
Connection 1> SELECT ID, Name, Population
              FROM world.city
              WHERE CountryCOde = 'BHS';
```

```
+-----+--------+------------+
| ID  | Name   | Population |
+-----+--------+------------+
| 148 | Nassau |     172000 |
+-----+--------+------------+
1 row in set (0.0006 sec)

Connection 1> UPDATE world.city
              SET Population = Population * 1.10
              WHERE CountryCOde = 'BHS';
Query OK, 2 rows affected (0.0012 sec)

Rows matched: 2  Changed: 2  Warnings: 0


Connection 1> SELECT ID, Name, Population
              FROM world.city
              WHERE CountryCOde = 'BHS';
+------+----------+------------+
| ID   | Name     | Population |
+------+----------+------------+
|  148 | Nassau   |     189200 |
| 4080 | Freeport |      55000 |
+------+----------+------------+
2 rows in set (0.0006 sec)
```

When Connection 1 queries all cities in the Bahamas (CountryCode = 'BHS') the first time, only the city of Nassau is returned. Then Connection 2 inserts a row for the city of Freeport and commits its transaction. When Connection 1 repeats its SELECT statement, it is still only Nassau that is returned. So far so good. This is what is expected of the consistent read feature. However, when Connection 1 increases the population of all cities in Bahamas with 10%, then two rows are updated, and a subsequent SELECT reveals that Freeport is now part of Connection 1's read view.

This behavior is not a bug! It happens because reads are non-locking in the REPEATABLE READ transaction isolation level. If you want to avoid this behavior, you either need to explicitly request a shared lock in Connection 1 using the FOR SHARE clause or you need to change to the SERIALIZABLE transaction isolation level.

The price to pay for consistent reads is a relatively large number of locks and that InnoDB must maintain several versions of the data. Remember from the discussion of undo logs that as long as there is still a read view that was started before a given transaction, then the undo log for the transaction must be kept, and that it is expensive to track of the versions of the same rows.

If you do not need consistent reads, the READ COMMITTED transaction isolation level is a good choice.

Read Committed

If you are used to other relational database systems such as Oracle DB or PostgreSQL, then you have probably been using the READ COMMITTED transaction isolation level. The NDBCluster storage engine in MySQL also uses READ COMMITTED. This isolation level is popular as it for many workloads provides strong enough isolation and it has reduced locking compared to the REPEATABLE READ and SERIALIZABLE isolation levels.

The main differences from REPEATABLE READ to READ COMMITTED are

- READ COMMITTED does not support consistent reads (though single statements still return consistent results). Because the lifetime of the read view is only that of the statement, InnoDB can faster purge old undo logs. This advantage is most significant for long-running transactions.

- The locks taken by DML statements on records that are examined but not modified are released as soon as the WHERE clause has been evaluated.

- READ COMMITTED will only take gap locks in connection with checking foreign keys and unique key constraints as well as in connection with page splits. A page split occurs when an InnoDB page is close to full and a record will have to be inserted in the middle of the page or an existing record grows, so there is no longer room in the page.

- For WHERE clauses resolved using a non-indexed column, the *semi-consistent* read feature allows transactions to use the last committed values of a row to match the filter even if the row is locked.

The lack of gap locks means that so-called phantom rows can occur. Phantom rows happen when the same statement is executed twice within the same transaction and it returns different rows even for locking statements such as SELECT ... FOR SHARE.

THE ILLUSIVE GAP LOCK

One of the more difficult hunts for a MySQL bug occurred in MySQL 5.7 and pre-GA MySQL 8. When using XA transactions in a replication setup, there were random occurring lock wait timeouts and deadlocks on the replicas caused solely by the replication traffic. How could that be when there were not any lock issues on the replication source?

The issue consisted of various parts. First, in MySQL 5.7 and later, XA transactions are written to the binary log when they are prepared, and they may not commit in the same order as they are prepared, which meant that even in single-threaded replication, the replica could have multiple write transactions open at the same time.

Second, the issue was mostly resolved by enforcing row-based replication and always using the READ COMMITTED transaction isolation level. However, very puzzling, occasionally – seemingly at random – there would still be lock conflicts on the replicas. In the end it turned out to be gap locks caused by page splits that were the culprit. Page splits do not occur at the same time on the source and replica, so that there could end up being additional locks on the replica. The issue was eventually solved in the 5.7.22 and 8.0.4 releases by releasing the gap locks taken by the replication threads when the XA transactions reach the prepare stage.

If you try the recurring UPDATE statement example in the READ COMMITTED transaction isolation level, you will see how it takes fewer locks than before. This is shown in Listing 12-6.

Listing 12-6. Locking in the READ COMMITTED transaction isolation level

```
-- Connection    Processlist ID    Thread ID    Event ID
-- -------------------------------------------------------
--           1            980          1582          6
--           2            981          1583          6

-- Connection 1
Connection 1> SET transaction_isolation = 'READ-COMMITTED';
Query OK, 0 rows affected (0.0002 sec)
```

```
Connection 1> START TRANSACTION;
Query OK, 0 rows affected (0.0002 sec)

Connection 1> UPDATE world.city
                SET Population = Population * 1.10
              WHERE CountryCode = 'SVK'
                AND District = 'Bratislava';
Query OK, 1 row affected (0.0007 sec)

Rows matched: 1  Changed: 1  Warnings: 0

-- Connection 2
Connection 2> SELECT index_name, lock_type,
                lock_mode, lock_data
              FROM performance_schema.data_locks
              WHERE object_schema = 'world'
                AND object_name = 'city'
                AND lock_type = 'RECORD'
                AND thread_id = 1582
              ORDER BY index_name, lock_data DESC;
+-------------+-----------+---------------+-------------+
| index_name  | lock_type | lock_mode     | lock_data   |
+-------------+-----------+---------------+-------------+
| CountryCode | RECORD    | X,REC_NOT_GAP | 'SVK', 3209 |
| PRIMARY     | RECORD    | X,REC_NOT_GAP | 3209        |
+-------------+-----------+---------------+-------------+
2 rows in set (0.0008 sec)

-- Connection 1
Connection 1> ROLLBACK;
Query OK, 0 rows affected (0.0754 sec)
```

Whereas the SERIALIZABLE and REPEATABLE READ isolation levels held seven record and gap locks, READ COMMITTED only holds one on the CountryCode index and one on the primary key – though for a while, locks were held on the other index and row records that were examined, but they have at the time of the output been released again. This greatly reduces the potential for lock waits and deadlocks.

A less known feature of the READ COMMITTED isolation level is semi-consistent reads which allow a statement to use the last committed value of a column to compare against its WHERE clause. If it is determined the row will not be affected by the statement, no lock conflict occurs even if another transaction holds a lock. If the row will be updated, the condition is re-evaluated, and a lock prevents conflicting changes. Listing 12-7 shows an example of this. There are two investigations available that you can explore if you want to take a look at the locks held.

Listing 12-7. READ COMMITTED Semi-consistent reads

```
-- Connection   Processlist ID   Thread ID   Event ID
-- ------------------------------------------------------
--          1          986          1592          6
--          2          987          1593          6

-- Connection 1
Connection 1> SET transaction_isolation = 'READ-COMMITTED';
Query OK, 0 rows affected (0.0004 sec)

Connection 1> START TRANSACTION;
Query OK, 0 rows affected (0.0004 sec)

Connection 1> UPDATE world.city
                 SET Population = Population * 1.10
               WHERE Name = 'San Jose'
                 AND District = 'Southern Tagalog';
Query OK, 1 row affected (0.0106 sec)

Rows matched: 1  Changed: 1  Warnings: 0

-- Connection 2
Connection 2> SET transaction_isolation = 'READ-COMMITTED';
Query OK, 0 rows affected (0.0004 sec)

Connection 2> START TRANSACTION;
Query OK, 0 rows affected (0.0065 sec)

Connection 2> UPDATE world.city
                 SET Population = Population * 1.10
               WHERE Name = 'San Jose'
```

```
                          AND District = 'Central Luzon';
Query OK, 1 row affected (0.0060 sec)

Rows matched: 1  Changed: 1  Warnings: 0
```

Both transactions update cities named San Jose, but in different districts. Neither the Name nor the District column is indexed. Even though the second transaction does examine the row with Name = 'San Jose' AND District = 'Southern Tagalog', there is no lock conflict as the transaction based on the district determines it will not update the row. However, if an index is added to the Name column, then there will be a lock conflict, so the feature is currently of limited value for large tables.

You may from this discussion get the impression that READ COMMITTED always performs better than REPEATABLE READ. This is the most logical conclusion, however as it often is, things are more complex than as such. The caveat is that in order to start a read view, the trx_sys mutex (the wait/synch/mutex/innodb/trx_sys_mutex Performance Schema instrument) is required, and since READ COMMITTED starts a new read view for each statement, it will end up obtaining the trx_sys mutex much more frequently than REPEATABLE READ. In the end, if you have a lot of quick transactions and statements, you can in READ COMMITTED end up with so much activity on the mutex that it becomes a severe bottleneck and you are better off using REPEATABLE READ. For longer-running transactions and statements, the balance shifts toward READ COMMITTED.

Tip: If you are interested in seeing some benchmark showing how the trx_sys mutex impacts the performance, see http://dimitrik.free.fr/blog/archives/2015/02/mysql-performance-impact-of-innodb-transaction-isolation-modes-in-mysql-57.html.

Read Uncommitted

The last transaction isolation level is READ UNCOMMITTED. As the name suggests, a transaction using this isolation level is allowed to read data that has not yet been committed; this is also called a *dirty read*. This may sound very dangerous, and in most cases, it is an absolute no-go. However, in a few special cases, it can be useful. Other than the dirty reads, the behavior is the same as for READ COMMITTED. The main advantage of READ UNCOMMITTED over READ COMMITTED is that InnoDB never needs to keep more than one version of the data to fulfill the query.

The main uses of READ UNCOMMITTED are for cases where only approximate values are needed, for bulk inserts, and for investigations where you want to take a peek at what changes have been made by another transaction. An example of only requiring approximate values is the calculation of index statistics for which InnoDB uses READ UNCOMMITTED. For bulk inserts, then MySQL Shell's parallel table data import feature (util.importTable() in JavaScript or util.import_table() in Python) switches to READ UNCOMMITTED during the bulk load.

Summary

This chapter has examined the four transaction isolation levels that InnoDB supports. The strictest isolation level is SERIALIZABLE which takes locks for all statements except auto-committing single-statement SELECT transactions. The REPEATABLE READ isolation level supports non-locking reads but keeps support for consistent reads. One gotcha is that if a transaction updates a row that was committed after the read view was established, then the updated row is added to the view.

The next level is READ COMMITTED which abandons consistent reads and always includes all committed rows. It does open up for phantom rows, but on the other hand, READ COMMITTED needs fewer locks and holds them for shorter and in that way greatly reduces the potential for lock conflicts. The final isolation level is READ UNCOMMITTED which behaves like READ COMMITTED but allows for dirty reads, that is, reading changes that have not yet been committed.

That concludes the theory part of the book. The remaining chapters go through six case studies with the first analyzing an issue involving flush locks.

CHAPTER 13

Case Study: Flush Locks

Lock issues are one of the common causes of performance issues, and the impact can be severe. In the worst cases, queries can fail, and connections pile up so no new connections can be made. Therefore, it is important to know how to investigate lock issues and remediate the problems.

This and the following chapters will discuss six categories of lock issues:

- Flush locks

- Metadata and schema locks

- Record-level locks including gap locks

- Deadlocks

- Foreign keys

- Semaphores

Apart from the foreign keys case study, each category of locks uses different techniques to determine the cause of the lock contention. When you read the examples, you should have in mind that similar techniques can be used to investigate lock issues that do not 100% match the example. For the first four case studies (Chapters 13–16), the discussion has been split into six parts:

- **The symptoms:** These enable you to identify the kind of lock issue encountered.

- **The cause:** The underlying reason you encounter this kind of lock issues. This is related to the general discussion of the locks earlier in the book, particularly Chapters 6 and 7.

© Jesper Wisborg Krogh 2021
J. W. Krogh, *MySQL Concurrency*, https://doi.org/10.1007/978-1-4842-6652-6_13

- **The setup:** This includes the steps to set up the lock issue if you want to try it yourself. As lock contention requires multiple connections, the prompt, for example, `Connection 1>`, is used to tell which connection should be used for which statements. If you want to follow the investigation with no more information than you would have in a real-world case, you can skip this section and go back and review it after getting through the investigation.

- **The investigation:** The details of the investigation. This draws on the discussion about monitoring in Chapter 2–4.

- **The solution:** How you resolve the immediate lock problem, so you minimize the outage caused by it.

- **The prevention:** A discussion of how to reduce the chance of encountering the issue. This is closely related to the discussion about reducing locking issues in Chapter 9.

The last two case studies for foreign keys and semaphores follow a similar pattern.

Enough talk, the first lock category that will be discussed is flush locks which is one of the most difficult lock issues to investigate.

The Symptoms

The main symptom of a flush lock issue is that the database comes to a grinding halt where all new queries using some or all tables end up waiting for the flush lock. The telltale signs to look for include the following:

- The query state of new queries is "Waiting for table flush." This may occur for all new queries or only for queries accessing specific tables.

- More and more connections are created.

- Eventually, new connections fail as MySQL is out of connection. The error received for new connections is `ER_CON_COUNT_ERROR: ERROR 1040 (HY000): Too many connections`. (When using the X protocol in 8.0.19 or earlier, the error is `MySQL Error 5011: Could not open session`.)

- There is at least one query that has been running later than the oldest request for a flush lock.

- There may be a FLUSH TABLES statement in the process list, but this is not always the case.

- When the FLUSH TABLES statement has waited for lock_wait_ timeout, an ER_LOCK_WAIT_TIMEOUT error occurs: ERROR: 1205: Lock wait timeout exceeded; try restarting transaction. Since the default value for lock_wait_timeout is 365 days, this is only likely to occur if the timeout has been reduced.

- If you connect with the mysql command-line client with a default schema set, the connection may seem to hang before you get to the prompt. The same can happen if you change the default schema with a connection open.

Tip   The issue that the mysql command-line client is blocking does not occur if you start the client with the -A option which disables collecting the autocompletion information. A better solution is to use MySQL Shell that fetches the autocompletion information in a way that does not block due to the flush lock.

If you see these symptoms, it is time to understand what is causing the lock issue.

The Cause

When a connection requests a table to be flushed, it requires all references to the table to be closed which means no active queries can be using the table. So, when a flush request arrives, it must wait for all queries using the tables that are to be flushed to finish. Note that unless you explicitly specify which tables to flush, it is just the query and not the entire transaction that must finish. Obviously, the case where all tables are flushed, for example, due to FLUSH TABLES WITH READ LOCK, is the most severe as it means all active queries must finish before the flush statement can proceed.

When the wait for the flush lock becomes a problem, it means that there are one or more queries preventing the FLUSH TABLES statement from obtaining the flush lock. Since the FLUSH TABLES statement requires an exclusive lock, it in turn stops subsequent queries from acquiring the shared lock they need.

This issue is often seen in connection with backups where the backup process needs to flush all tables and get a read lock in order to create a consistent backup.

A special case can occur when the FLUSH TABLES statement has timed out or has been killed, but the subsequent queries are not proceeding. When that happens, it is because the low-level table definition cache (TDC) version lock is not released. This is a case that can cause confusion as it is not obvious why the subsequent queries are still waiting for the table flush. A similar case happens when an ANALYZE TABLE statement triggers an implicit flush of the table or tables that were analyzed.

The Setup

The lock situation that will be investigated involves three connections (not including the connection used for the investigation). The first connection executes a slow query, the second flushes all tables with a read lock, and the last connection executes a quick query. The statements are shown in Listing 13-1.

Listing 13-1. Triggering flush lock contention

```
-- Connection   Processlist ID   Thread ID   Event ID
-- ----------------------------------------------------
--          1              668        1106          6
--          2              669        1107          6
--          3              670        1108          6

-- Connection 1
Connection 1> SELECT city.*, SLEEP(3600) FROM world.city WHERE ID = 130;

-- Connection 2
Connection 2> FLUSH TABLES WITH READ LOCK;

-- Connection 3
Connection 3> SELECT * FROM world.city WHERE ID = 3805;
```

The use of SLEEP(3600) in the first query means you have an hour (3600 seconds) to execute the two other queries and perform the investigation. If you want to stop the lock situation, you can kill the query:

```
-- Investigation #6
-- Connection 4
```

```
Connection 4> KILL 668;
Query OK, 0 rows affected (0.0004 sec)
```

You are now ready to start the investigation.

The Investigation

The investigation of flush locks requires you to look at the list of queries running on the instance. Unlike other lock contentions, there are no Performance Schema tables or InnoDB monitor report that can be used to query for the blocking query directly.

Listing 13-2 shows an example of the output using the sys.session view. Similar results will be produced using the alternative ways to get a list of queries. The thread and connection ids as well as the statement latencies will vary.

Listing 13-2. Investigating flush lock contention using sys.session

```
-- Investigation #1
-- Connection 4
Connection 4> SELECT thd_id, conn_id, state,
                     current_statement,
                     statement_latency
               FROM sys.session
              WHERE command = 'Query'\G
*************************** 1. row ***************************
          thd_id: 1106
         conn_id: 668
           state: User sleep
current_statement: SELECT city.*, SLEEP(3600) FROM world.city WHERE ID = 130
statement_latency: 1.48 min
*************************** 2. row ***************************
          thd_id: 1107
         conn_id: 669
           state: Waiting for table flush
current_statement: FLUSH TABLES WITH READ LOCK
statement_latency: 1.44 min
```

```
************************** 3. row **************************
            thd_id: 1108
           conn_id: 670
             state: Waiting for table flush
 current_statement: SELECT * FROM world.city WHERE ID = 3805
 statement_latency: 1.41 min
************************** 4. row **************************
            thd_id: 1105
           conn_id: 667
             state: NULL
 current_statement: SELECT thd_id, conn_id, state, ... on      WHERE command
 = 'Query'
 statement_latency: 40.63 ms
 4 rows in set (0.0419 sec)
```

There are four queries in the output. The sys.session and sys.processlist views by default sort the queries according to the execution time in descending order. This makes it easy to investigate issues like contention around the flush lock where the query time is the primary thing to consider when looking for the cause.

You start out looking for the FLUSH TABLES statement (the case where there is no FLUSH TABLES statement will be discussed shortly). In this case, that is thd_id = 1107 (the second row). Notice that the state of the FLUSH statement is "Waiting for table flush." You then look for queries that have been running for a longer time. In this case, there is only one query: the one with thd_id = 1106. This is the query that blocks the FLUSH TABLES WITH READ LOCK from completing. In general, there may be more than one query.

The two remaining queries are a query being blocked by the FLUSH TABLES WITH READ LOCK and the query to obtain the output. Together, the three first queries form a typical example of a long-running query blocking a FLUSH TABLES statement which in turn blocks other queries.

You can also get the process list from MySQL Workbench and in some cases also from your monitoring solution (MySQL Enterprise Monitor is an example). In MySQL Workbench, you can use the *Client Connections* report by choosing the Administration tab in the navigator as shown in Figure 13-1.

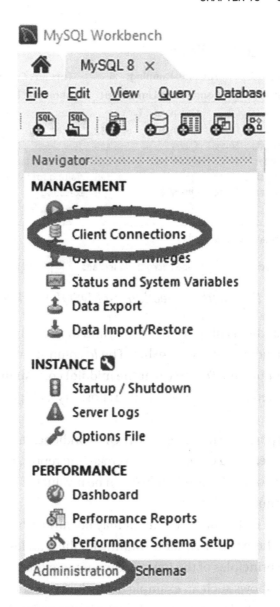

Figure 13-1. *Navigating to the Client Connection report*

You open the report by selecting *Client Connections* in the *Management* section.

The report fetches the process information from the performance_schema.threads table with a LEFT JOIN on the performance_schema.session_connect_attrs table to get the program name. You can choose whether to filter out background threads as well as sleeping connections, and MySQL Workbench allows you to change the ordering without re-executing the statement that generates the report. Optionally, you can also refresh the report. An example for this case study is shown in Figure 13-2.

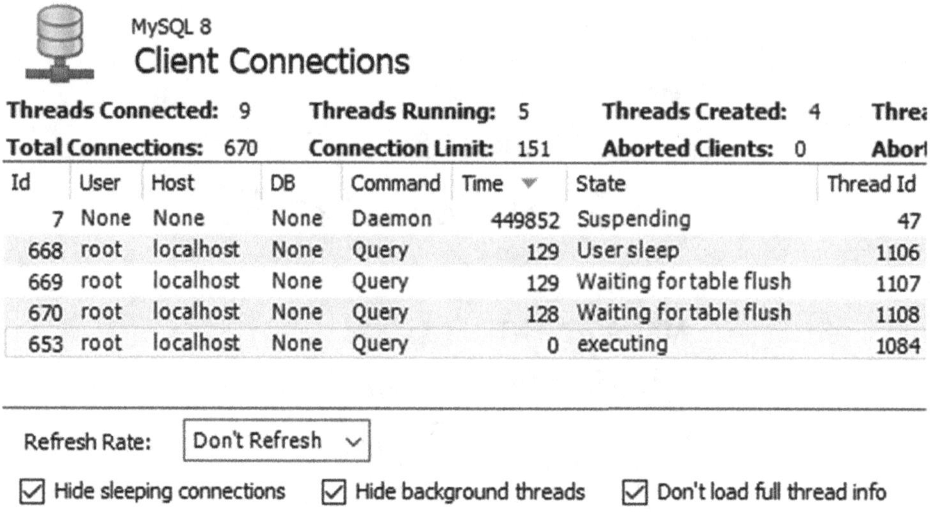

MySQL 8
Client Connections

Threads Connected:	9		Threads Running:	5		Threads Created:	4	Threa
Total Connections:	670		Connection Limit:	151		Aborted Clients:	0	Abort

Id	User	Host	DB	Command	Time ▼	State	Thread Id
7	None	None	None	Daemon	449852	Suspending	47
668	root	localhost	None	Query	129	User sleep	1106
669	root	localhost	None	Query	129	Waiting for table flush	1107
670	root	localhost	None	Query	128	Waiting for table flush	1108
653	root	localhost	None	Query	0	executing	1084

Refresh Rate: [Don't Refresh ▾]

☑ Hide sleeping connections   ☑ Hide background threads   ☑ Don't load full thread info

Figure 13-2. *Showing the client connections in MySQL Workbench*

You cannot choose which columns to include, and to make the text readable, only part of the report is included in the screenshot. The *Id* column corresponds to conn_id in the sys.session output, and *Thread* (near the middle) corresponds to thd_id. The full screenshot is included in this book's GitHub repository as figure_13_2_workbench_flush_lock.png.

An advantage of reports like the ones in MySQL Workbench and MySQL Enterprise Monitor is that they use existing connections to create the report. In cases where the lock issue causes all connections to be used, then it can be invaluable to be able to get the list of queries using a monitoring solution.

As mentioned, the FLUSH TABLES statement may not always be present in the list of queries. The reason there still are queries waiting for flush tables is the low-level TDC version lock. The principles of the investigation remain the same, but it can seem confusing. Listing 13-3 shows such an example using the same setup but killing the connection executing the flush statement before the investigation (Ctrl+C can be used in MySQL Shell in the connection executing FLUSH TABLES WITH READ LOCK if you are executing it interactively).

Listing 13-3. Flush lock contention without a FLUSH TABLES statement

```
-- Investigation #7
Connection 4> KILL 669;
Query OK, 0 rows affected (0.0004 sec)
```

```
-- Investigation #1
Connection 4> SELECT thd_id, conn_id, state,
                     current_statement,
                     statement_latency
                FROM sys.session
               WHERE command = 'Query'\G
*************************** 1. row ***************************
          thd_id: 1106
         conn_id: 668
           state: User sleep
current_statement: SELECT city.*, SLEEP(3600) FROM world.city WHERE ID = 130
statement_latency: 3.88 min
*************************** 2. row ***************************
          thd_id: 1108
         conn_id: 670
           state: Waiting for table flush
current_statement: SELECT * FROM world.city WHERE ID = 3805
statement_latency: 3.81 min
*************************** 3. row ***************************
          thd_id: 1105
         conn_id: 667
           state: NULL
current_statement: SELECT thd_id, conn_id, state, ... on        WHERE command
= 'Query'
statement_latency: 39.53 ms
3 rows in set (0.0406 sec)
```

This situation is identical to the previous except the FLUSH TABLES statement is gone. In this case, find the query that has been waiting the longest with the state "Waiting for table flush." Queries that have been running longer than this query has been waiting are the ones preventing the TDC version lock from being released. In this case, that means thd_id = 668 is the blocking query.

Once you have identified the issue and the principal queries involved, you need to decide what to do about the issue.

The Solution

There are two levels of solving the issue. First of all, you need to resolve the immediate problem of queries not executing. Second, you need to work at avoiding the issue in the future. This subsection will discuss the immediate solution, and the next will consider how to reduce the chance of the issue occurring.

To resolve the immediate issue, you have the option of waiting for the queries to complete or starting to kill queries. If you can redirect the application to use another instance while the flush lock contention is ongoing, you may be able to let the situation resolve itself by letting the long-running queries complete. If there are data changing queries among those running or waiting, you do in that case need to consider whether it will leave the system in a consistent state after all queries have completed. One option may be to continue in read-only mode with the read queries executing on a different instance.

Tip   If the long-running query is a rogue query with missing join clauses, it can take a very long time to complete. The author of this book has experienced a query that ran for months. When deciding whether to wait, you want to try to estimate how long the query will take. A good option is to use the EXPLAIN FOR CONNECTION <processlist id> command to examine the query plan of the long-running query.

If you decide to kill queries, you can try to kill the FLUSH TABLES statement. If that works, it is the simplest solution. However, as discussed, that will not always help, and in that case, the only solution is to kill the queries that were preventing the FLUSH TABLES statement from completing. If the long-running queries look like runaway queries and the application/client that executed them anyway is not waiting for them any longer, you may want to kill them without trying to kill the FLUSH TABLES statement first.

One important consideration when looking to kill a query is how much data has been changed. For a pure SELECT query (not involving stored routines), that is always nothing, and from the perspective of work done, it is safe to kill it. For INSERT, UPDATE, DELETE, and similar queries, however, the changed data must be rolled back if the query is killed. It will usually take longer to roll back changes than making them in the first place, so be prepared to wait a long time for the rollback if there are many changes. You can use the `information_schema.INNODB_TRX` view to estimate the amount of work done by looking at the `trx_rows_modified` column. If there is a lot of work to roll back, it is usually better to let the query complete.

Caution   When a DML statement is killed, the work it has done must be rolled back. The rollback will usually take longer than creating the change, sometimes much longer. You need to factor that in, if you consider killing a long-running DML statement.

Of course, optimally you prevent the issue from happening at all.

The Prevention

The flush lock contention happens because of the combination of a long-running query and a `FLUSH TABLES` statement. So, to prevent the issue, you need to look at what you can do to avoid these two conditions to be present at the same time.

Finding, analyzing, and handling long-running queries are beyond the scope of this book. However, one option of particular interest is to set a timeout for the query which is supported for `SELECT` statements using the `max_execution_time` system variable and the `MAX_EXECUTION_TIME(N)` optimizer hint and is a great way to protect against runaway queries. Some connectors also have support for timing out queries.

Tip   To avoid long-running `SELECT` queries, you can configure the `max_execution_time` option or set the `MAX_EXECUTION_TIME(N)` optimizer hint. This will make the `SELECT` statement time out after the specified period and help prevent issues like flush lock waits.

Some long-running queries cannot be prevented. It may be a reporting job, building a cache table, or another task that must access a lot of data. In that case, the best you can do is to try to avoid them running, while it is also necessary to flush the tables. One option is to schedule the long-running queries to run at different times than when it is necessary to flush tables. Another option is to have the long-running queries run on a different instance than the jobs that require flushing tables.

A common task that requires flushing the tables is taking a backup. In MySQL 8, you can avoid that issue by using the backup and log locks. For example, MySQL Enterprise Backup (MEB) does this in version 8.0.16 and later, so InnoDB tables are never flushed. Alternatively, you can perform the backup at a period with low usage, so the potential for conflicts is lower, or you can even do the backup while the system is in read-only mode and avoid the FLUSH TABLES WITH READ LOCK altogether.

Summary

This chapter has studied a situation where a long-running query prevented a FLUSH TABLES WITH READ LOCK statement from acquiring the flush lock which subsequently prevented queries started later to execute. A situation like this is among the hardest to investigate as there is no help to get from the lock tables in the Performance Schema. Instead you need to look at the process list and look for queries that are older than the FLUSH TABLES statement or, if that is not present, the connection that has waited for a flush lock the longest.

In most cases, you have the option of waiting for the long-running query to complete or to kill it in order to resolve the issue. Whether killing the query is acceptable depends on the purpose of the query and how many changes have been made by the transaction. To prevent the issue, you can try to separate tasks so long-running queries and FLUSH TABLE statements are not executing at the same time or they are executing on different MySQL instances. For SELECT statements, you can also use the max_execution_time option or the MAX_EXECUTION_TIME(N) optimizer switch to automatically kill long-running queries.

Another lock type that often causes confusion is the metadata lock. A case study involving metadata locks will be discussed in the next chapter.

## CHAPTER 14

Case Study: Metadata and Schema Locks

In MySQL 5.7 and earlier, metadata locks were often a source of confusion. The problem is that it is not obvious who holds the metadata lock. In MySQL 5.7, instrumentation of the metadata locks was added to the Performance Schema, and in MySQL 8.0, it is enabled by default. With the instrumentation enabled, it becomes easy to determine who is blocking the connection trying to obtain the lock. This chapter goes through an example of a situation with metadata locks and examines it. First the symptoms are discussed.

The Symptoms

The symptoms of metadata lock contention are similar to those of flush lock contention. In a typical situation, there will be a long-running query or transaction, a DDL statement waiting for the metadata lock, and possibly queries pilling up. The symptoms to look out for are as follows:

- A DDL statement and possibly other queries are stuck in the state "Waiting for table metadata lock."

- Queries may be pilling up. The queries that are waiting all use the same table. (There may potentially be more than one group of queries waiting if there are DDL statements for multiple tables waiting for the metadata lock.)

- When the DDL statement has waited for `lock_wait_timeout`, an `ER_LOCK_WAIT_TIMEOUT` error occurs: `ERROR: 1205: Lock wait timeout exceeded; try restarting transaction`. Since the default value for `lock_wait_timeout` is 365 days, this is only likely to occur if the timeout has been reduced.

© Jesper Wisborg Krogh 2021
J. W. Krogh, *MySQL Concurrency*, https://doi.org/10.1007/978-1-4842-6652-6_14

- There is a long-running query or a long-running transaction. In the latter case, the transaction may be idle or executing a query that does not use the table that the DDL statement acts on.

What makes the situation potentially confusing is the last point: there may not be any long-running queries that are the clear candidates for causing the lock issue. So, what is the cause of the metadata lock contention?

The Cause

Remember that the metadata locks exist to protect the schema definition (as well as being used with explicit locks). The schema protection will exist for as long as a transaction is active, so when a transaction queries a table, the metadata lock will last until the end of the transaction. Therefore, you may not see any long-running queries. In fact, the transaction holding the metadata lock may not be doing anything at all.

In short, the metadata lock exists as one or more connections may rely on the schema for a given table not changing, or they have explicitly locked the table either using the LOCK TABLES or FLUSH TABLES WITH READ LOCK statement.

The Setup

The example investigation of metadata locks uses three connections like in the example in the previous chapter. The first connection is in the middle of a transaction, the second connection tries to add an index to the table used by the transaction, and the third connection attempts to execute a query against the same table. The queries are shown in Listing 14-1.

Listing 14-1. Triggering metadata lock contention

```
-- Connection   Processlist ID   Thread ID   Event ID
-- ----------------------------------------------------
--         1              713         1181          6
--         2              714         1182          6
--         3              715         1183          6
```

```
-- Connection 1
Connection 1> START TRANSACTION;
Query OK, 0 rows affected (0.0003 sec)

Connection 1> SELECT * FROM world.city WHERE ID = 3805\G
*************************** 1. row ***************************
        ID: 3805
      Name: San Francisco
CountryCode: USA
  District: California
 Population: 776733
1 row in set (0.0007 sec)

Connection 1> SELECT Code, Name FROM world.country WHERE Code = 'USA'\G
*************************** 1. row ***************************
Code: USA
Name: United States
1 row in set (0.0005 sec)

-- Connection 2
Connection 2> ALTER TABLE world.city ADD INDEX (Name);

-- Connection 3
Connection 3> SELECT * FROM world.city WHERE ID = 130;
```

At this point, you can start the investigation. The situation will not resolve itself (unless you have a low value for lock_wait_timeout or you are prepared to wait a year), so you have all the time you want. When you want to resolve the block, you can start terminating the ALTER TABLE statement in Connection 2 to avoid modifying the world. city table. Then commit or roll back the transaction in Connection 1.

The Investigation

If you have the wait/lock/metadata/sql/mdl Performance Schema instrument enabled (the default in MySQL 8), it is straightforward to investigate metadata lock issues. You can use the metadata_locks table in the Performance Schema to list the granted and pending locks. However, a simpler way to get a summary of the lock situation is to use the schema_table_lock_waits view in the sys schema.

As an example, consider the metadata lock wait issue that can be seen in Listing 14-2 where three connections are involved. The WHERE clause has been chosen to just include the rows of interest for this investigation.

Listing 14-2. A metadata lock wait issue

```
-- Investigation #1
-- Connection 4
Connection 4> SELECT thd_id, conn_id, state,
                     current_statement,
                     statement_latency
                FROM sys.session
               WHERE command = 'Query' OR trx_state = 'ACTIVE'\G
*************************** 1. row ***************************
          thd_id: 1181
         conn_id: 713
           state: NULL
current_statement: SELECT Code, Name FROM world.country WHERE Code = 'USA'
statement_latency: NULL
*************************** 2. row ***************************
          thd_id: 1182
         conn_id: 714
           state: Waiting for table metadata lock
current_statement: ALTER TABLE world.city ADD INDEX (Name)
statement_latency: 26.68 s
*************************** 3. row ***************************
          thd_id: 1183
         conn_id: 715
           state: Waiting for table metadata lock
current_statement: SELECT * FROM world.city WHERE ID = 130
statement_latency: 24.68 s
*************************** 4. row ***************************
          thd_id: 1180
         conn_id: 712
           state: NULL
```

```
current_statement: SET @sys.statement_truncate_le ... ('statement_truncate_
len', 64)
statement_latency: 50.42 ms
4 rows in set (0.0530 sec)
```

Two connections are waiting for a metadata lock (on the world.city table). There
is a third connection included (conn_id = 713) which is idle and can be seen from the
NULL for the statement latency (in some versions earlier than 8.0.18 and after 8.0.21, you
may also see that the current statement is NULL). In this case, the list of queries is limited
to those with an active query or an active transaction, but usually you will start out with
a full process list. However, to make it easy to focus on the important parts, the output is
filtered.

Once you know there is a metadata lock issue, you can use the sys.schema_table_
lock_waits view to get information about the lock contention. Listing 14-3 shows an
example of the output corresponding to the just discussed process list.

Listing 14-3. Finding metadata lock contention

```
-- Investigation #3
Connection 4> SELECT *
                FROM sys.schema_table_lock_waits\G
*************************** 1. row ***************************
              object_schema: world
                object_name: city
            waiting_thread_id: 1182
                waiting_pid: 714
            waiting_account: root@localhost
          waiting_lock_type: EXCLUSIVE
      waiting_lock_duration: TRANSACTION
              waiting_query: ALTER TABLE world.city ADD INDEX (Name)
          waiting_query_secs: 128
  waiting_query_rows_affected: 0
  waiting_query_rows_examined: 0
            blocking_thread_id: 1181
                blocking_pid: 713
            blocking_account: root@localhost
          blocking_lock_type: SHARED_READ
```

```
      blocking_lock_duration: TRANSACTION
       sql_kill_blocking_query: KILL QUERY 713
  sql_kill_blocking_connection: KILL 713
*************************** 2. row ***************************
                object_schema: world
                  object_name: city
             waiting_thread_id: 1183
                   waiting_pid: 715
               waiting_account: root@localhost
             waiting_lock_type: SHARED_READ
         waiting_lock_duration: TRANSACTION
                 waiting_query: SELECT * FROM world.city WHERE ID = 130
            waiting_query_secs: 126
    waiting_query_rows_affected: 0
    waiting_query_rows_examined: 0
            blocking_thread_id: 1181
                  blocking_pid: 713
              blocking_account: root@localhost
            blocking_lock_type: SHARED_READ
        blocking_lock_duration: TRANSACTION
       sql_kill_blocking_query: KILL QUERY 713
  sql_kill_blocking_connection: KILL 713
*************************** 3. row ***************************
                object_schema: world
                  object_name: city
             waiting_thread_id: 1182
                   waiting_pid: 714
               waiting_account: root@localhost
             waiting_lock_type: EXCLUSIVE
         waiting_lock_duration: TRANSACTION
                 waiting_query: ALTER TABLE world.city ADD INDEX (Name)
            waiting_query_secs: 128
    waiting_query_rows_affected: 0
    waiting_query_rows_examined: 0
            blocking_thread_id: 1182
```

```
              blocking_pid: 714
          blocking_account: root@localhost
        blocking_lock_type: SHARED_UPGRADABLE
    blocking_lock_duration: TRANSACTION
     sql_kill_blocking_query: KILL QUERY 714
sql_kill_blocking_connection: KILL 714
*************************** 4. row ***************************
             object_schema: world
               object_name: city
          waiting_thread_id: 1183
               waiting_pid: 715
           waiting_account: root@localhost
         waiting_lock_type: SHARED_READ
     waiting_lock_duration: TRANSACTION
             waiting_query: SELECT * FROM world.city WHERE ID = 130
         waiting_query_secs: 126
  waiting_query_rows_affected: 0
  waiting_query_rows_examined: 0
          blocking_thread_id: 1182
              blocking_pid: 714
          blocking_account: root@localhost
        blocking_lock_type: SHARED_UPGRADABLE
    blocking_lock_duration: TRANSACTION
     sql_kill_blocking_query: KILL QUERY 714
sql_kill_blocking_connection: KILL 714
4 rows in set (0.0041 sec)
```

The output shows that there are four cases of queries waiting and blocking. This
may be surprising, but it happens because there are several locks involved and there
is a chain of waits. Each row is a pair of a waiting and blocking connection. The output
uses "pid" for the process list id which is the same as the connection id used in earlier
outputs. The information includes what the lock is on, details about the waiting
connection, details about the blocking connection, and two queries that can be used to
kill the blocking query or connection.

The third row shows process list id 714 waiting on itself. That sounds like a deadlock, but it is not. The reason is that the ALTER TABLE first took a shared lock that can be upgraded and then tried to get the exclusive lock which is waiting. Because there is no explicit information on which existing lock is actually blocking the new lock, this information ends up being included.

The fourth row shows that the SELECT statement is waiting for process list id 714 which is the ALTER TABLE. This is the reason that connections can start to pile up as the DDL statement requires an exclusive lock, so it will block requests for shared locks.

The first and second rows are where the underlying issue for the lock contention is revealed. Process list id 713 is blocking for both of the other connections which shows that this is the main culprit that is blocking the DDL statement. So, when you are investigating an issue like this, look for a connection waiting for an exclusive metadata lock that is blocked by another connection. If there is a large number of rows in the output, you can also look for the connection causing the most blocks and use that as a starting point. Listing 14-4 shows an example of how you can do this.

Listing 14-4. Looking for the connection causing the metadata lock block

```
-- Investigation #4
Connection 4> SELECT *
               FROM sys.schema_table_lock_waits
              WHERE waiting_lock_type = 'EXCLUSIVE'
                AND waiting_pid <> blocking_pid\G
*************************** 1. row ***************************
              object_schema: world
                object_name: city
           waiting_thread_id: 1182
                 waiting_pid: 714
             waiting_account: root@localhost
           waiting_lock_type: EXCLUSIVE
       waiting_lock_duration: TRANSACTION
              waiting_query: ALTER TABLE world.city ADD INDEX (Name)
          waiting_query_secs: 678
  waiting_query_rows_affected: 0
  waiting_query_rows_examined: 0
          blocking_thread_id: 1181
               blocking_pid: 713
```

```
              blocking_account: root@localhost
            blocking_lock_type: SHARED_READ
        blocking_lock_duration: TRANSACTION
        sql_kill_blocking_query: KILL QUERY 713
   sql_kill_blocking_connection: KILL 713
1 row in set (0.0025 sec)

-- Investigation #5
Connection 4> SELECT blocking_pid, COUNT(*)
                FROM sys.schema_table_lock_waits
                WHERE waiting_pid <> blocking_pid
                GROUP BY blocking_pid
                ORDER BY COUNT(*) DESC;
+--------------+----------+
| blocking_pid | COUNT(*) |
+--------------+----------+
|          713 |        2 |
|          714 |        1 |
+--------------+----------+
2 rows in set (0.0023 sec)
```

The first query looks for a wait for an exclusive metadata lock where the blocking process list id is not itself. In this case, that immediately gives the main block contention. The second query determines the number of blocking queries triggered by each process list id. It may not be as simple as shown in this example, but using queries as shown here will help narrow down where the lock contention is.

Once you have determined where the lock contention originates, you need to determine what the transaction is doing. In this case, the root of the lock contention is the connection with process list id 713. Going back to the process list output, you can see that it is not doing anything in this case:

```
*************************** 1. row ***************************
             thd_id: 1181
             conn_id: 713
              state: NULL
  current_statement: SELECT Code, Name FROM world.country WHERE Code = 'USA'
  statement_latency: NULL
```

What did this connection do to take the metadata lock? The fact that there is no current statement that involves the world.city table suggests the connection has an active transaction open. In this case, the transaction is idle (as seen by statement_latency = NULL), but it could also be that there was a query executing that is unrelated to the metadata lock on the world.city table. In either case, you need to determine what the transaction was doing prior to the current state. You can use the Performance Schema and Information Schema for this. Listing 14-5 shows an example of investigating the status and recent history of a transaction.

Listing 14-5. Investigating a transaction

```
-- Investigation #6
Connection 4> SELECT *
                FROM information_schema.INNODB_TRX
               WHERE trx_mysql_thread_id = 713\G
*************************** 1. row ***************************
                  trx_id: 284186648310752
               trx_state: RUNNING
             trx_started: 2020-08-06 19:57:33
   trx_requested_lock_id: NULL
         trx_wait_started: NULL
              trx_weight: 0
       trx_mysql_thread_id: 713
               trx_query: NULL
      trx_operation_state: NULL
        trx_tables_in_use: 0
        trx_tables_locked: 0
         trx_lock_structs: 0
   trx_lock_memory_bytes: 1136
          trx_rows_locked: 0
        trx_rows_modified: 0
   trx_concurrency_tickets: 0
      trx_isolation_level: REPEATABLE READ
        trx_unique_checks: 1
    trx_foreign_key_checks: 1
```

```
 trx_last_foreign_key_error: NULL
  trx_adaptive_hash_latched: 0
  trx_adaptive_hash_timeout: 0
           trx_is_read_only: 0
 trx_autocommit_non_locking: 0
        trx_schedule_weight: NULL
1 row in set (0.0010 sec)

-- Investigation #7
Connection 4> SELECT *
                FROM performance_schema.events_transactions_current
                WHERE thread_id = 1181\G
*************************** 1. row ***************************
                    THREAD_ID: 1181
                     EVENT_ID: 8
                 END_EVENT_ID: NULL
                   EVENT_NAME: transaction
                        STATE: ACTIVE
                       TRX_ID: NULL
                         GTID: AUTOMATIC
                 XID_FORMAT_ID: NULL
                     XID_GTRID: NULL
                     XID_BQUAL: NULL
                     XA_STATE: NULL
                       SOURCE: transaction.cc:209
                  TIMER_START: 456761974401600000
                    TIMER_END: 457816781775400000
                   TIMER_WAIT: 1054807373800000
                  ACCESS_MODE: READ WRITE
              ISOLATION_LEVEL: REPEATABLE READ
                   AUTOCOMMIT: NO
          NUMBER_OF_SAVEPOINTS: 0
NUMBER_OF_ROLLBACK_TO_SAVEPOINT: 0
    NUMBER_OF_RELEASE_SAVEPOINT: 0
          OBJECT_INSTANCE_BEGIN: NULL
              NESTING_EVENT_ID: 7
```

```
            NESTING_EVENT_TYPE: STATEMENT
1 row in set (0.0010 sec)

-- Investigation #8
Connection 4> SELECT event_id, current_schema, sql_text
              FROM performance_schema.events_statements_history
            WHERE thread_id = 1181
                  AND nesting_event_id = 8
                  AND nesting_event_type = 'TRANSACTION'\G
*************************** 1. row ***************************
     event_id: 9
current_schema: NULL
     sql_text: SELECT * FROM world.city WHERE ID = 3805
*************************** 2. row ***************************
     event_id: 10
current_schema: NULL
     sql_text: SELECT Code, Name FROM world.country WHERE Code = 'USA'
2 rows in set (0.0010 sec)

-- Investigation #9
Connection 4> SELECT attr_name, attr_value
              FROM performance_schema.session_connect_attrs
            WHERE processlist_id = 713
            ORDER BY attr_name;
+-----------------+-----------------+
| attr_name       | attr_value      |
+-----------------+-----------------+
| _client_license | GPL             |
| _client_name    | libmysqlxclient |
| _client_version | 8.0.21          |
| _os             | Win64           |
| _pid            | 27832           |
| _platform       | x86_64          |
| _thread         | 31396           |
| program_name    | mysqlsh         |
+-----------------+-----------------+
8 rows in set (0.0007 sec)
```

The first query uses the INNODB_TRX view in the Information Schema. It, for example, shows when the transaction was started, so you can determine how long it has been active. The trx_rows_modified column is also useful to know how much data has been changed by the transaction in case it is decided to roll back the transaction. Note that what InnoDB calls the MySQL thread id (the trx_mysql_thread_id column) is actually the connection id.

The second query uses the events_transactions_current table from the Performance Schema to get more transaction information. You can use the timer_wait column to determine the age of the transaction. The value is in picoseconds, so it can be easier to understand what the value is by using the FORMAT_PICO_TIME() function:

```
mysql> SELECT FORMAT_PICO_TIME(1054807373800000) AS Age;
+-----------+
| Age       |
+-----------+
| 17.58 min |
+-----------+
1 row in set (0.0006 sec)
```

If you are using MySQL 8.0.15 or earlier, use the sys.format_time() function instead.

The third query uses the events_statements_history table to find the previous queries executed in the transaction. The nesting_event_id column is set to the value of the event_id from the output of the events_transactions_current table, and the nesting_event_type column is set to match a transaction. This ensures that only events that are children of the ongoing transaction are returned. The result is ordered by the event_id (of the statement) to get the statements in the order they were executed. By default, the events_statements_history table will include at most the ten latest queries for the connection.

In this example, the investigation shows that the transaction has executed two queries: one selecting from the world.city table and one selecting from the world.country table. It is the first of these queries causing the metadata lock contention.

The fourth query uses the session_connect_attrs table to find the attributes submitted by the connection. Not all clients and connectors submit attributes, or they may be disabled, so this information is not always available. When the attributes are available, they can be useful to find out where the offending transaction is executed from. In this example, you can see the connection is from MySQL Shell (mysqlsh).

243

When you are done investigating the issue, you can roll back the transaction for process list id 713. This will cause the ALTER TABLE to execute, so you should also drop the Name index again if you want to leave the schema as it was before this example:

```
-- Connection 1
Connection 1> ROLLBACK;
Query OK, 0 rows affected (0.0006 sec)

-- Connection 2
Query OK, 0 rows affected (35 min 34.2938 sec)

Records: 0  Duplicates: 0  Warnings: 0

-- Connection 3
+-----+--------+-------------+-----------------+------------+
| ID  | Name   | CountryCode | District        | Population |
+-----+--------+-------------+-----------------+------------+
| 130 | Sydney | AUS         | New South Wales |    3276207 |
+-----+--------+-------------+-----------------+------------+
1 row in set (35 min 31.1277 sec)

-- Connection 2
Connection 2> ALTER TABLE world.city DROP INDEX Name;
Query OK, 0 rows affected (0.1890 sec)

Records: 0  Duplicates: 0  Warnings: 0
```

The Solution

For a metadata lock contention, you essentially have two options to resolve the issue: make the blocking transaction complete or kill the DDL statement. To complete the blocking transaction, you will need to either commit it or roll it back. If you kill the connection, it triggers a rollback of the transaction, so you need to take into consideration how much work will need to be rolled back. In order to commit the transaction, you must find where the connection is executed and commit it that way. You cannot commit a transaction owned by a different connection.

Killing the DDL statement will allow the other queries to proceed, but it does not solve the issue in the long term if the lock is held by an abandoned but still active transaction. For cases where there is an abandoned transaction holding the metadata lock, it can however be an option to kill both the DDL statement and the connection with the abandoned transaction. That way, you avoid the DDL statement to continue blocking subsequent queries while the transaction rolls back. Then when the rollback has completed, you can retry the DDL statement.

The Prevention

The key to avoiding metadata lock contention is to avoid long-running transactions at the same time as you need to execute DDL statements for the tables used by the transaction. You can, for example, execute DDL statements at times when you know there are no long-running transactions. You can also set the lock_wait_timeout option to a low value which makes the DDL statement abandon after lock_wait_timeout seconds. While that does not avoid the lock problem, it mitigates the issue by avoiding the DDL statement stopping other queries from executing. You can then find the root cause without the stress of having a large part of the application not working.

You can also aim at reducing how long transactions are active. One option is to split a large transaction into several smaller transactions, if it is not required that all operations are performed as an atomic unit. You should also make sure that the transaction is not kept open for unnecessarily long time by making sure you are not doing interactive work, file I/O, transferring data to the end user, and so on while the transaction is active.

One common cause of long-running transactions is that the application or client does not commit or roll back the transaction at all. This is particularly likely to happen with the autocommit option disabled. When autocommit is disabled, any query – even a plain read-only SELECT statement – will start a new transaction when there is not already an active transaction. This means that an innocent-looking query may start a transaction, and if the developer is not aware that autocommit is disabled, then the developer may not think about explicitly ending the transaction. The autocommit setting is enabled by default in MySQL Server, but some connectors disable it by default.

Summary

In this chapter you investigated a situation where an abandoned transaction caused an ALTER TABLE statement to block and subsequently prevent other queries on the same table to execute. The key to determining the cause of the contention is the sys.schema_table_lock_waits view which is based on the performance_schema.metadata_locks table. As the number of pairs of waiting and blocking lock requests quickly can add up, you may want to filter the rows looking, for example, for a waiting request for an exclusive lock, or you can aggregate the information to find the connection blocking the most requests.

The solution is to commit or roll back the transaction or kill the DDL statement waiting for the exclusive metadata lock. Optionally you can also kill both the transaction and the DDL statement which can be useful if the transaction has to roll back many changes. A good way to prevent pileups of queries is to use a low value for lock_wait_timeout and retry the DDL statement if you experience lock wait timeouts.

In the next chapter, you will analyze a situation with InnoDB record lock requests timing out.

## CHAPTER 15

Case Study: Record-Level Locks

Record lock contention is the most frequently encountered, but usually also the least intrusive as the default lock wait timeout is just 50 seconds, so there is not the same potential for queries pilling up. That said, there are cases – as will be shown – where record locks can cause MySQL to come to a grinding halt. This chapter will look into investigating InnoDB record lock issues in general and in more detail lock wait timeout issues. Investigating the specifics of deadlocks is deferred until the next chapter.

The Symptoms

The symptoms of InnoDB record lock contention are often very subtle and not easily recognizable. In severe cases, you will get a lock wait timeout or a deadlock error, but in many cases, there may be no direct symptoms. Rather the symptom is that queries are slower than normal. This may range from being a fraction of a second slower to being many seconds slower.

For cases where there is a lock wait timeout, you will see an ER_LOCK_WAIT_TIMEOUT error like the one in the following example:

```
ERROR: 1205: Lock wait timeout exceeded; try restarting transaction
```

When the queries are slower than they would be without lock contention, the most likely way to detect the issue is through monitoring, either using something similar to the Query Analyzer in MySQL Enterprise Monitor or detecting lock contention using the

247

© Jesper Wisborg Krogh 2021
J. W. Krogh, *MySQL Concurrency*, https://doi.org/10.1007/978-1-4842-6652-6_15

sys.innodb_lock_waits view. Figure 15-1 shows an example of a query in the Query Analyzer. The sys schema view will be used when discussing the investigation of record lock contention. The figure is also available in full size in this book's GitHub repository as figure_15_1_quan.png.

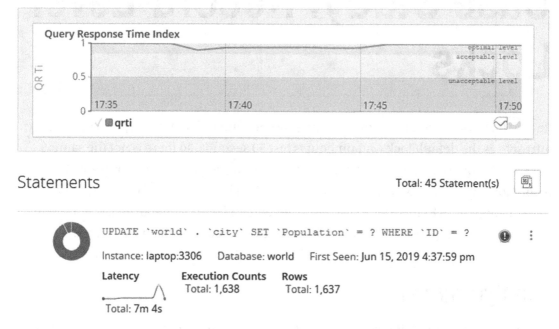

Figure 15-1. *Example of a lock contention detected in the Query Analyzer*

In the figure, notice how the latency graph for the query increases toward the end of the period and then suddenly drops again. There is also a red icon to the right of the normalized query – that icon means the query has returned errors. In this case the error is a lock wait timeout, but that cannot be seen from the figure. The donut-shaped chart to the left of the normalized query also shows a red area indicating the Query Response Time index[1] for the query at times is considered poor. The large graph at the top shows a small dip showing there were enough issues in the instance to cause a general degradation of the performance of the instance.

---

[1]https://dev.mysql.com/doc/mysql-monitor/en/mem-features-qrti.html

There are also several instance-level metrics that show how much locking is occurring for the instance. These can be very useful to monitor the general lock contention over time. Listing 15-1 shows the available metrics using the sys.metrics view.

Listing 15-1. InnoDB lock metrics

```
mysql> SELECT Variable_name,
              Variable_value AS Value,
              Enabled
         FROM sys.metrics
        WHERE Variable_name LIKE 'innodb_row_lock%'
              OR Type = 'InnoDB Metrics - lock';
+-------------------------------+--------+---------+
| Variable_name                 | Value  | Enabled |
+-------------------------------+--------+---------+
| innodb_row_lock_current_waits | 0      | YES     |
| innodb_row_lock_time          | 480628 | YES     |
| innodb_row_lock_time_avg      | 1219   | YES     |
| innodb_row_lock_time_max      | 51066  | YES     |
| innodb_row_lock_waits         | 394    | YES     |
| lock_deadlock_false_positives | 0      | YES     |
| lock_deadlock_rounds          | 193790 | YES     |
| lock_deadlocks                | 0      | YES     |
| lock_rec_grant_attempts       | 218    | YES     |
| lock_rec_lock_created         | 0      | NO      |
| lock_rec_lock_removed         | 0      | NO      |
| lock_rec_lock_requests        | 0      | NO      |
| lock_rec_lock_waits           | 0      | NO      |
| lock_rec_locks                | 0      | NO      |
| lock_rec_release_attempts     | 7522   | YES     |
| lock_row_lock_current_waits   | 0      | YES     |
| lock_schedule_refreshes       | 193790 | YES     |
| lock_table_lock_created       | 0      | NO      |
```

```
| lock_table_lock_removed         | 0      | NO       |
| lock_table_lock_waits           | 0      | NO       |
| lock_table_locks                | 0      | NO       |
| lock_threads_waiting            | 0      | YES      |
| lock_timeouts                   | 193    | YES      |
+--------------------------------+--------+---------+
23 rows in set (0.0089 sec)
```

For this discussion, the innodb_row_lock_% and lock_timeouts metrics are the most interesting. The three time variables are in milliseconds. It can be seen there have been 193 lock wait timeouts which on its own is not necessarily a cause for concern (at least you need to consider over how long those timeouts occurred). You can also see there have been 394 cases when a lock could not be granted immediately (innodb_row_lock_waits) and there have been waits up to more than 51 seconds (innodb_row_lock_time_max). When the general level of lock contention increases, you will see these metrics increase as well.

Even better than monitoring the metrics manually, ensure your monitoring solution record the metrics and can plot them over time in timeseries graphs. Figure 15-2 shows an example of the metrics plotted for the same incident that was found in Figure 15-1.

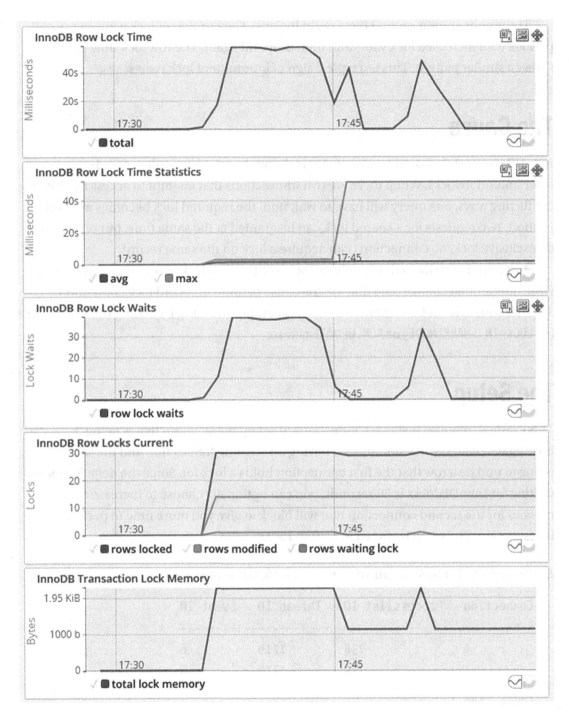

Figure 15-2. *Timeseries graphs for InnoDB row lock metrics*

The graphs show a general increase in locking. The number of lock waits has two periods with increased lock waits and then drops off again. The row lock time graph shows a similar pattern. This is a typical sign of intermittent lock issues.

The Cause

InnoDB works with shared and exclusive locks on the row data, index records, gaps, and insert intention locks. When there are two transactions that attempt to access the data in conflicting ways, one query will have to wait until the required lock becomes available. In short, two requests for a shared lock can be granted at the same time, but once there is an exclusive lock, no connections can acquire a lock on the same record.

As it is exclusive locks that are the most likely to cause lock contention, it is usually DML queries that change data that are the cause of InnoDB record lock contention. Another source is SELECT statements doing preemptive locking by adding the FOR SHARE (or LOCK IN SHARE MODE) or FOR UPDATE clause.

The Setup

This example requires just two connections to set up the scenario that is being investigated with the first connection having an ongoing transaction and the second trying to update a row that the first connection holds a lock for. Since the default timeout waiting for InnoDB locks is 50 seconds, you can optionally choose to increase this timeout for the second connection that will block to give you more time to perform the investigation. The setup is shown in Listing 15-2.

Listing 15-2. Triggering InnoDB record lock contention

```
-- Connection   Processlist ID   Thread ID   Event ID
-- ----------------------------------------------------
--          1              738        1219          6
--          2              739        1220          6

-- Connection 1
Connection 1> START TRANSACTION;
Query OK, 0 rows affected (0.0002 sec)
```

```
Connection 1> UPDATE world.city
              SET Population = 5000000
              WHERE ID = 130;
Query OK, 1 row affected (0.0248 sec)

Rows matched: 1  Changed: 1  Warnings: 0

-- Connection 2
Connection 2> SET SESSION innodb_lock_wait_timeout = 3600;
Query OK, 0 rows affected (0.0004 sec)

Connection 2> START TRANSACTION;
Query OK, 0 rows affected (0.0002 sec)

Connection 2> UPDATE world.city SET Population = Population * 1.10 WHERE
CountryCode = 'AUS';
```

In this example, the lock wait timeout for Connection 2 is set to 3600 seconds to give you an hour to investigate the issue. The START TRANSACTION for Connection 2 is not required but allows you to roll both transactions back when you are done to avoid making changes to the data.

The Investigation

The investigation of record locks is very similar to investigating metadata locks. You can query the data_locks and data_lock_waits tables in the Performance Schema which will show the raw lock data and pending locks, respectively. There is also the sys. innodb_lock_waits view which queries the two tables to find pairs of locks with one being blocked by the other.

Note   The data_locks and data_lock_waits tables are new in MySQL 8. In MySQL 5.7 and earlier, there were two similar tables in the Information Schema named INNODB_LOCKS and INNODB_LOCK_WAITS. An advantage of using the innodb_lock_waits view is that it works the same (but with some extra information in MySQL 8) across the MySQL versions.

In most cases, it is easiest to start the investigation using the innodb_lock_waits view and only dive into the Performance Schema tables as needed. Listing 15-3 shows an example of the output from innodb_lock_waits for a lock wait situation.

Listing 15-3. Retrieving lock information from the innodb_lock_waits view

```
-- Investigation #1
-- Connection 3
Connection 3> SELECT * FROM sys.innodb_lock_waits\G
*************************** 1. row ***************************
                wait_started: 2020-08-07 18:04:56
                    wait_age: 00:00:16
               wait_age_secs: 16
                locked_table: `world`.`city`
         locked_table_schema: world
           locked_table_name: city
      locked_table_partition: NULL
   locked_table_subpartition: NULL
                locked_index: PRIMARY
                 locked_type: RECORD
              waiting_trx_id: 537516
         waiting_trx_started: 2020-08-07 18:04:56
             waiting_trx_age: 00:00:16
     waiting_trx_rows_locked: 2
   waiting_trx_rows_modified: 0
                 waiting_pid: 739
               waiting_query: UPDATE world.city SET Populati ... 1.10 WHERE
                  CountryCode = 'AUS'
             waiting_lock_id: 2711671601760:1923:7:44:2711634704240
           waiting_lock_mode: X,REC_NOT_GAP
             blocking_trx_id: 537515
                blocking_pid: 738
              blocking_query: NULL
            blocking_lock_id: 2711671600928:1923:7:44:2711634698920
          blocking_lock_mode: X,REC_NOT_GAP
```

```
       blocking_trx_started: 2020-08-07 18:04:56
           blocking_trx_age: 00:00:16
    blocking_trx_rows_locked: 1
  blocking_trx_rows_modified: 1
      sql_kill_blocking_query: KILL QUERY 738
sql_kill_blocking_connection: KILL 738
1 row in set (0.0805 sec)
```

The columns in the output can be divided into five sections based on the prefix of the column name. The groups are

- **wait_:** These columns show some general information around the age of the lock wait.

- **locked_:** These columns show what is locked ranging from the schema to the index as well as the lock type.

- **waiting_:** These columns show details of the transaction that is waiting for the lock to be granted including the query and the lock mode requested.

- **blocking_:** These columns show details of the transaction that is blocking the lock request. Note that in the example, the blocking query is NULL. This means the transaction is idle at the time the output was generated. Even when there is a blocking query listed, the query may not have anything to do with the lock that there is contention for – other than the query is executed by the same transaction that holds the lock.

- **sql_kill_:** These two columns provide the KILL queries that can be used to kill the blocking query or connection.

Note   The column blocking_query is the query currently executed (if any) for the blocking transaction. It does not mean that the query itself is necessarily causing the lock request to block.

The case where the `blocking_query` column is NULL is a common situation. It means that the blocking transaction is currently not executing a query. This may be because it is between two queries. If this period is an extended period, it suggests the application is doing work that ideally should be done outside the transaction. More commonly, the transaction is not executing a query because it has been forgotten about, either in an interactive session where the human has forgotten to end the transaction or an application flow that does not ensure transactions are committed or rolled back.

The Solution

The solution depends on the extent of the lock waits. If it is a few queries having short lock waits, it may very well be acceptable to just let the affected queries wait for the lock to become available. Remember locks are there to ensure the integrity of the data, so locks are not inherently a problem. Locks are only a problem when they cause a significant impact on the performance or cause queries to fail to an extent where it is not feasible to retry them.

If the lock situation lasts for an extended period – particularly if the blocking transaction has been abandoned – you can consider killing the blocking transaction. As always you need to consider that the rollback may take a significant amount of time if the blocking transaction has performed a large amount of work.

For queries that fail because of a lock wait timeout error, the application should retry them. Remember that by default a lock wait timeout only rolls back the query that was executing when the timeout occurred. The rest of the transaction is left as it were before the query. A failure to handle the timeout may thus leave an unfinished transaction with its own locks that can cause further lock issues. Whether just the query or the whole transaction will be rolled back is controlled by the `innodb_rollback_on_timeout` option.

Caution   It is very important that a lock wait timeout is handled as otherwise it may leave the transaction with locks that are not released. If that happens, other transactions may not be able to acquire the locks they require.

The Prevention

Preventing significant record-level lock contention largely follows the guidelines that were discussed in Chapter 9, "Reduce Locking Issues." To recapitulate the discussion, the way to reduce lock wait contention is largely about reducing the size and duration of transactions, using indexes to reduce the number of records accessed, and possibly switching the transaction isolation level to READ COMMITTED to release locks earlier and reduce the number of gap locks.

Summary

In this chapter a case study with InnoDB record locks has been discussed. The symptoms were that a query that was expected to be quick took a long time to complete. The key to determine which connections are involved in the lock contention is to use the sys.innodb_lock_waits view which directly shows information for the waiting and blocking connections. For more details you can dive into the data_locks and data_lock_waits tables in the Performance Schema.

The solution depends on the extent of the lock waits. If they are short and infrequent, you may be able to ignore them and just let the waiting queries wait for the lock request to become available. If the lock waits are caused by excessively long-running queries or forgotten transactions, you may need to kill the offending query or connection but taking the effort to roll back the changes into account. To prevent the issues in the future, work to reduce the size and duration of your transactions, review the indexes, and consider the READ COMMITTED transaction isolation level.

In the next case study, a related issue where two transactions have a circular lock wait graph – better known as a deadlock – will be examined.

CHAPTER 16

Case Study: Deadlocks

One of the lock issues causing the most concerns for database administrators is deadlocks. This is partly because of the name and partly because they unlike the other lock issues discussed always cause an error. However, there is as such nothing especially worrying about deadlocks compared to other locking issues. On the contrary, that they cause an error means that you know about them sooner and the lock issue resolves itself.

This chapter sets up a deadlock scenario and completes an investigation to work backward from the deadlock information in the InnoDB monitor output to determine the transactions involved in the deadlock.

The Symptoms

The symptoms are straightforward. The victim of a deadlock receives an error and the `lock_deadlocks` InnoDB metric increments. The error that will be returned to the transaction that InnoDB chooses as the victim is `ER_LOCK_DEADLOCK`:

```
ERROR: 1213: Deadlock found when trying to get lock; try restarting
transaction
```

The `lock_deadlocks` metric is very useful to keep an eye on how often deadlocks occur. A convenient way to track the value of `lock_deadlocks` is to use the `sys.metrics` view:

```
mysql> SELECT *
         FROM sys.metrics
        WHERE Variable_name = 'lock_deadlocks'\G
*************************** 1. row ***************************
  Variable_name: lock_deadlocks
 Variable_value: 2
          Type: InnoDB Metrics - lock
        Enabled: YES
1 row in set (0.0096 sec)
```

259

J. W. Krogh, *MySQL Concurrency*, https://doi.org/10.1007/978-1-4842-6652-6_16

Alternatively, you can use the events_errors_summary_global_by_error table in the Performance Schema and query for the ER_LOCK_DEADLOCK error:

```
mysql> SELECT *
          FROM performance_schema.events_errors_summary_global_by_error
          WHERE error_name = 'ER_LOCK_DEADLOCK'\G
*************************** 1. row ***************************
     ERROR_NUMBER: 1213
       ERROR_NAME: ER_LOCK_DEADLOCK
        SQL_STATE: 40001
 SUM_ERROR_RAISED: 5
SUM_ERROR_HANDLED: 0
       FIRST_SEEN: 2020-08-01 13:09:29
        LAST_SEEN: 2020-08-07 18:28:20
1 row in set (0.0083 sec)
```

Do however be aware that this includes all cases of a deadlock returning error 1213 irrespective of the lock type, whereas the lock_deadlocks metric only includes InnoDB deadlocks.

You can also check the LATEST DETECTED DEADLOCK section in the output of the InnoDB monitor, for example, by executing SHOW ENGINE INNODB STATUS. This will show when the last deadlock last occurred, and thus you can use that to judge how frequently deadlocks occur. If you have the innodb_print_all_deadlocks option enabled, the error lock will have many outputs of deadlock information. The details of the InnoDB monitor output for deadlocks will be covered in the section "The Investigation" after the cause of deadlocks and the setup have been discussed.

The Cause

Deadlocks are caused by locks being obtained in different orders for two or more transactions. Each transaction ends up holding a lock that the other transaction needs. This lock may be a record lock, gap lock, predicate lock, or insert intention lock. Figure 16-1 shows an example of a circular dependency that triggers a deadlock.

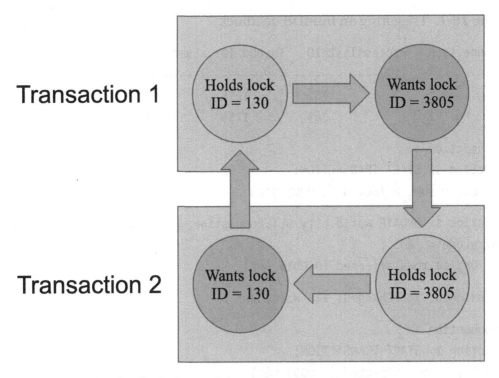

Figure 16-1. *A circular lock dependency triggering a deadlock*

The deadlock shown in the figure is due to two record locks on the primary keys of a table. That is one of the simplest deadlocks that can occur. As shown when investigating a deadlock, the circle can be more complex than this.

The Setup

This example uses two connections as the example in the previous chapter, but this time both make changes before Connection 1 ends up blocking until Connection 2 rolls back its changes with an error. Connection 1 updates the population of Australia and its cities with 10%, whereas Connection 2 updates the Australian population with that of the city of Darwin and adds the city. The statements are shown in Listing 16-1.

Listing 16-1. Triggering an InnoDB deadlock

```
-- Connection    Processlist ID    Thread ID    Event ID
-- ---------------------------------------------------------
--           1             762          1258           6
--           2             763          1259           6
```

```
-- Connection 1
Connection 1> START TRANSACTION;
Query OK, 0 rows affected (0.0005 sec)

Connection 1> UPDATE world.city SET Population = Population * 1.10 WHERE
CountryCode = 'AUS';
Query OK, 14 rows affected (0.0016 sec)

Rows matched: 14  Changed: 14  Warnings: 0

-- Connection 2
Connection 2> START TRANSACTION;
Query OK, 0 rows affected (0.0005 sec)

Connection 2> UPDATE world.country SET Population = Population + 146000
WHERE Code = 'AUS';
Query OK, 1 row affected (0.2683 sec)

Rows matched: 1  Changed: 1  Warnings: 0

-- Connection 1
Connection 1> UPDATE world.country SET Population = Population * 1.10 WHERE
Code = 'AUS';

-- Connection 2
Connection 2> INSERT INTO world.city VALUES (4080, 'Darwin', 'AUS',
'Northern Territory', 146000);
ERROR: 1213: Deadlock found when trying to get lock; try restarting
transaction

-- Connection 1
Query OK, 1 row affected (0.1021 sec)

Rows matched: 1  Changed: 1  Warnings: 0
```

```
-- Connection 2
Connection 2> ROLLBACK;
Query OK, 0 rows affected (0.0003 sec)

-- Connection 1
Connection 1> ROLLBACK;
Query OK, 0 rows affected (0.0545 sec)
```

The key is that the two transactions update both the `city` and `country` tables but in opposite order. The setup completes by explicitly rolling back both transactions to ensure the tables are left without changes.

The Investigation

The main tool to analyze deadlocks is the section with information about the latest detected deadlock in the InnoDB monitor output. If you have the `innodb_print_all_deadlocks` option enabled (`OFF` by default), you may also have the deadlock information from the error log; however, the information is the same, so it does not change the analysis.

The deadlock information contains four parts describing the deadlock and the result. The parts are

- When the deadlock occurred.

- Information for the first of the transactions involved in the deadlock.

- Information for the second of the transactions involved in the deadlock.

- Which of the transactions that was rolled back. This information is not included in the error log when `innodb_print_all_deadlocks` is enabled.

The numbering of the two transactions is arbitrary, and the main purpose is to be able to refer to one transaction or the other. The two parts with transaction information are the most important ones. They include how long the transaction was active, some statistics about the size of the transactions in terms of locks taken and undo log entries and similar, the query that was blocking waiting for a lock, and information about the locks involved in the deadlock.

The lock information is not as easy to interpret as when you use the data_locks and data_lock_waits tables and the sys.innodb_lock_waits view. However, it is not too difficult once you have tried to perform the analysis a few times.

Tip   Create some deadlocks on purpose in a test system, and study the resulting deadlock information. Then work your way through the information to determine why the deadlock occurred. Since you know the queries, it is easier to interpret the lock data.

For this deadlock investigation, consider the deadlock section from the InnoDB monitor that is shown in Listing 16-2. The listing is rather long and the lines wide, so the information is also available in this book's GitHub repository as listing_16_2_ deadlock.txt, so you can open the output in a text editor of your choice.

Listing 16-2. Example of the information for a detected deadlock

```
-- Investigation #1
-- Connection 3
Connection 3> SHOW ENGINE INNODB STATUS\G
*************************** 1. row ***************************
...
------------------------
LATEST DETECTED DEADLOCK
------------------------
2020-08-07 20:08:55 0x9f0
*** (1) TRANSACTION:
TRANSACTION 537544, ACTIVE 0 sec starting index read
mysql tables in use 1, locked 1
LOCK WAIT 6 lock struct(s), heap size 1136, 30 row lock(s), undo log
entries 14
MySQL thread id 762, OS thread handle 10344, query id 3282590 localhost ::1
root updating
UPDATE world.country SET Population = Population * 1.10 WHERE Code = 'AUS'
```

*** (1) HOLDS THE LOCK(S):

RECORD LOCKS space id 1923 page no 14 n bits 1272 index CountryCode of table `world`.`city` trx id 537544 lock_mode X locks gap before rec
Record lock, heap no 603 PHYSICAL RECORD: n_fields 2; compact format; info bits 0

 0: len 3; hex 415554; asc AUT;;
 1: len 4; hex 800005f3; asc   ;;

*** (1) WAITING FOR THIS LOCK TO BE GRANTED:

RECORD LOCKS space id 1924 page no 5 n bits 120 index PRIMARY of table `world`.`country` trx id 537544 lock_mode X locks rec but not gap waiting
Record lock, heap no 16 PHYSICAL RECORD: n_fields 17; compact format; info bits 0

 0: len 3; hex 415553; asc AUS;;
 1: len 6; hex 0000000833c9; asc   3 ;;
 2: len 7; hex 02000001750a3c; asc   u <;;
 3: len 30; hex 4175737472616c69612020202020202020202020202020202020202020
    0; asc Australia   ; (total 52 bytes);
 4: len 1; hex 05; asc ;;
 5: len 26; hex 4175737472616c696120616e64204e6577205a65616c616e6420; asc
    Australia and New Zealand ;;
 6: len 5; hex 80761f2400; asc v $;;
 7: len 2; hex 876d; asc m;;
 8: len 4; hex 812267c0; asc "g ;;
 9: len 2; hex cf08; asc   ;;
 10: len 5; hex 80055bce00; asc [;;
 11: len 5; hex 8005fecf00; asc   ;;
 12: len 30; hex 4175737472616c69612020202020202020202020202020202020202020
    2020; asc Australia   ; (total 45 bytes);
 13: len 30; hex 436f6e737469747574696f6e616c204d6f6e61726368792c20466
    5646572; asc Constitutional Monarchy, Feder; (total 45 bytes);
 14: len 30; hex 456c69736162657468204949492020202020202020202020202020202020
    2020; asc Elisabeth II   ; (total 60 bytes);
 15: len 4; hex 80000087; asc   ;;
 16: len 2; hex 4155; asc AU;;

*** (2) TRANSACTION:
TRANSACTION 537545, ACTIVE 0 sec inserting
mysql tables in use 1, locked 1
LOCK WAIT 4 lock struct(s), heap size 1136, 2 row lock(s), undo log entries 2
MySQL thread id 763, OS thread handle 37872, query id 3282591 localhost ::1
root update
INSERT INTO world.city VALUES (4080, 'Darwin', 'AUS', 'Northern Territory',
146000)

*** (2) HOLDS THE LOCK(S):
RECORD LOCKS space id 1924 page no 5 n bits 120 index PRIMARY of table
`world`.`country` trx id 537545 lock_mode X locks rec but not gap
Record lock, heap no 16 PHYSICAL RECORD: n_fields 17; compact format; info
bits 0
 0: len 3; hex 415553; asc AUS;;
 1: len 6; hex 0000000833c9; asc   3 ;;
 2: len 7; hex 02000001750a3c; asc   u <;;
 3: len 30; hex 4175737472616c69612020202020202020202020202020202020202020
    020; asc Australia   ; (total 52 bytes);
 4: len 1; hex 05; asc ;;
 5: len 26; hex 4175737472616c696120616e64204e6577205a65616c616e6420; asc
    Australia and New Zealand ;;
 6: len 5; hex 80761f2400; asc v $;;
 7: len 2; hex 876d; asc m;;
 8: len 4; hex 812267c0; asc "g ;;
 9: len 2; hex cf08; asc   ;;
10: len 5; hex 80055bce00; asc   [;;
11: len 5; hex 8005fecf00; asc   ;;
12: len 30; hex 4175737472616c6961202020202020202020202020202020202020202020
    2020; asc Australia   ; (total 45 bytes);
13: len 30; hex 436f6e737469747574696f6e616c204d6f6e61726368792c204665
    646572; asc Constitutional Monarchy, Feder; (total 45 bytes);
14: len 30; hex 456c697361626574682049492020202020202020202020202020202020
    2020; asc Elisabeth II   ; (total 60 bytes);
15: len 4; hex 80000087; asc   ;;
16: len 2; hex 4155; asc AU;;

```
*** (2) WAITING FOR THIS LOCK TO BE GRANTED:
RECORD LOCKS space id 1923 page no 14 n bits 1272 index CountryCode of
table `world`.`city` trx id 537545 lock_mode X locks gap before rec insert
intention waiting
Record lock, heap no 603 PHYSICAL RECORD: n_fields 2; compact format; info
bits 0
 0: len 3; hex 415554; asc AUT;;
 1: len 4; hex 800005f3; asc     ;;

*** WE ROLL BACK TRANSACTION (2)
```

The deadlock occurred on August 7, 2020, at 20:08:55 in the server time zone. You can use this information to see if the information is for the same deadlock as the deadlock reported by a user.

The interesting part is the information for the two transactions. You can see that transaction 1 was updating the population of the country with Code = 'AUS':

```
UPDATE world.country SET Population = Population * 1.10 WHERE Code = 'AUS'
```

Transaction 2 was attempting to insert a new city:

```
INSERT INTO world.city VALUES (4080, 'Darwin', 'AUS', 'Northern Territory',
146000)
```

This is a case where the deadlock involved multiple tables. While the two queries work on different tables, it cannot on its own prove that there are more queries involved as a foreign key can trigger one query to take locks on two tables. In this case though, the Code column is the primary key of the country table, and the only foreign key involved is from the CountryCode column on the city table to the Code column of the country table (showing this is left as an exercise for the reader using the world sample database). So it is not likely that two queries deadlock on their own.

Note   In MySQL 8.0.17 and earlier, the deadlock information contained less information about the locks involved. If you are still using an earlier release, upgrading will make it easier to investigate deadlocks.

The next thing to observe is what locks are being waited on. Transaction 1 waits for an exclusive lock on the primary key of the country table:

```
RECORD LOCKS space id 1924 page no 5 n bits 120 index PRIMARY of table
`world`.`country` trx id 537544 lock_mode X locks rec but not gap waiting
```

The value of the primary key can be found in the information that follows this information. It can seem a little overwhelming as InnoDB includes all the information related to the record. Since it is a primary key record, the whole row is included. This is useful to understand what data is in the row, particularly if the primary key does not carry that information on its own, but it can be confusing when you see it the first time. The primary key of the country table is the first column of the table, so it is the first line of the record information that contains the value of the primary key the lock is requesting:

```
 0: len 3; hex 415553; asc AUS;;
```

InnoDB includes the value in hexadecimal notation, but also tries to decode it as a string, so here it is clear that the value is "AUS", which is not surprising since that is also in the WHERE clause of the query. It is not always that obvious, so you should always confirm the value from the lock output. You can also see from the information that the column is sorted in ascending order in the index.

Transaction 2 waits for an insert intention lock on the CountryCode index of the city table:

```
RECORD LOCKS space id 1923 page no 14 n bits 1272 index CountryCode of
table `world`.`city` trx id 537545 lock_mode X locks gap before rec insert
intention waiting
```

You can see the lock request involves a gap before record. The lock information is simpler in this case as there are only two columns in the CountryCode index – the CountryCode column and the primary key (ID column) since the CountryCode index is a nonunique secondary index. The index is effectively (CountryCode, ID), and the values for the gap before record are as follows:

```
 0: len 3; hex 415554; asc AUT;;
 1: len 4; hex 800005f3; asc     ;;
```

This shows that the value of the CountryCode is "AUT" which is not all that surprising given it is the next value after "AUS" when sorting in alphabetical ascending order. The value for the ID column is the hex value 0x5f3 which in decimal is 1523. If you query for cities with CountryCode = AUT and sort them in order of the CountryCode index, you can see that ID = 1523 is the first city found:

```
-- Investigation #3
Connection 3> SELECT *
              FROM world.city
              WHERE CountryCode = 'AUT'
              ORDER BY CountryCode, ID
              LIMIT 1;
+------+------+-------------+----------+------------+
| ID   | Name | CountryCode | District | Population |
+------+------+-------------+----------+------------+
| 1523 | Wien | AUT         | Wien     |    1608144 |
+------+------+-------------+----------+------------+
1 row in set (0.2673 sec)
```

So far, so good. Since the transactions are waiting for these locks, it can of course be inferred that the other transaction holds the lock. In version 8.0.18 and later, InnoDB includes the full list of locks held by both transactions; in earlier versions, InnoDB only includes this explicitly for one of the transactions, so you need to determine what other queries the transactions have executed.

From the information available, you can make some educated guesses. For example, the INSERT statement is blocked by a gap lock on the CountryCode index. An example of a query that would take that gap lock is a query using the condition CountryCode = 'AUS'. The deadlock information also includes information about the two connections owning the transactions which may help you:

```
MySQL thread id 762, OS thread handle 10344, query id 3282590 localhost ::1
root updating

MySQL thread id 763, OS thread handle 37872, query id 3282591 localhost ::1
root update
```

You can see both connections were made using the root@localhost account. If you ensure to have different users for each application and role, the account may help you to narrow down who executed the transactions.

If the connections still exist, you can also use the events_statements_history table in the Performance Schema to find the latest queries executed by the connection. This may not be those involved in the deadlock, depending on whether the connection has been used for more queries, but may nevertheless provide a clue to what the connection is used for. If the connections no longer exist, you may in principle be able to find the queries in the events_statements_history_long table, but you will need to map the "MySQL thread id" (the connection ID) to the Performance Schema thread ID which there is no trivial way to do. Also, the events_statements_history_long consumer is not enabled by default.

In this particular case, both connections are still present, and they have not done anything other than rolling back the transactions. Listing 16-3 shows how you can find the queries involved in the transactions. Be aware that in real-world cases, the queries may return more rows than shown here as it is not possible to add a filter on the event_id.

Listing 16-3. Finding the queries involved in the deadlock

```
-- Investigation #4
Connection 3> SELECT sql_text, nesting_event_id,
                    nesting_event_type, mysql_errno,
                    IFNULL(error_name, '') AS error,
                    message_text
              FROM performance_schema.events_statements_history
                   LEFT OUTER JOIN performance_schema.events_errors_
                   summary_global_by_error
                        ON error_number = mysql_errno
              WHERE thread_id = PS_THREAD_ID(762)
                    AND event_id > 6
              ORDER BY event_id\G
*************************** 1. row ***************************
        sql_text: start transaction
  nesting_event_id: NULL
nesting_event_type: NULL
```

```
      mysql_errno: 0
            error:
     message_text: NULL
*************************** 2. row ***************************
         sql_text: UPDATE world.city SET Population = Population * 1.10
         WHERE CountryCode = 'AUS'
  nesting_event_id: 8
nesting_event_type: TRANSACTION
      mysql_errno: 0
            error:
     message_text: Rows matched: 14  Changed: 14  Warnings: 0
*************************** 3. row ***************************
         sql_text: UPDATE world.country SET Population = Population * 1.10
         WHERE Code = 'AUS'
  nesting_event_id: 8
nesting_event_type: TRANSACTION
      mysql_errno: 0
            error:
     message_text: Rows matched: 1  Changed: 1  Warnings: 0
*************************** 4. row ***************************
         sql_text: rollback
  nesting_event_id: 8
nesting_event_type: TRANSACTION
      mysql_errno: 0
            error:
     message_text: NULL
4 rows in set (0.0016 sec)

-- Investigation #5
Connection 3> SELECT sql_text, nesting_event_id,
                     nesting_event_type, mysql_errno,
                     IFNULL(error_name, '') AS error,
                     message_text
                FROM performance_schema.events_statements_history
                     LEFT OUTER JOIN performance_schema.events_errors_
                     summary_global_by_error
```

```
                         ON error_number = mysql_errno
            WHERE thread_id = PS_THREAD_ID(763)
                    AND event_id > 6
            ORDER BY event_id\G
*************************** 1. row ***************************
        sql_text: start transaction
  nesting_event_id: NULL
nesting_event_type: NULL
      mysql_errno: 0
            error:
    message_text: NULL
*************************** 2. row ***************************
        sql_text: UPDATE world.country SET Population = Population +
        146000 WHERE Code = 'AUS'
  nesting_event_id: 8
nesting_event_type: TRANSACTION
      mysql_errno: 0
            error:
    message_text: Rows matched: 1  Changed: 1  Warnings: 0
*************************** 3. row ***************************
        sql_text: INSERT INTO world.city VALUES (4080, 'Darwin', 'AUS',
        'Northern Territory', 146000)
  nesting_event_id: 8
nesting_event_type: TRANSACTION
      mysql_errno: 1213
            error: ER_LOCK_DEADLOCK
    message_text: Deadlock found when trying to get lock; try restarting
    transaction
*************************** 4. row ***************************
        sql_text: SHOW WARNINGS
  nesting_event_id: NULL
nesting_event_type: NULL
      mysql_errno: 0
            error:
    message_text: NULL
```

```
*************************** 5. row ***************************
          sql_text: rollback
   nesting_event_id: NULL
 nesting_event_type: NULL
        mysql_errno: 0
              error:
       message_text: NULL
5 rows in set (0.0010 sec)
```

Notice that for connection id 763 (the second of the transactions), the MySQL error number is included, and the third row has it set to 1213 – a deadlock. MySQL Shell automatically executes a SHOW WARNINGS statement when an error is encountered which is the statement in row 4. Notice also that the nesting event is NULL for the ROLLBACK for transaction 2, but not for the ROLLBACK of transaction 1. That is because the deadlock triggered the whole transaction to be rolled back (so the ROLLBACK for transaction 2 did not do anything).

The deadlock was triggered by transaction 1 first updating the population of the city table and then of the country table. Transaction 2 first updated the population of the country table and then tried to insert a new city into the city table. This is a typical example of two workflows updating records in different orders and thus being prone to deadlocks.

Summarizing the investigation, it consists of two steps:

1. Analyze the deadlock information from InnoDB to determine the locks involved in the deadlock, and get as much information as possible about the connections.

2. Use other sources such as the Performance Schema to find more information about the queries in the transactions. Often it is necessary to analyze the application to get the list of queries.

Now that you know what triggered the deadlock, what is required to solve the issue?

The Solution

Deadlocks are the easiest lock situation to resolve as InnoDB automatically chooses one of the transactions as the victim and rolls it back. In the deadlock examined in the previous discussion, transaction 2 was chosen as the victim which can be seen from the deadlock output:

```
*** WE ROLL BACK TRANSACTION (2)
```

This means that for transaction 1, there is nothing to do. After transaction 2 has been rolled back, transaction 1 can continue and complete its work.

For transaction 2, InnoDB has rolled back the whole transaction, so all you need to do is to retry the transaction. Remember to execute all queries again instead of relying on values returned during the first attempt; otherwise, you may be using outdated values.

Tip   Always be prepared to handle deadlocks and lock wait timeouts. For deadlocks or when the transaction has been rolled back after a lock wait timeout, retry the entire transaction. For lock wait timeouts where only the query has been rolled back, retry the query possibly adding a delay.

If deadlocks occur relatively rarely, you do not really need to do anything more. Deadlocks are a fact of life, so do not be alarmed by encountering a few of them. If deadlocks cause a significant impact, you need to look at making changes to prevent some of the deadlocks.

The Prevention

Reducing deadlocks is very similar to reducing record lock contention in general with the addition that acquiring the locks in the same order throughout the application is very important. It is recommended to read Chapter 9 about reducing locking issues again:

- Reduce the work done by each transaction by splitting large transactions into several smaller ones and adding indexes to reduce the number of locks taken.

- Consider the READ COMMITTED transaction isolation level if it is suitable for your application to reduce the number of locks and how long they are held.

- Make sure transactions are only held open for as short time as possible.

- Access records in the same order, if necessary by executing SELECT ... FOR UPDATE or SELECT ... FOR SHARE queries to take the locks preemptively.

The main points to reduce deadlocks are to reduce the number of locks and how long they are held and to take them in the same order.

Summary

In this case study, a deadlock was generated by simulating a workload updating the population of all cities in a country followed by updating the population of the country. Simultaneously, another connection added a new city to the same country but first updated the country's population and then inserted the new city. This is a classic example of why deadlocks occur with two different workflows using the same tables but in opposite order.

The deadlock was investigated primarily using the LATEST DETECTED DEADLOCK section of the InnoDB monitor output. From this it could be seen which connections were involved, the last statement they executed, the locks they held, and the locks they were waiting for. Additionally, the Performance Schema tables with the statement history were used to find the exact statements involved in the transaction; however, often, you do not have that luxury and will have to analyze the application to determine the statements involved.

The good news when a deadlock occurs is that it automatically resolves itself by rolling back one of the transactions so the other can continue. You will then have to retry the victim transaction. If you have too many deadlocks, the key points are to reduce the number of locks and the duration of them and to ensure you take the locks in the same order for different tasks.

In the next chapter, you will study a case where foreign keys cause lock contention.

CHAPTER 17

Case Study: Foreign Keys

One of the more difficult lock contention cases to investigate happens when foreign keys are involved as you can have queries on different table content for the same locks. This case study investigates an example where both metadata and InnoDB record locks occur due to foreign keys. As the symptoms and the cause are the same as for the case study discussing metadata locks in Chapter 14 and the case study of the InnoDB record locks in Chapter 15, these are skipped in this discussion.

The Setup

This case study is more complex than the previous ones, and there is not a simple way to reproduce it on your own. However, the Listing 17-1 workload in the concurrency_ book module for MySQL Shell will allow you to reproduce the contention. The workload consists of five connections:

- Two connections that update the sakila.customer table in such a way that there is always a transaction ongoing with a metadata and record lock on the table. There is a sleep before the COMMIT to ensure the duration is long enough to avoid race conditions. The duration of the sleep can be configured during the execution of the workload.

- One connection that executes ALTER TABLE on the sakila.inventory table. This uses lock_wait_timeout = 1.

- One connection that updates the sakila.film_category table.

- One connection that updates the sakila.category table. This uses innodb_lock_wait_timeout = 1.

© Jesper Wisborg Krogh 2021

J. W. Krogh, *MySQL Concurrency*, https://doi.org/10.1007/978-1-4842-6652-6_17

When you execute the workload, after entering the password, you will be asked to enter the runtime of the test and how long the two connections updating the sakila.customer table should sleep for committing their transactions. The sleep is specified as a factor that is multiplied with 0.1 second.

Note   The test is not deterministic in the sense that you should expect to see different data even when reproducing the same issue.

Once the test has started, various monitoring outputs will be displayed so you can investigate the issue.

Listing 17-1 shows part of the output of an example execution of the workload (the exact number of locks encountered and values of the various metrics will differ from execution to execution). The complete output is available in listing_17-1.txt in this book's GitHub repository. Several parts of the output will also be used in the discussion in the remainder of the chapter.

Listing 17-1. Locks and foreign keys

```
Specify the number of seconds to run for (10-3600) [15]:
Specify the sleep factor (0-30) [15]:

-- Connection    Processlist ID    Thread ID    Event ID
-- ---------------------------------------------------------
--           1              462          792           6
--           2              463          793           6
--           3              464          794           6
--           4              465          795           6
--           5              466          796           6

mysql> SELECT error_number, error_name, sum_error_raised
          FROM performance_schema.events_errors_summary_global_by_error
         WHERE error_name IN ('ER_LOCK_WAIT_TIMEOUT', 'ER_LOCK_DEADLOCK');
```

```
+--------------+----------------------+-------------------+
| error_number | error_name           | sum_error_raised  |
+--------------+----------------------+-------------------+
|         1205 | ER_LOCK_WAIT_TIMEOUT |               310 |
|         1213 | ER_LOCK_DEADLOCK     |                12 |
+--------------+----------------------+-------------------+
```

...

```
mysql> UPDATE sakila.category SET name = IF(name = 'Travel', 'Exploring',
'Travel') WHERE category_id = 16;
ERROR: 1205: Lock wait timeout exceeded; try restarting transaction

mysql> ALTER TABLE sakila.inventory FORCE;
ERROR: 1205: Lock wait timeout exceeded; try restarting transaction --
Metrics reported by rate collected during the test:
time,innodb_row_lock_time,innodb_row_lock_waits,lock_deadlocks,lock_
timeouts
2020-08-02 14:17:12.168000,0.0,0.0,0.0,0.0
2020-08-02 14:17:13.180000,0.0,0.0,0.0,0.0
2020-08-02 14:17:14.168000,0.0,1.0121457489878543,0.0,0.0
2020-08-02 14:17:15.177000,0.0,0.0,0.0,0.0
2020-08-02 14:17:16.168000,2019.1725529767912,1.0090817356205852,0.0,1.0090
817356205852
2020-08-02 14:17:17.169000,0.0,0.0,0.0,0.0
2020-08-02 14:17:18.180000,1541.0484668644908,0.0,0.0,0.9891196834817014
2020-08-02 14:17:19.180000,0.0,0.0,0.0,0.0
2020-08-02 14:17:20.168000,0.0,0.0,0.0,0.0
2020-08-02 14:17:21.180000,0.0,0.0,0.0,0.0
2020-08-02 14:17:22.168000,82.99595141700405,2.0242914979757085,0.0,0.0
2020-08-02 14:17:23.179000,0.0,0.0,0.0,0.0
2020-08-02 14:17:24.180000,1997.0029970029973,0.9990009990009991,0.0,0.9990
009990009991
2020-08-02 14:17:25.179000,0.0,0.0,0.0,0.0
2020-08-02 14:17:26.182000,2115.6530408773683,0.9970089730807579,0.0,0.9970
089730807579
2020-08-02 14:17:27.180000,0.0,0.0,0.0,0.0
```

```
2020-08-02 14:17:28.168000,0.0,0.0,0.0,0.0
2020-08-02 14:17:29.180000,0.0,0.0,0.0,0.0
2020-08-02 14:17:30.168000,66.80161943319838,2.0242914979757085,0.0,0.0

mysql> SELECT error_number, error_name, sum_error_raised
        FROM performance_schema.events_errors_summary_global_by_error
        WHERE error_name IN ('ER_LOCK_WAIT_TIMEOUT', 'ER_LOCK_DEADLOCK');
+--------------+----------------------+-------------------+
| error_number | error_name           | sum_error_raised  |
+--------------+----------------------+-------------------+
|         1205 | ER_LOCK_WAIT_TIMEOUT |               317 |
|         1213 | ER_LOCK_DEADLOCK     |                12 |
+--------------+----------------------+-------------------+

...


2020-08-02 14:17:30.664018  0 [INFO] Stopping the threads.

2020-08-02 14:17:33.818122  0 [INFO] Completing the workload Listing 17-1
2020-08-02 14:17:33.820075  0 [INFO] Disconnecting for the workload Listing 17-1
2020-08-02 14:17:33.820075  0 [INFO] Completed the workload Listing 17-1
```

First, questions for the runtime and sleep factor are prompted. For this discussion, the default values will work, but you are encouraged to try other settings for your own testing. Particularly, lowering the sleep factor to 8 or lower will make the ALTER TABLE start to succeed, and you will see the ER_LOCK_DEADLOCK counter increment; this is a metadata deadlock.

Note   As concurrent workloads in MySQL Shell are not entirely thread safe, it can occasionally be necessary to retry the test.

Second, some initial monitoring information is printed. The same monitoring is performed at the end of the test, so you can get information about the number of errors that occurred and other metrics. The monitoring information at the end of the test also includes information in CSV format that you can copy into a spreadsheet and, for example, create a graph for.

Otherwise, the output contains information about metadata locks and lock waits as well as the statements experiencing lock wait timeouts.

The Discussion

The investigation will usually go through several steps. First, the errors logged by the application and the monitoring will be covered. Second, the lock metrics are discussed. Third, the metadata locks are covered, and finally the InnoDB lock contention is discussed.

Errors and High-Level Monitoring

The first thing you are likely to notice is that the application is experiencing errors; in this case they are lock wait timeouts. In a real-world case, you may not get the errors as directly as in this case study. If you do not handle the errors, you may see the application error out or even crash. It is important always to handle the errors and preferably log the errors, so you can keep track of the issues the application experiences, and log analyzers such as Splunk[1] can be used to analyze the frequency of the errors. Examples of the errors from this case study include

```
mysql> UPDATE sakila.category SET name = IF(name = 'Travel', 'Exploring',
'Travel') WHERE category_id = 16;
ERROR: 1205: Lock wait timeout exceeded; try restarting transaction

mysql> ALTER TABLE sakila.inventory FORCE;
ERROR: 1205: Lock wait timeout exceeded; try restarting transaction
```

You can also look at your monitoring which should include information about InnoDB lock waits similar to what is shown in Figure 17-1, that is, the number of InnoDB lock waits, the number of InnoDB lock wait timeouts, and the InnoDB lock time in milliseconds measured during the test.

---

[1]https://www.splunk.com/

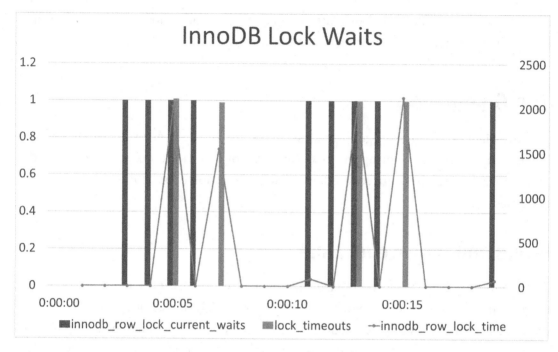

Figure 17-1. *InnoDB lock wait metrics*

The current waits are the direct measurements, whereas the lock timeouts and lock time are the difference compared to the previous measurement. The current waits and lock timeouts use the y-axis on the left and are represented by bars, whereas the lock time is shown in a line graph using the y-axis on the right. The x-axis is the time into the test.

From the graphs you can see the locking issue is intermittent, and you can use it to determine when the issue happens. If you have a monitoring solution that allows you to see which queries are running during a given interval, you can use that to investigate the workload causing the lock waits. Examples of monitoring solutions that support this are MySQL Enterprise Monitor (also known as MEM)[2], Solarwinds Database Performance Monitor (DPM, formerly VividCortex)[3], and Percona Monitoring and Management (PMM).[4]

---

[2]https://www.mysql.com/products/enterprise/monitor.html

[3]https://www.solarwinds.com/database-performance-monitor

[4]https://www.percona.com/software/database-tools/percona-monitoring-and-management

Lock Metrics

The monitoring of the lock metrics makes it easy to spot periods with increased
lock contention, and it is worth discussing the metrics some more. For InnoDB, it is
straightforward to monitor the lock waits as just shown, but unfortunately, there are no
metrics that can easily give the same kind of information for metadata locks. You can
use the error statistics from the Performance Schema to track the number of lock wait
timeouts and deadlocks:

```
mysql> SELECT error_number, error_name, sum_error_raised
       FROM performance_schema.events_errors_summary_global_by_error
       WHERE error_name IN ('ER_LOCK_WAIT_TIMEOUT', 'ER_LOCK_DEADLOCK');
+--------------+----------------------+------------------+
| error_number | error_name           | sum_error_raised |
+--------------+----------------------+------------------+
|         1205 | ER_LOCK_WAIT_TIMEOUT |              310 |
|         1213 | ER_LOCK_DEADLOCK     |               12 |
+--------------+----------------------+------------------+

...

mysql> SELECT error_number, error_name, sum_error_raised
       FROM performance_schema.events_errors_summary_global_by_error
       WHERE error_name IN ('ER_LOCK_WAIT_TIMEOUT', 'ER_LOCK_DEADLOCK');
+--------------+----------------------+------------------+
| error_number | error_name           | sum_error_raised |
+--------------+----------------------+------------------+
|         1205 | ER_LOCK_WAIT_TIMEOUT |              317 |
|         1213 | ER_LOCK_DEADLOCK     |               12 |
+--------------+----------------------+------------------+
```

This shows that during this test, there were seven lock wait timeouts and no
deadlocks. The problem with this information is that it does not tell you whether
it is metadata locks, InnoDB locks, or some third lock type that experienced a lock
wait timeout or deadlock. That said, since InnoDB has its own lock wait timeout and
deadlock statistics, you can derive the numbers for non-InnoDB locks by subtracting the
two statistics. The InnoDB lock statistics for the test are shown in Listing 17-2.

Listing 17-2. The InnoDB lock statistics for the test

```
mysql> SELECT Variable_name, Variable_value
       FROM sys.metrics
       WHERE Variable_name IN (
               'innodb_row_lock_current_waits',
               'lock_row_lock_current_waits',
               'innodb_row_lock_time',
               'innodb_row_lock_waits',
               'lock_deadlocks',
               'lock_timeouts'
           );
+-------------------------------+----------------+
| Variable_name                 | Variable_value |
+-------------------------------+----------------+
| innodb_row_lock_current_waits | 0              |
| innodb_row_lock_time          | 409555         |
| innodb_row_lock_waits         | 384            |
| lock_deadlocks                | 0              |
| lock_row_lock_current_waits   | 0              |
| lock_timeouts                 | 188            |
+-------------------------------+----------------+

...

mysql> SELECT Variable_name, Variable_value
       FROM sys.metrics
       WHERE Variable_name IN (
               'innodb_row_lock_current_waits',
               'lock_row_lock_current_waits',
               'innodb_row_lock_time',
               'innodb_row_lock_waits',
               'lock_deadlocks',
               'lock_timeouts'
           )
```

```
+--------------------------------+----------------+
| Variable_name                  | Variable_value |
+--------------------------------+----------------+
| innodb_row_lock_current_waits  | 1              |
| innodb_row_lock_time           | 417383         |
| innodb_row_lock_waits          | 392            |
| lock_deadlocks                 | 0              |
| lock_row_lock_current_waits    | 1              |
| lock_timeouts                  | 192            |
+--------------------------------+----------------+
```

Here you can see there were a total of four InnoDB lock wait timeouts (the lock_
timeouts status counter) out of the total seven ER_LOCK_WAIT_TIMEOUT errors, so you can
conclude there were three non-InnoDB lock wait timeouts. In this case study, these are
all metadata lock wait timeouts.

Metadata Lock Contention

In practice it is best if you can catch the lock contention while it is ongoing as shown
in the earlier case studies. In the output of this example, there are outputs from the
performance_schema.metadata_locks table as well as the schema_table_lock_waits
and innodb_lock_waits sys schema views. The metadata_locks table highlights the
extent of the spread of metadata locks as it can be seen from Listing 17-3.

Listing 17-3. The metadata locks found during the test

```
mysql> SELECT object_name, lock_type, lock_status,
              owner_thread_id, owner_event_id
         FROM performance_schema.metadata_locks
        WHERE object_type = 'TABLE'
          AND object_schema = 'sakila'
        ORDER BY owner_thread_id, object_name, lock_type\G
*************************** 1. row ***************************
    object_name: category
      lock_type: SHARED_READ
    lock_status: GRANTED
owner_thread_id: 792
 owner_event_id: 9
```

```
*************************** 2. row ***************************
    object_name: film
      lock_type: SHARED_READ
    lock_status: GRANTED
owner_thread_id: 792
 owner_event_id: 9
*************************** 3. row ***************************
    object_name: film_category
      lock_type: SHARED_WRITE
    lock_status: GRANTED
owner_thread_id: 792
 owner_event_id: 9
*************************** 4. row ***************************
    object_name: category
      lock_type: SHARED_WRITE
    lock_status: GRANTED
owner_thread_id: 793
 owner_event_id: 9
*************************** 5. row ***************************
    object_name: film
      lock_type: SHARED_READ
    lock_status: GRANTED
owner_thread_id: 793
 owner_event_id: 9
*************************** 6. row ***************************
    object_name: film_category
      lock_type: SHARED_WRITE
    lock_status: GRANTED
owner_thread_id: 793
 owner_event_id: 9
*************************** 7. row ***************************
    object_name: address
      lock_type: SHARED_READ
    lock_status: GRANTED
owner_thread_id: 794
 owner_event_id: 10
```

```
*************************** 8. row ***************************
    object_name: customer
      lock_type: SHARED_WRITE
    lock_status: GRANTED
owner_thread_id: 794
 owner_event_id: 10
*************************** 9. row ***************************
    object_name: inventory
      lock_type: SHARED_READ
    lock_status: GRANTED
owner_thread_id: 794
 owner_event_id: 10
*************************** 10. row ***************************
    object_name: payment
      lock_type: SHARED_WRITE
    lock_status: GRANTED
owner_thread_id: 794
 owner_event_id: 10
*************************** 11. row ***************************
    object_name: rental
      lock_type: SHARED_WRITE
    lock_status: GRANTED
owner_thread_id: 794
 owner_event_id: 10
*************************** 12. row ***************************
    object_name: staff
      lock_type: SHARED_READ
    lock_status: GRANTED
owner_thread_id: 794
 owner_event_id: 10
*************************** 13. row ***************************
    object_name: store
      lock_type: SHARED_READ
    lock_status: GRANTED
owner_thread_id: 794
 owner_event_id: 10
```

```
*************************** 14. row ***************************
    object_name: address
      lock_type: SHARED_READ
    lock_status: GRANTED
owner_thread_id: 795
 owner_event_id: 10
*************************** 15. row ***************************
    object_name: customer
      lock_type: SHARED_WRITE
    lock_status: GRANTED
owner_thread_id: 795
 owner_event_id: 10
*************************** 16. row ***************************
    object_name: inventory
      lock_type: SHARED_READ
    lock_status: PENDING
owner_thread_id: 795
 owner_event_id: 10
*************************** 17. row ***************************
    object_name: payment
      lock_type: SHARED_WRITE
    lock_status: GRANTED
owner_thread_id: 795
 owner_event_id: 10
*************************** 18. row ***************************
    object_name: rental
      lock_type: SHARED_WRITE
    lock_status: GRANTED
owner_thread_id: 795
 owner_event_id: 10
*************************** 19. row ***************************
    object_name: staff
      lock_type: SHARED_READ
    lock_status: GRANTED
owner_thread_id: 795
 owner_event_id: 10
```

```
*************************** 20. row ***************************
    object_name: store
      lock_type: SHARED_READ
    lock_status: GRANTED
owner_thread_id: 795
 owner_event_id: 10
*************************** 21. row ***************************
    object_name: #sql-35e8_1d2
      lock_type: EXCLUSIVE
    lock_status: GRANTED
owner_thread_id: 796
 owner_event_id: 9
*************************** 22. row ***************************
    object_name: film
      lock_type: SHARED_UPGRADABLE
    lock_status: GRANTED
owner_thread_id: 796
 owner_event_id: 9
*************************** 23. row ***************************
    object_name: inventory
      lock_type: EXCLUSIVE
    lock_status: PENDING
owner_thread_id: 796
 owner_event_id: 9
*************************** 24. row ***************************
    object_name: inventory
      lock_type: SHARED_UPGRADABLE
    lock_status: GRANTED
owner_thread_id: 796
 owner_event_id: 9
*************************** 25. row ***************************
    object_name: rental
      lock_type: SHARED_UPGRADABLE
    lock_status: GRANTED
owner_thread_id: 796
 owner_event_id: 9
```

```
*************************** 26. row ***************************
    object_name: store
      lock_type: SHARED_UPGRADABLE
    lock_status: GRANTED
owner_thread_id: 796
 owner_event_id: 9
```

The two pending locks (rows 16 and 23) are for the ALTER TABLE and one of the UPDATE statements on the customer table.

At the point in time where this output was collected, there are 26 granted or pending metadata locks by just five threads. All the statements just query a single table (technically the ALTER TABLE has a second table – the one named #sql-35e8_1d2 in this example, but that is the temporary table name used for rebuilding the inventory table). Grouping the locks by the table name, you can see there are metadata locks for 11 tables including the temporary table (the numbers may not add up with the previous output as they are not made on the exact same time):

```
mysql> SELECT object_name, COUNT(*)
         FROM performance_schema.metadata_locks
        WHERE object_type = 'TABLE'
          AND object_schema = 'sakila'
        GROUP BY object_name
        ORDER BY object_name;
+----------------+----------+
| object_name    | COUNT(*) |
+----------------+----------+
| #sql-35e8_1d2  |        1 |
| address        |        2 |
| category       |        2 |
| customer       |        2 |
| film           |        3 |
| film_category  |        2 |
| inventory      |        4 |
| payment        |        2 |
| rental         |        3 |
```

```
| staff          |        2 |
| store          |        3 |
+----------------+----------+
```

The reason for all of these tables being affected is that the sakila schema is a heavy user of foreign keys. Figure 17-2 shows the tables and their foreign key relationships. In the figure, only the columns that are part of the table's primary key or are part of a foreign key are included.

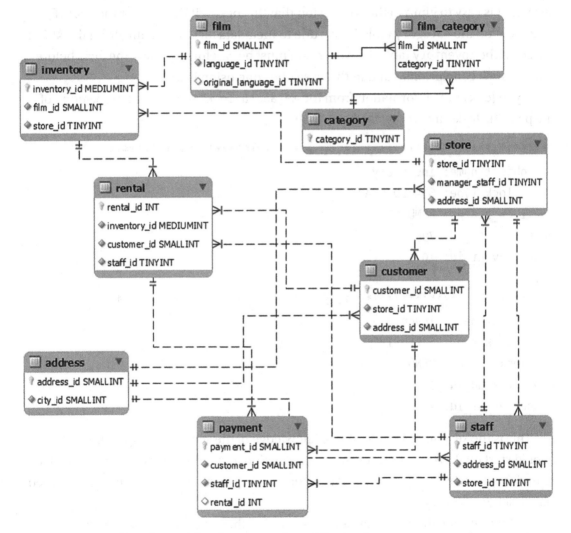

Figure 17-2. *The relationship between the tables in the test*

For finding the statements that cause the lock wait timeouts for the ALTER TABLE, the simplest is to use the sys.schema_table_lock_waits view as discussed in Chapter 14. The steps are left as an exercise for the reader. The conflicting statements are the updates on the customer table and the ALTER TABLE on the inventory table.

InnoDB Lock Contention

When you consider the foreign key relationships between the tables in the previous section, it is easy to jump to the conclusion that the lock wait timeout for the UPDATE statement on the category table is also due to metadata locks cascading from the ALTER TABLE on the inventory table. However, you must be careful and study the facts before making such conclusions – and in this case, the conclusion is wrong.

If you look at the information from the metadata_locks table, you can see none of the pending locks are for the category table:

```
*************************** 16. row ***************************
    object_name: inventory
      lock_type: SHARED_READ
    lock_status: PENDING
owner_thread_id: 795
 owner_event_id: 10
...
*************************** 23. row ***************************
    object_name: inventory
      lock_type: EXCLUSIVE
    lock_status: PENDING
owner_thread_id: 796
 owner_event_id: 9
```

This is the key message here. While knowledge of the schema is important, you should start out looking at the lock wait information and then use the schema knowledge to understand why the locks occur rather than try to guess at what locks may exist based on the schema knowledge.

The monitoring discussed earlier did show that there were InnoDB lock wait timeouts, and the sys.innodb_lock_waits output in Listing 17-4 shows which are the conflicting locks and statements.

Listing 17-4. The InnoDB lock waits during the test

```
mysql> SELECT * FROM sys.innodb_lock_waits\G
*************************** 1. row ***************************
                wait_started: 2020-08-02 14:17:13
                    wait_age: 00:00:02
               wait_age_secs: 2
                locked_table: `sakila`.`category`
         locked_table_schema: sakila
           locked_table_name: category
      locked_table_partition: None
   locked_table_subpartition: None
                locked_index: PRIMARY
                 locked_type: RECORD
               waiting_trx_id: 535860
          waiting_trx_started: 2020-08-02 14:17:13
              waiting_trx_age: 00:00:02
       waiting_trx_rows_locked: 1
     waiting_trx_rows_modified: 0
                 waiting_pid: 463
               waiting_query: UPDATE sakila.category SET name = IF(name =
               'Travel', 'Exploring', 'Travel') WHERE category_id = 16
             waiting_lock_id: 2711671600928:1795:4:282:2711634698920
           waiting_lock_mode: X,REC_NOT_GAP
              blocking_trx_id: 535859
                blocking_pid: 462
              blocking_query: None
            blocking_lock_id: 2711671600096:1795:4:282:2711634694976
          blocking_lock_mode: S,REC_NOT_GAP
         blocking_trx_started: 2020-08-02 14:17:13
             blocking_trx_age: 00:00:02
      blocking_trx_rows_locked: 5
    blocking_trx_rows_modified: 2
       sql_kill_blocking_query: KILL QUERY 462
  sql_kill_blocking_connection: KILL 462
1 row in set (0.0017 sec)
```

The lock contention is on the primary key of the `category` table with process list id 462 being the blocking connection. This connection is idle at the time of the output, so you need to use the Performance Schema statement history tables or the query analysis in your monitoring solution or study the application or a combination of them to determine which queries were executed by the transaction. In this case, it is the update of the `film_category` table (formatted for readability):

```
UPDATE sakila.film_category
   SET category_id = IF(category_id = 7, 16, 7)
 WHERE film_id = 64;
```

The reason this causes a lock on the `category` table is that there is a foreign key between the `category_id` column in the `film_category` and `category` tables, so when the connection with process list id 463 tries to update the row in the `category` table with the same id as connection 462 has updated, it will block until 462 is committed or rolled back.

The Solution and Prevention

The solutions and preventions discussed in Chapters 14 and 15 also apply in the case where foreign keys are involved. This means that the most effective way to avoid the issues in the first place is to avoid long-running transactions, and as a quick way to unblock metadata lock waits, you can kill the DDL statement requesting exclusive locks.

Note   Foreign keys are a bigger issue with metadata locks than for InnoDB record locks as the latter only affect cases where the columns used in foreign keys are involved.

When foreign keys are present, it can be particularly useful to keep a low value for `lock_wait_timeout` to avoid a large number of metadata lock requests across many tables to be requested or held for extended periods while waiting for all the requests to be granted. This can potentially be combined with reducing the value of `max_write_lock_count` to avoid stalling requests for shared metadata locks requested through foreign keys on busy tables. (Reducing `max_write_lock_count` will not change this case study.)

If you have severe problems with lock contention due to foreign keys, one possibility is to move the responsibility of keeping the data consistent into the application. You should however be aware this does remove the insurance at the MySQL level to keep the data consistent (the C in ACID), so it is not recommended. That said, in some cases, it may be the only way to avoid excessive locking in high concurrency systems.

Caution   While handling foreign key relations in the application can help reduce locking in the database, be careful as it also weakens the consistency guarantees.

Additionally, some general solutions exist that are not special to foreign keys:

- If the locks are held for too long, for example, because of an abandoned transaction, consider killing the blocking transaction, but remember to take into account the number of changes that will have to be rolled back.

- Remember to handle a transaction that has a query failing with a lock wait timeout, so the transaction does not stay around with the locks taken before the statement that failed.

- Consider what you can do to reduce the duration and size of your transactions.

- Use indexes to reduce the number of records accessed.

- Consider the READ COMMITTED transaction isolation level, if it is suitable for your application.

Summary

This chapter went through a case study with simultaneous metadata lock and InnoDB lock contention caused by foreign keys. The main discussion point was how the locks spread to other tables than the ones used by the queries. This is particularly the case for metadata locks, whereas the effect is less for InnoDB record locks as extra locks are only taken when columns used for the foreign keys are involved.

The principles of investigating the lock issues are the same as when foreign keys are not involved; however, it is more difficult due to the number of locks involved; for the metadata locks in the example, there were 26 lock requests returned by `performance_schema.metadata_locks`. It is thus particularly useful to use the `sys` schema views to help with the analysis.

In addition to the usual methods to reduce lock issues, for metadata locks, you can consider combining a low `lock_wait_timeout` with a relatively low value of `max_write_lock_count`. Another option that can help for both metadata and InnoDB locks is to leave the responsibility of guaranteeing the consistency of the foreign keys to the application; however, be very careful if you do that as it will not provide as strong a guarantee as when MySQL handles it.

There remains one case study left which covers a case where there are semaphore waits in InnoDB as it will be discussed in the next chapter.

CHAPTER 18

Case Study: Semaphores

Mutex and semaphore contention is one of the most elusive kinds of contention you can come across as except for extreme situations, you will not directly notice any issues. Instead, the contention tends to materialize as an overall added latency and throughput reduction that can be hard to put your finger on. Then out of the blue, you may have crossed a load threshold, and the contention causes your server to come to a grinding halt.

This chapter goes through a case study of investigating contention on the adaptive hash index rw-semaphore. However, do be aware that semaphore contention differs depending on the mutex or semaphore where the contention occurs, and so does the investigation required to solve it. In high-severity cases, you may also find that you have contention on multiple semaphore waits at the same time.

The Symptoms

The two most common ways to notice that there is contention on an InnoDB mutex or semaphore are through the InnoDB monitor and the innodb_rwlock_% InnoDB metrics.

In the InnoDB monitor output, you will see ongoing waits in the SEMAPHORES section near the top of the output, for example

```
----------
SEMAPHORES
----------
OS WAIT ARRAY INFO: reservation count 77606
--Thread 19304 has waited at btr0sea.ic line 122 for 0 seconds the
semaphore:
S-lock on RW-latch at 00000215E6DC12F8 created in file btr0sea.cc line 202
a writer (thread id 11100) has reserved it in mode exclusive
number of readers 0, waiters flag 1, lock_word: 0
```

297

© Jesper Wisborg Krogh 2021
J. W. Krogh, *MySQL Concurrency*, https://doi.org/10.1007/978-1-4842-6652-6_18

```
Last time read locked in file btr0sea.ic line 122
Last time write locked in file G:\ade\build\sb_0-39697839-1592332179.68\
mysql-8.0.21\storage\innobase\btr\btr0sea.cc line 1197
--Thread 26128 has waited at btr0sea.ic line 92 for 0 seconds the
semaphore:
X-lock on RW-latch at 00000215E6DC12F8 created in file btr0sea.cc line 202
a writer (thread id 11100) has reserved it in mode exclusive
number of readers 0, waiters flag 1, lock_word: 0
Last time read locked in file btr0sea.ic line 122
Last time write locked in file G:\ade\build\sb_0-39697839-1592332179.68\
mysql-8.0.21\storage\innobase\btr\btr0sea.cc line 1197
OS WAIT ARRAY INFO: signal count 93040
RW-shared spins 18200, rounds 38449, OS waits 20044
RW-excl spins 22345, rounds 1121445, OS waits 38469
RW-sx spins 3684, rounds 100410, OS waits 2886
Spin rounds per wait: 2.11 RW-shared, 50.19 RW-excl, 27.26 RW-sx
```

The more waits and the longer they have been waiting, the more severe the issue is.

You may also notice in your monitoring that the number of rw-lock waits is high and possibly spiky at the time of high load. In one real-world example where there was severe contention on the adaptive hash index, there were tens of thousands of OS waits per second for extended periods of time.

The Cause

The issue is that requests for a shared resource, such as access to the adaptive hash index, arrive faster than they can be handled. These resources are protected inside the source code using mutexes and rw-locks. Contention indicates that either you have hit the concurrency limit of the MySQL version you are using for your workload or that your need to split the resource into more parts or similar.

The Setup

Reproducing semaphore contention at will can be difficult to do at will. The more CPUs you have available on your system, the more likely it is that you generate a workload that experiences semaphore waits.

The outputs for the discussion in this chapter have been generated with the Listing 8-1 workload on a laptop with eight CPUs and the buffer pool set to the default size of 128 MiB. If you try to reproduce the case, then you may need to experiment with the number of connections. The script prompts you for these defaulting to 1 read-write thread and using one connection per remaining CPU for read-only connections.

Note   MySQL Shell's session objects are not entirely thread safe even with each thread having its own session. For this reason, it can be necessary to attempt the test a couple of times. The issue is particularly seen on Microsoft Windows with multiple read-write connections.

You can also try to change the size of the buffer pool. An option is also to reduce the flushing when committing transactions which particularly can help if your disk has poor flush performance:

```
SET GLOBAL innodb_flush_log_at_trx_commit = 0,
    GLOBAL sync_binlog = 0;
```

Caution   Reducing flushing is fine on a test system, but you should not do that on a production system as you may end up losing committed transactions in case of a crash.

Running for a longer time can also increase the chance of seeing contention at least once.

The test also allows you to request MySQL to be restarted before the test, and you can choose whether to delete the indexes that the test creates. Restarting MySQL allows you to see the difference of starting out with a cold InnoDB buffer pool (though the workload does do its own warmup of the buffer pool).

Note   Restarting MySQL from the test only works if you have started MySQL under a supervisor process. This, for example, happens when you start MySQL as a service on Microsoft Windows, using `mysqld_safe`, or through `systemd` on Linux.

If you want to run the test several times, it can be an advantage to tell the test not to delete its indexes as that allows the test to skip the creation on the next execution.

An example of executing the test case is shown in Listing 18-1. The full output of the execution is included in the file `listing_18-1.txt` that is available from this book's GitHub repository.

Listing 18-1. Semaphore waits

```
Specify the number of read-write connections (0-31) [1]:
Specify the number of read-only connections (1-31) [7]:
Specify the number of seconds to run for (1-3600) [10]:
Restart MySQL before executing the test? (Y|Yes|N|No) [No]:
Delete the test specific indexes after executing the test? (Y|Yes|N|No)
[Yes]:

2020-07-25 15:56:33.928772  0 [INFO] Adding 1 index to the dept_emp table
2020-07-25 15:56:43.238872  0 [INFO] Adding 1 index to the employees table
2020-07-25 15:56:54.202735  0 [INFO] Adding 1 index to the salaries table
2020-07-25 15:57:47.050114  0 [INFO] Warming up the InnoDB buffer pool.
2020-07-25 15:58:04.543354  0 [INFO] Waiting 2 seconds to let the
monitoring collect some information before starting the test.
2020-07-25 15:58:06.544765  0 [INFO] Starting the work connections.
2020-07-25 15:58:07.556126  0 [INFO] Completed   10%
…

-- Total mutex and rw-semaphore waits during test:
+----------------+-------+
| File:Line      | Waits |
+----------------+-------+
| btr0sea.cc:202 | 13368 |
+----------------+-------+
```

```
-- Total execution time: 25.685603 seconds

2020-07-25 15:58:34.374196  0 [INFO] Dropping indexes on the dept_emp table.
2020-07-25 15:58:35.651209  0 [INFO] Dropping indexes on the employees table.
2020-07-25 15:58:36.344171  0 [INFO] Dropping indexes on the salaries table.
```

Notice that at the start of the example, there are five prompts for information on how to run the test.

When the test reproduces the issue, you will see one or more outputs of the SEMAPHORES section from the InnoDB monitor output, and at the end, some diagnostics data is generated. This data includes

- RW-lock metrics collected every second during the test. This is printed in CSV format, so you can copy it into a spreadsheet and plot it.

- Adaptive hash index metrics collected every second during the test. This is also printed in CSV format.

- The total number of pages as well as the rate made young or not made young in the InnoDB buffer pool.

- The INSERT BUFFER AND ADAPTIVE HASH INDEX section as it looks at the end of the test.

- The total mutex and rw-semaphore waits during test.

The read-only workload consists of a join between three tables in the employees database which includes a large number of secondary index lookups:

```
SELECT dept_name, MIN(salary) min_salary,
       AVG(salary) AS avg_salary, MAX(salary) AS max_salary
  FROM employees.departments
       INNER JOIN employees.dept_emp USING (dept_no)
       INNER JOIN employees.salaries USING (emp_no)
 WHERE dept_emp.to_date = '9999-01-01'
       AND salaries.to_date = '9999-01-01'
 GROUP BY dept_no
 ORDER BY dept_name;
```

The read-write workload chooses a random last name from the `employees.employees` table and gives all employees with that surname a pay rise. With placeholders, the steps are

```
SELECT last_name
  FROM employees.employees
 WHERE emp_no = ?;

SELECT emp_no, salary, from_date + INTERVAL 1 DAY
  FROM employees.employees
       INNER JOIN employees.salaries USING (emp_no)
 WHERE employees.last_name = ?
       AND to_date = '9999-01-01';

# For each employee found in the previous query,
# execute the insert and update:
INSERT INTO employees.salaries
VALUES (?, ?, ?, '9999-01-01');

UPDATE employees.salaries
   SET to_date = ?
 WHERE emp_no = ? AND to_date = '9999-01-01';
```

This means that the data in the `employees` database is modified. You do not need to reload the data between each test, but you may want to reset it when you are done testing if you want to have the original data returned.

Three indexes have been added to the tables to ensure the necessary secondary indexes are present to cause the contention (remember the adaptive hash index is only used for secondary indexes):

```
ALTER TABLE employees.dept_emp
  ADD INDEX idx_concurrency_book_0 (dept_no, to_date);

ALTER TABLE employees.employees
  ADD INDEX idx_concurrency_book_1 (last_name, first_name);

ALTER TABLE employees.salaries
  ADD INDEX idx_concurrency_book_2 (emp_no, to_date, salary);
```

The indexes are dropped again at the end of the test unless you request to keep them.

Finally, to avoid premature eviction of the pages read into the buffer pool during the test, the old blocks time is set to 0 for the duration of the test:

```
SET GLOBAL innodb_old_blocks_time = 0;
```

This helps putting the buffer pool under higher pressure than it otherwise would be which makes it more likely to reproduce the contention. The variable is set back to 1000 (the default value) at the end of the test.

Note   The test will take longer than the runtime you specify as the runtime is only checked at the start of each loop of queries. So, all pending queries in a loop will complete.

Now that the workload causing the issue has been established, it is time to start the investigation.

The Investigation

When you encounter semaphore contention, the first port of call is usually your monitoring system where you can get an overview of the contention. While you can query the metrics yourself, the semaphore waits tend to fluctuate, and you may well have periods with no contention and only see the issue during the busiest periods or when specific workloads are executed. Viewing the metrics in a graph makes it much easier to determine when the contention occurs.

This section discusses how you can monitor the innodb_rwlock_% metrics, the SEMAPHORES section of the InnoDB monitor, the InnoDB mutex monitor, and determining the workload.

The InnoDB RW-Lock Metrics

One option is to start your investigation by looking at the innodb_rwlock_% metrics from information_schema.INNODB_METRICS or sys.metrics. There are three groups of metrics: for shared, for shared-exclusive, and for exclusive rw-locks. Each group has three metrics: number of spin waits, number of spin rounds, and number of operating system waits. The CSV output at the end of the test includes the metrics for the shared and exclusive groups. (The shared-exclusive rw-locks are not of interest in this investigation.) Figure 18-1 shows an example of the metrics for the shared rw-locks plotted with the time into the test on the x-axis.

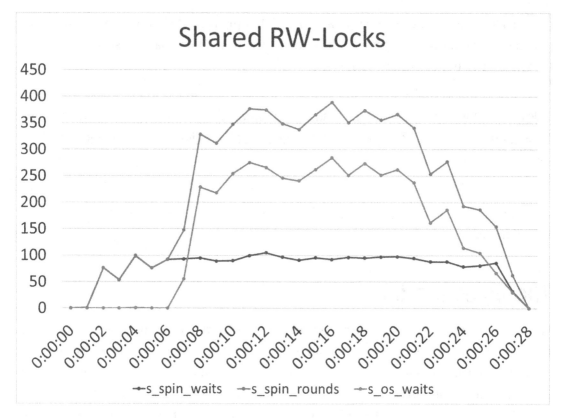

Figure 18-1. *The number of waits and spin rounds for shared rw-locks*

Here the number of spin waits is almost constant during the test, but the number of spin rounds (the top line in the graph) greatly increases around 7 seconds into the test. This also causes the number of OS waits to increase. That the OS waits jump up means that the spin rounds for a spin wait exceed `innodb_sync_spin_loops` (defaults to 30).

The picture for the exclusive rw-locks is similar except that the number of spin rounds is much higher as shown in Figure 18-2.

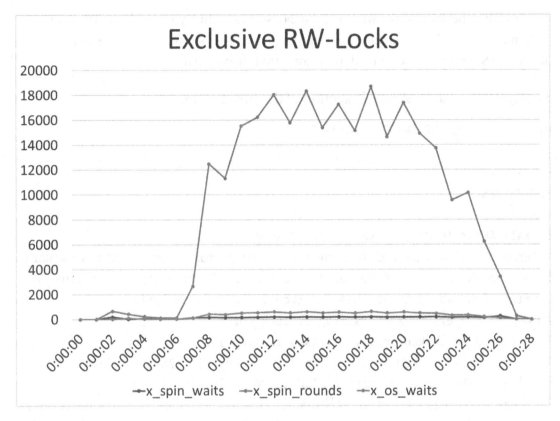

Figure 18-2. *The number of waits and spin rounds for exclusive rw-locks*

While it is hard to see because the number of spin rounds dwarfs the spin and OS waits, they do follow the same pattern as for the shared rw-locks, and the absolute numbers for the waits are around twice that of the shared locks. The number of waits that is cause of concern depends on your workload, and the more concurrent queries you have, the larger the number of waits there is in general. You should particularly keep an eye on the OS waits as those increase when the waits happen for so long that the thread is suspended.

InnoDB Monitor and Mutex Monitor

When you have established when the contention occurs, you need to determine which rw-lock the contention is for (there may be more than one rw-lock). There are two main tools to determine where the contention occurs of which the first is the InnoDB monitor. Unless you have enabled it so it automatically outputs to the error log or the contention is so bad that the semaphore waits exceed 240 seconds, then you need to catch your system in the act of experiencing contention. Listing 18-2 shows an example of the SEMAPHORES section of the InnoDB monitor output from the test.

Listing 18-2. The SEMAPHORES section of the InnoDB monitor

```
mysql> SHOW ENGINE INNODB STATUS\G
...
----------
SEMAPHORES
----------
OS WAIT ARRAY INFO: reservation count 36040
--Thread 35592 has waited at btr0sea.ic line 92 for 0 seconds the semaphore:
X-lock on RW-latch at 000001BD277CCFF8 created in file btr0sea.cc line 202
a writer (thread id 25492) has reserved it in mode exclusive
number of readers 0, waiters flag 1, lock_word: 0
Last time read locked in file btr0sea.ic line 122
Last time write locked in file G:\ade\build\sb_0-39697839-1592332179.68\
mysql-8.0.21\storage\innobase\include\btr0sea.ic line 92
--Thread 27836 has waited at btr0sea.ic line 92 for 0 seconds the semaphore:
X-lock on RW-latch at 000001BD277CCFF8 created in file btr0sea.cc line 202
a writer (thread id 25492) has reserved it in mode exclusive
number of readers 0, waiters flag 1, lock_word: 0
Last time read locked in file btr0sea.ic line 122
Last time write locked in file G:\ade\build\sb_0-39697839-1592332179.68\
mysql-8.0.21\storage\innobase\include\btr0sea.ic line 92
--Thread 25132 has waited at btr0sea.ic line 92 for 0 seconds the semaphore:
X-lock on RW-latch at 000001BD277CCFF8 created in file btr0sea.cc line 202
a writer (thread id 25492) has reserved it in mode exclusive
number of readers 0, waiters flag 1, lock_word: 0
Last time read locked in file btr0sea.ic line 122
Last time write locked in file G:\ade\build\sb_0-39697839-1592332179.68\
mysql-8.0.21\storage\innobase\include\btr0sea.ic line 92
--Thread 22512 has waited at btr0sea.ic line 92 for 0 seconds the semaphore:
X-lock on RW-latch at 000001BD277CCFF8 created in file btr0sea.cc line 202
a writer (thread id 25492) has reserved it in mode exclusive
number of readers 0, waiters flag 1, lock_word: 0
```

```
Last time read locked in file btr0sea.ic line 122
Last time write locked in file G:\ade\build\sb_0-39697839-1592332179.68\
mysql-8.0.21\storage\innobase\include\btr0sea.ic line 92
--Thread 22184 has waited at btr0sea.ic line 122 for 0 seconds the semaphore:
S-lock on RW-latch at 000001BD277CCFF8 created in file btr0sea.cc line 202
a writer (thread id 25492) has reserved it in mode exclusive
number of readers 0, waiters flag 1, lock_word: 0
Last time read locked in file btr0sea.ic line 122
Last time write locked in file G:\ade\build\sb_0-39697839-1592332179.68\
mysql-8.0.21\storage\innobase\include\btr0sea.ic line 92
--Thread 32236 has waited at btr0sea.ic line 92 for 0 seconds the semaphore:
X-lock on RW-latch at 000001BD277CCFF8 created in file btr0sea.cc line 202
a writer (thread id 25492) has reserved it in mode exclusive
number of readers 0, waiters flag 1, lock_word: 0
Last time read locked in file btr0sea.ic line 122
Last time write locked in file G:\ade\build\sb_0-39697839-1592332179.68\
mysql-8.0.21\storage\innobase\include\btr0sea.ic line 92
OS WAIT ARRAY INFO: signal count 68351
RW-shared spins 9768, rounds 21093, OS waits 11109
RW-excl spins 13012, rounds 669111, OS waits 24669
RW-sx spins 16, rounds 454, OS waits 15
Spin rounds per wait: 2.16 RW-shared, 51.42 RW-excl, 28.38 RW-sx
...
```

In this example, all the waits are on the semaphore created in line 202 in btr0sea. cc (the line number may differ depending on the platform and MySQL release, e.g., on Linux, the line will be 201 for 8.0.21). If you look at the source code for MySQL 8.0.21 in the file storage/innobase/btr/btr0sea.cc, then the code around line 202 is

```
186 /** Creates and initializes the adaptive search system at a database
    start.
187 @param[in]      hash_size       hash table size. */
188 void btr_search_sys_create(ulint hash_size) {
189   /* Search System is divided into n parts.
190   Each part controls access to distinct set of hash buckets from
191   hash table through its own latch. */
```

```
192
193    /* Step-1: Allocate latches (1 per part). */
194    btr_search_latches = reinterpret_cast<rw_lock_t **>(
195        ut_malloc(sizeof(rw_lock_t *) * btr_ahi_parts, mem_key_ahi));
196
197    for (ulint i = 0; i < btr_ahi_parts; ++i) {
198      btr_search_latches[i] = reinterpret_cast<rw_lock_t *>(
199          ut_malloc(sizeof(rw_lock_t), mem_key_ahi));
200
201      rw_lock_create(btr_search_latch_key, btr_search_latches[i],
202                       SYNC_SEARCH_SYS);
203    }
...
```

This is the code for the adaptive hash index, so this proves that the adaptive hash index is where the contention is. (It also shows that lines 201 and 202 are for the same statement, so the difference in the line numbers between Microsoft Windows and Linux is whether the first or last line of the statement is chosen as the creation of the rw-lock.)

You can also use the mutex monitor to get statistics of which locks are the ones most frequently experiencing waits. An example of the output of the mutex monitor from the end of this test is

```
mysql> SHOW ENGINE INNODB MUTEX;
```

Type	Name	Status
InnoDB	rwlock: fil0fil.cc:3206	waits=11
InnoDB	rwlock: dict0dict.cc:1035	waits=12
InnoDB	rwlock: btr0sea.cc:202	waits=7730
InnoDB	rwlock: btr0sea.cc:202	waits=934
InnoDB	rwlock: btr0sea.cc:202	waits=5445
InnoDB	rwlock: btr0sea.cc:202	waits=889
InnoDB	rwlock: btr0sea.cc:202	waits=9076
InnoDB	rwlock: btr0sea.cc:202	waits=13608
InnoDB	rwlock: btr0sea.cc:202	waits=1050

```
| InnoDB | rwlock: hash0hash.cc:171    | waits=4   |
| InnoDB | sum rwlock: buf0buf.cc:778 | waits=86  |
+--------+----------------------------+-----------+
```

11 rows in set (0.0008 sec)

If you create the mutex monitor report with regular intervals, you can sum the waits and group by file and line number and then monitor the difference where the waits occur at which time. (The author of this book is not aware of any monitoring solution that does this out of the box.) For this example, the test itself calculates the number of waits for each file and line number which will primarily show waits for btr0sea.cc line 202 (remember the line number depends in the exact release and compiler/platform):

```
-- Total mutex and rw-semaphore waits during test:
+-----------------+--------+
| File:Line       | Waits  |
+-----------------+--------+
| btr0sea.cc:202  | 13368  |
+-----------------+--------+
```

The most likely other file and line you will see is hash0hash:171 (for 8.0.21 on Windows or line 170 on Linux for 8.0.21) which is related to InnoDB's implementation of hash tables. It shows that it was not a coincidence that the semaphore waits in the InnoDB monitor output were all for btr0sea.cc line 202.

Determining the Workload

The final step of the investigation is to determine the workload causing the contention. This is also the most difficult task. The best is if you have a monitoring solution that collects information about the queries that are executed and aggregates statistics for them. With such monitoring, you can directly see what queries are executed which can help you determine what causes the contention. If you do not have access monitoring data for the queries executed during the time of contention, you can try to monitor the queries using sys.session or the Performance Schema tables with statement information (threads, events_statements_current, events_statements_history, and events_statements_history_long). An option is also to use the statement_performance_analyzer() procedure in the sys schema which takes two snapshots of the events_statements_summary_by_digest table and calculates the difference and returns one or more reports showing information about the queries executed between the two snapshots.

Tip   The `statement_performance_analyzer()` procedure in the `sys` schema can be used to generate a "poor man's query analyzer" with the queries executed between two snapshots. See `https://dev.mysql.com/doc/refman/en/sys-statement-performance-analyzer.html` for the documentation and an example.

This sounds easy, but in practice, it is not so simple. Even with good monitoring, it may be near impossible to determine which queries are the problem. In a real-world production system, you may have peaks at more than 100000 queries per second and more than 10000 unique query digests each minute. Trying to find the combinations of queries causing the contention among those makes finding a needle in a haystack seems easy.

If you are lucky, you may be able to guess what kind of queries you are looking for based on the contented mutexes and semaphores. In this case, the contention is on the adaptive hash index which is exclusively used for secondary indexes. So, you know that the queries of interest must be using secondary indexes, and the larger the number of index lookups and index modifications a query performs, the more likely it is to be part of the issue. In this case, the read-only query uses two secondary indexes as it can be seen from the query plan as shown in Listing 18-3.

Listing 18-3. The query plan for the read-only query in the test

```
EXPLAIN
 SELECT dept_name, MIN(salary) min_salary,
        AVG(salary) AS avg_salary, MAX(salary) AS max_salary
   FROM employees.departments
        INNER JOIN employees.dept_emp USING (dept_no)
        INNER JOIN employees.salaries USING (emp_no)
  WHERE dept_emp.to_date = '9999-01-01'
        AND salaries.to_date = '9999-01-01'
  GROUP BY dept_no
  ORDER BY dept_name
```

```
*************************** 1. row ***************************
           id: 1
  select_type: SIMPLE
        table: departments
   partitions: NULL
         type: index
possible_keys: PRIMARY,dept_name
          key: PRIMARY
      key_len: 16
          ref: NULL
         rows: 9
     filtered: 100
        Extra: Using temporary; Using filesort
*************************** 2. row ***************************
           id: 1
  select_type: SIMPLE
        table: dept_emp
   partitions: NULL
         type: ref
possible_keys: PRIMARY,dept_no,idx_concurrency_book_0
          key: idx_concurrency_book_0
      key_len: 19
          ref: employees.departments.dept_no,const
         rows: 9
     filtered: 100
        Extra: Using index
*************************** 3. row ***************************
           id: 1
  select_type: SIMPLE
        table: salaries
   partitions: NULL
         type: ref
possible_keys: PRIMARY,idx_concurrency_book_2
          key: idx_concurrency_book_2
      key_len: 7
```

```
            ref: employees.dept_emp.emp_no,const
           rows: 1
       filtered: 100
          Extra: Using index
3 rows in set, 1 warning (0.0009 sec)
```

The joins on the dept_emp and salaries tables are both performed using a secondary index, the idx_concurrency_book_0 and idx_concurrency_book_2 indexes, respectively. Likewise, the queries executed by the read-write connection use secondary indexes; it is left as an exercise for the reader to verify that.

With the investigation completed, you need to decide how to handle the contention.

The Solution and Prevention

Unlike the previous case studies, there is in general no straightforward way to solve and prevent the issue. Instead, you will need to test and verify the effect of various possible changes to your system. For this reason, the solution and prevention sections are combined.

- Disabling the adaptive hash index altogether

- Increasing the number of partitions

- Increasing the number of spin rounds before suspending the thread

- Splitting the workload to different replicas

These options will be discussed in the remainder of this section.

Disabling the Adaptive Hash Index

For contention on the adaptive hash index, the most straightforward solution is to disable the feature. Before you do so, you need to consider whether the reported contention is really a performance issue. Remember, mutex and semaphore waits are not by themselves a sign of problems; in fact, they are a natural part of MySQL. The spin waits counter increments as soon as a request cannot be fulfilled immediately. If the query only waits a few spin rounds before the request is fulfilled, it is not necessarily an issue. One thing you can look at is the average number of spin rounds per wait and use that to estimate how long the waits are. This is illustrated in Figure 18-3.

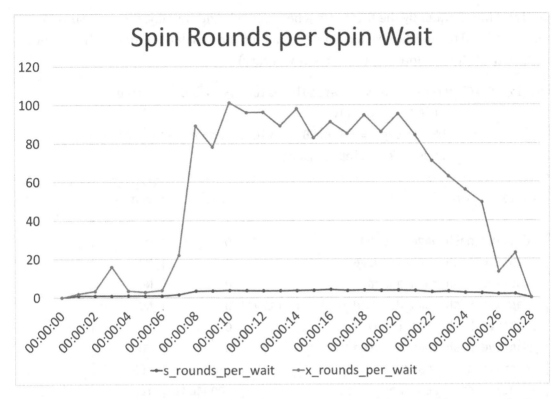

Figure 18-3. *The average spin rounds per wait for shared and exclusive rw-locks*

The figure shows that for exclusive locks, on average, each wait spends 80 to 100 rounds waiting. That is significant as there is a delay between each poll (the innodb_ spin_wait_delay and innodb_spin_wait_pause_multiplier options). Additionally, by default, after 30 rounds (the innodb_sync_spin_loops option), InnoDB suspends the thread to make it become available for other purposes which makes waking up the query again more expensive. For shared locks, the average is less than five and thus more manageable.

You should also consider how often the adaptive hash index can be used to find the rows and save a B-tree search. Hash index lookups are fast compared with B-tree searches, so the more searches that can be fulfilled by the adaptive hash index, the more overhead it justifies. InnoDB has two metrics that track how frequently the hash index is used and how frequently the B-tree must be accessed. Additionally, there are six other metrics related to the adaptive hash index, but these are disabled by default (the values include work done before this test, so they will vary):

```
mysql> SELECT variable_name, variable_value AS value, enabled
              FROM sys.metrics
              WHERE type = 'InnoDB Metrics - adaptive_hash_index'
              ORDER BY variable_name;
```

variable_name	value	enabled
adaptive_hash_pages_added	0	NO
adaptive_hash_pages_removed	0	NO
adaptive_hash_rows_added	0	NO
adaptive_hash_rows_deleted_no_hash_entry	0	NO
adaptive_hash_rows_removed	0	NO
adaptive_hash_rows_updated	0	NO
adaptive_hash_searches	51488882	YES
adaptive_hash_searches_btree	10904682	YES

```
8 rows in set (0.0097 sec)
```

This shows that more than 51 million searches (adaptive_hash_searches) have been fulfilled by the hash index and less than 11 million searches required using the B-tree. That gives a hit rate of

$$Hit\ Rate = 100\% * \frac{adaptive\_hash\_searches}{adaptive\_hash\_searches + adaptive\_hash\_searches\_btree} = 82.5\%$$

A hit rate of 82.5% may seem good, but it is likely (depending on the workload) on the low side for the adaptive hash index to be beneficial. Remember that the hash index also takes up memory in the buffer pool. If you disable the adaptive hash index, that memory can be used for caching B-tree indexes instead. You also need to take into consideration how long the metrics cover and whether there are fluctuations in the usefulness of the hash index. For the latter, a graph in your monitoring software is a good way to look at the data over time. Figure 18-4 shows an example based on the metrics collected during this test.

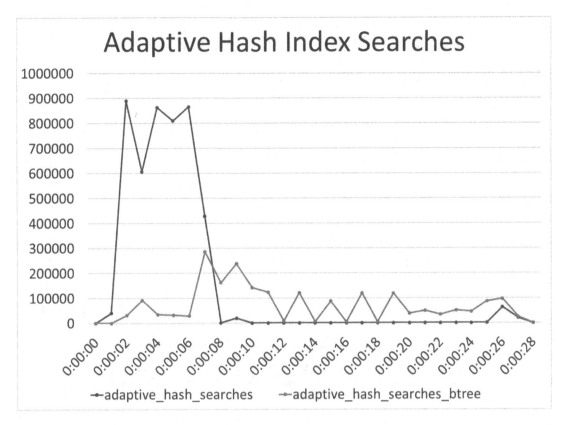

Figure 18-4. *The adaptive hash index search metrics during the test*

Here you can see that initially, the adaptive hash index is effective with the majority of searches being fulfilled using the hash index. However, 6 seconds into the test, the `adaptive_hash_searches` metric starts to plummet, and after the 9-second mark and until near the end of the test, it does not get above 250 matches per second. You can also see that the sum of the two is much lower during that period than in the start which may be due to contention causing the overall query performance to suffer. However, you will need to confirm whether that is the case using other sources; this is left as an exercise.

Alternative, you can plot the hit rate directly as it is shown in Figure 18-5.

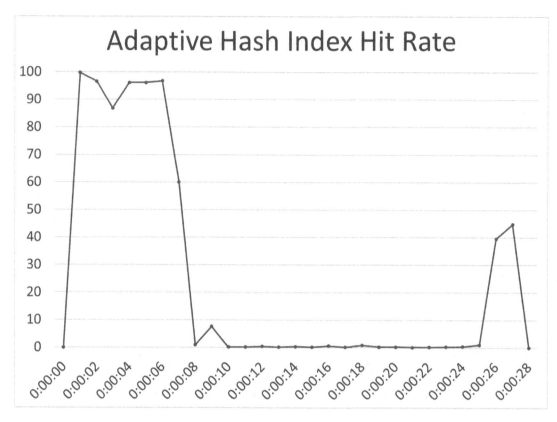

Figure 18-5. *The adaptive hash index hit rate during the test*

This clearly shows that initially, the adaptive hash index is quite effective but then becomes useless. Based on this, it seems likely that it is worth disabling the adaptive hash index which you can do by setting `innodb_adaptive_hash_index` to OFF or 0, for example

```
SET GLOBAL innodb_adaptive_hash_index = OFF;
Query OK, 0 rows affected (0.1182 sec)
```

While you can test disabling the hash index dynamically, do be aware that as soon as you do so, the hash index in the buffer pool is purged, so if you later re-enable the feature, you will need for the hashes to be rebuilt. For large instances, the adaptive hash index may use 25 GiB or more memory, so it will take a while to rebuild. Thus, when you disable the adaptive hash index in a production system, you may want to keep a replica ready with it enabled, so you can fail over to the replica should the disablement of `innodb_adaptive_hash_index` turn out to cause a performance regression.

Tip Ultimately, for semaphore contention issues, you will need to verify the effect of your changes using benchmarks or testing in a production-like environment or by having replicas with different settings. While some estimates of the effect can be made like in this discussion, the interactions between the involved parts are complex, and you cannot be sure of the overall effect before you measure it.

While disabling the adaptive hash index is a straightforward solution, there are other changes you can consider that may allow you to continue using the adaptive hash index at least partially.

Increase the Number of Hash Index Parts

If the contention is caused by too many connections hitting the same hash partition, then an option is to increase the number of parts the adaptive hash index is split into. This is done with the innodb_adaptive_hash_index_parts option. There is no direct way to determine whether increasing the number of hash index parts will help, though you can take a look at INSERT BUFFER AND ADAPTIVE HASH INDEX section in the InnoDB monitor output and see the size and number of buffers in each part, for example

```
mysql> SHOW ENGINE INNODB STATUS\G
...
-------------------------------------
INSERT BUFFER AND ADAPTIVE HASH INDEX
-------------------------------------
Ibuf: size 1, free list len 13, seg size 15, 0 merges
merged operations:
 insert 0, delete mark 0, delete 0
discarded operations:
 insert 0, delete mark 0, delete 0
Hash table size 34679, node heap has 1 buffer(s)
Hash table size 34679, node heap has 3880 buffer(s)
Hash table size 34679, node heap has 1 buffer(s)
Hash table size 34679, node heap has 1 buffer(s)
Hash table size 34679, node heap has 1 buffer(s)
```

```
Hash table size 34679, node heap has 1 buffer(s)
Hash table size 34679, node heap has 1 buffer(s)
Hash table size 34679, node heap has 1 buffer(s)
0.00 hash searches/s, 0.00 non-hash searches/s
...
```

This output is from the end of the test, and you can see that it is mostly one of the parts that is in use (which part may differ for you). So, in this case, it likely does not help to add more hash index parts. In a more realistic production usage with many indexes, you are more likely to benefit from more parts.

Other Solutions

It was discussed earlier in this section that it was a problem so many of the spin waits were converted into OS waits. Particularly if you do not use all of your CPUs, you can consider increasing the value of the innodb_sync_spin_loops option to allow InnoDB to keep polling for the rw-lock to become available. This can reduce the number of context switches and the overall wait time.

Finally, you can consider dividing your queries into those that benefit from the adaptive hash index and those that do not and direct each group of queries to separate replicas. That way, you can execute the queries that benefit from the adaptive hash index on a replica where the feature is enabled and those that do not benefit on a replica with it disabled. This obviously is mostly a solution for read-only tasks.

Summary

This case study has investigated an example of semaphore contention on the adaptive hash index. The symptoms include an elevated number of waits reported by the innodb_rwlock_% InnoDB metrics and the SEMAPHORES section of the InnoDB monitor caused by too many queries requiring conflicting access to the same latches.

The setup for this case study is more involved compared to most of the previous case studies and is easiest reproduced using the concurrency_book module for MySQL Shell. The workload for this chapter prompts for various settings for the test, so you can try and adapt the test for your system.

The investigation started out using the `innodb_rwlock_%` metrics to determine when the contention is a problem. You can both look at the raw metrics and the spin rounds per spin wait. Then the InnoDB monitor and mutex monitor were used to determine where the contention is, in this case, on the adaptive hash index. Finally, it was discussed how you may be able to determine the workload causing the contention.

The solution is in general not simple and deterministic when working with mutex and semaphore contention. For the adaptive hash index, the most straightforward option is to disable it, but before you do that, you need to consider the overall effectiveness of the feature including the hit rate. An alternative is to split the hash index into more parts; however, that only works if the contention affects several of your existing partitions. Other solutions include increasing the number of spin loops allowed to reduce how often InnoDB suspends the polling and to use multiple read replicas with different configurations.

That concludes the journey through the world of MySQL concurrency with focus on locks and transactions. Remember that practice makes perfect, and this is particularly true with the topics discussed in this book. The remainder of the book consists of two appendixes of which Appendix A contains various references for Performance Schema tables, the InnoDB monitor, and more. Appendix B is a reference for the `concurrency_book` module for MySQL Shell.

Good luck with your continued MySQL concurrency performance journey.

APPENDIX A

References

MySQL includes several views and tables in the Performance Schema, sys schema, and Information Schema that provide information that you can use when investigating issues. This appendix includes a quick reference to the resources most useful in connection with this book. For the object and lock types in the performance_schema.metadata_locks table, lists of possible values are also included. Finally, there is a brief description of each of the sections of the InnoDB monitor.

Tip MySQL Workbench includes several performance reports that are based on the sys schema views. This allows you to use a graphical user interface to obtain the information discussed here. The interface also allows you to change the ordering of the rows.

Tables and Views

The Performance Schema is the primary resource for information related to locks and transactions. Additionally, the Information Schema provides a couple of views, and the sys schema makes the information available as reports.

Tip Most of the sys schema views are also available with x$ prefixed, for example, x$statement_analysis. The views with x$ prefixed do not add the formatting making them better if you want to add additional filters on the formatted columns, change the ordering, or similar.

© Jesper Wisborg Krogh 2021
J. W. Krogh, *MySQL Concurrency*, https://doi.org/10.1007/978-1-4842-6652-6

This section first lists the resources with lock information, then the possible values of the OBJECT_TYPE and LOCK_TYPE columns of the performance_schema.metadata_locks table, and then resources with transaction, statement, waits, table and file I/O, and error information. Finally, the tables and views with the status variables and InnoDB metrics are covered.

Lock Information

The information is available through four Performance Schema tables:

- **data_locks:** This table contains details of table and records locks at the InnoDB level. It shows all locks currently held or are pending.

- **data_lock_waits:** Like the data_locks table, it shows locks related to InnoDB, but only those waiting to be granted with information on which threads is blocking the request.

- **metadata_locks:** This table contains information about user-level locks, metadata locks, and similar. To record information, the wait/lock/metadata/sql/mdl Performance Schema instrument must be enabled (it is enabled by default in MySQL 8). The OBJECT_TYPE column shows which kind of lock is held, and the LOCK_TYPE column shows the access level.

- **table_handles:** This table holds information about which table locks are currently in effect. The wait/lock/table/sql/handler Performance Schema instrument must be enabled for data to be recorded (this is the default). This table is less frequently used than the other tables.

The sys schema includes two invaluable views showing details of ongoing lock waits. The views are

- **innodb_lock_waits:** This view shows ongoing InnoDB row lock waits. It uses the data_locks and data_lock_waits tables.

- **schema_table_lock_waits:** This view shows ongoing metadata and user lock waits. It uses the metadata_locks table.

Metadata Object Types

The OBJECT_TYPE column shows which kind of lock is held with the possible values defined in sql/mdl.h in the source code.[1] Table A-1 summarizes the possible values of the OBJECT_TYPE column in alphabetical order with a brief explanation of the locks each value represents.

Table A-1. *Object types in the performance_schema.metadata_locks table*

Object Type	Description
ACL_CACHE	For the access control list (ACL) cache.
BACKUP_LOCK	For the backup lock.
CHECK_CONSTRAINT	For the names of CHECK constraints.
COLUMN_STATISTICS	For histograms and other column statistics.
COMMIT	For blocking commits. It is related to the global read lock.
EVENT	For stored events.
FOREIGN_KEY	For the foreign key names.
FUNCTION	For stored functions.
GLOBAL	For the global read lock (triggered by FLUSH TABLES WITH READ LOCK).
LOCKING_SERVICE	For locks acquired using the locking service interface.
PROCEDURE	For stored procedures.
RESOURCE_GROUPS	For the resource groups.
SCHEMA	For schema/databases. These are similar to the metadata locks for tables except they are for a schema.
SRID	For the spatial reference systems (SRIDs).
TABLE	For tables and views. This includes what is called metadata locks in this book.
TABLESPACE	For tablespaces.
TRIGGER	For triggers (on tables).
USER_LEVEL_LOCK	For user-level locks.

The most commonly encountered object types are GLOBAL and TABLE.

---

[1]https://github.com/mysql/mysql-server/blob/8.0/sql/mdl.h line 356 and onward in 8.0.21

Metadata Lock Types

The LOCK_TYPE column contains the access level of the lock. This is a variation of shared and exclusive combined with modifiers such as intention and the priority. Table A-2 summarizes the possible value.[2]

Table A-2. *The lock types in the* performance_schema.metadata_locks *table*

Lock Type	Description
INTENTION_EXCLUSIVE	An intention exclusive lock that can later be upgraded to an exclusive lock. This is also used when accessing the dictionary cache.
SHARED	For shared access to only the metadata of the object. For example, used with stored procedures and when preparing prepared statements.
SHARED_HIGH_PRIO	A high-priority shared lock which is used when only accessing the metadata, for example, when populating the Information Schema view with metadata for the tables.
SHARED_READ	A shared lock for cases where it is intended to read the data of the object.
SHARED_WRITE	A shared lock on the metadata for cases where the intention is to modify the data of the object.
SHARED_WRITE_LOW_ PRIO	The same as SHARED_WRITE but for statements that use the LOW_ PRIORITY clause. This is not supported by InnoDB.
SHARED_UPGRADABLE	A shared lock that allows concurrent read/write of the table data. It can later be upgraded to lock types preventing data changes. It is used by the first phase of ALTER TABLE statements.
SHARED_READ_ONLY	This lock type is used with LOCK TABLES … READ to take a shared lock while preventing modification of the table's metadata and data.
SHARED_NO_WRITE	Another upgradable shared lock which blocks writes to the data. It is also used with the first phase of ALTER TABLE statements.

(continued)

---

[2]https://github.com/mysql/mysql-server/blob/8.0/sql/mdl.h line 181 and onward in 8.0.21

Table A-2. (*continued*)

Lock Type	Description
SHARED_NO_READ_WRITE	An upgradable lock holding a shared lock on the metadata but prevents both reads and writes of the table data. This is used by LOCK TABLES ... WRITE.
EXCLUSIVE	No other access to neither the metadata nor table data is allowed. This is used with CREATE TABLE, DROP TABLE, and RENAME TABLE statements as well as some phases of other DDL statements.

Transaction Information

The transaction tables can be used to find information about individual transactions or aggregated data. The Performance Schema tables with information about individual transactions as well as the INNODB_TRX view in the Information Schema are

- **events_transactions_current:** Transactions that are ongoing as well as the latest transaction for threads that are still connected but that have not yet started a new transaction.

- **events_transactions_history:** The last ten transactions (can be changed with the performance_schema_events_transactions_history_size) for each existing thread.

- **events_transactions_history_long:** The last 10000 transactions (the performance_schema_events_transactions_history_long_size option) for the instance. It also includes transactions for disconnected threads. The consumer for this table is disabled by default.

- **INNODB_TRX:** This Information Schema view includes details for InnoDB transactions and is the best resource for studying ongoing InnoDB transactions.

There are five transaction summary tables grouping the data globally or by account, host, thread, or user. The tables are

- **events_transactions_summary_global_by_event_name:** All transactions aggregated. There is only a single row in this table.

- **events_transactions_summary_by_account_by_event_name:** The transactions grouped by username and hostname.

- **events_transactions_summary_by_host_by_event_name:** The transactions grouped by hostname of the account.

- **events_transactions_summary_by_thread_by_event_name:** The transactions grouped by thread. Only currently existing threads are included.

- **events_transactions_summary_by_user_by_event_name:** The events grouped by the username part of the account.

Statement Information

The statement tables follow the same pattern as the transaction tables with three tables with information about individual events and several summary tables with aggregate data. Additionally, there is the threads table. The tables for individual statements are

- **events_statements_current:** The statements currently executing or for idle connections the latest executed query. When executing stored programs, there may be more than one row per connection.

- **events_statements_history:** The last statements for each connection. The number of statements per connection is capped at performance_schema_events_statements_history_size (defaults to 10). The statements for a connection are removed when the connection is closed.

- **events_statements_history_long:** The latest queries for the instance irrespective of which connection executed it. This table also includes statements from connections that have been closed. The consumer for this table is disabled by default. The number of rows is capped at performance_schema_events_statements_history_long_size (defaults to 10000).

- **threads:** Information about all current threads in the instance, both background and foreground threads. You can use this table instead of the SHOW PROCESSLIST command. In addition to the process list information, there are columns showing whether the thread is instrumented, the operating system thread id, and more.

The statement summary tables group the data by the statement digest, event name, user, etc. The tables are

- **events_statements_summary_by_digest:** The statement statistics grouped by the default schema and digest.

- **events_statements_summary_by_account_by_event_name:** The statement statistics grouped by the account and event name. The event name shows what kind of statement is executed, for example, statement/sql/select for a SELECT statement executed directly (not executed through a stored program).

- **events_statements_summary_by_host_by_event_name:** The statement statistics grouped by the hostname of the account and the event name.

- **events_statements_summary_by_program:** The statement statistics grouped by the stored program (event, function, procedure, table, or trigger) that executed the statement. This is useful to find the stored programs that perform the most work.

- **events_statements_summary_by_thread_by_event_name:** The statement statistics grouped by thread and event name. Only threads currently connected are included.

- **events_statements_summary_by_user_by_event_name:** The statement statistics grouped by the username of the account and the event name.

- **events_statements_summary_global_by_event_name:** The statement statistics grouped by the event name.

- **events_statements_histogram_by_digest:** Histogram statistics grouped by the default schema and digest.

- **events_statements_histogram_global:** Histogram statistics where all queries are aggregated in one histogram.

- **prepared_statements_instances:** Statistics for prepared statements with one row per prepared statement (the same statement prepared by two threads count as two unique prepared statements).

Of these tables, the events_statements_summary_by_digest is the most used. One important thing to note is that queries executed as prepared statements are not included in the statement tables, and instead the prepared_statements_instances table must be used to get information about them.

The sys schema includes a view that serves as an advanced process list as well as views returning statements filtered by criteria such as whether they perform full tables scans, performs sorting, etc. The views are

- **session:** This view returns an advanced process list based on the threads and events_statements_current tables with some additional information from other Performance Schema tables. The view includes the current statement for active connections and the last executed statement for idle connections. The rows are returned in descending order according to the process list time and the duration of the previous statement. The session view is particularly useful to understand what is happening right now.

- **statement_analysis:** This view is a formatted version of the events_statements_summary_by_digest table ordered by the total latency in descending order.

- **statements_with_errors_or_warnings:** This view returns the statements that cause errors or warnings. The rows are ordered in descending order by the number of errors and then number of warnings.

- **statements_with_full_table_scans:** This view returns the statements that include a full table scan. The rows are first ordered by the percentage of times no index is used and then by the total latency, both in descending order.

- **statements_with_runtimes_in_95th_percentile:** This view returns the statements that are in the 95th percentile of all queries in the events_statements_summary_by_digest table. The rows are ordered by the average latency in descending order.

- **statements_with_sorting:** This view returns the statements that sort the rows in its result. The rows are ordered by the total latency in descending order.

- **statements_with_temp_tables:** This view returns the statements that use internal temporary tables. The rows are ordered in descending order by the number of internal temporary tables on disk and internal temporary tables in memory.

In addition to the views listed here, there is also the statement_performance_ analyzer() procedure which takes two snapshots of the events_statements_summary_ by_digest table and calculates the difference and returns one or more reports showing information about the queries executed between the two snapshots.

Wait Information

The wait tables are not used as frequently as the statement tables, and most wait events are disabled by default. Otherwise, the tables follow the same pattern as for transactions and statements. The tables with information about individual wait events are

- **events_waits_current:** The current ongoing or last completed wait events for each existing thread. This requires the events_waits_ current consumer to be enabled.

- **events_waits_history:** The last ten (the performance_schema_ events_waits_history_size option) wait events for each existing thread. This requires the events_waits_history consumer to be enabled in addition to the events_waits_current consumer.

- **events_waits_history_long:** The last 10,000 (the performance_ schema_events_waits_history_long_size option) events globally, including for threads that no longer exist. This requires the events_ waits_history_long consumer to be enabled in addition to the events_waits_current consumer.

Due to the sheer number of wait events that are executed, typically, the summary tables are the most useful for wait events. These are

- **events_waits_summary_by_account_by_event_name**: The wait events grouped by the username and hostname of the accounts (also called actors in the Performance Schema).

- **events_waits_summary_by_host_by_event_name**: The wait events grouped by the hostname of the account triggering the event and event name.

- **events_waits_summary_by_instance**: The wait events grouped by the event name as well as the memory address (OBJECT_INSTANCE_ BEGIN) of the object. This is useful for events with more than one instance to monitor whether the waits are evenly distributed among the instances. An example is the table cache mutex (wait/synch/ mutex/sql/LOCK_table_cache) which has one object per table cache instance (table_open_cache_instances).

- **events_waits_summary_by_thread_by_event_name**: The wait events for currently existing threads grouped by the thread id and event name.

- **events_waits_summary_by_user_by_event_name**: The wait events grouped by the username of the account triggering the event and event name.

- **events_waits_summary_global_by_event_name**: The wait events grouped by the event names. This table is useful to get an overview of how much time is spent waiting for a given type of event.

Table I/O Information

When studying concurrency issues, it can be useful to determine which are the most used tables. There are two tables in the Performance Schema that provides this information:

- **table_io_waits_summary_by_table**: The aggregate information for the table with details of read, write, fetch, insert, and update I/O.

- **table_io_waits_summary_by_index_usage:** The same information as for the `table_io_waits_summary_by_table` table except the statistics are per index or lack thereof.

The `sys` schema views for table I/O can be used to find information about the usage of tables and indexes. This includes finding indexes that are not used and tables where full table scans are executed. The views that base their information on the table I/O all have `schema_` as the prefix for the name. The views are

- **schema_index_statistics:** This view includes all the rows of the `table_io_waits_summary_by_index_usage` table where the index name is not NULL. The rows are ordered by the total latency in descending order. The view shows you how much each index is used for selecting, inserting, updating, and deleting data.

- **schema_table_statistics:** This view combines data from the `table_io_waits_summary_by_table` and `file_summary_by_instance` tables to return both the table I/O and the file I/O related to the table. The file I/O statistics are only included for tables in their own tablespace. The rows are ordered by the total table I/O latency in descending order.

- **schema_table_statistics_with_buffer:** This view is the same as the `schema_table_statistics` view except that is also includes buffer pool usage information from the `INNODB_BUFFER_PAGE` Information Schema view. Be aware that querying the `innodb_buffer_page` view can have a significant overhead and is best used on test systems.

- **schema_tables_with_full_table_scans:** This view queries the `table_io_waits_summary_by_index_usage` table for rows where the index name is NULL – that is, where an index was not used – and includes the rows where the read count is greater than 0. These are the tables where there are rows that are read without using an index – that is, through a full table scan. The rows are ordered by the total number of rows read in descending order.

- **schema_unused_indexes:** This view also uses the `table_io_waits_summary_by_index_usage` table but includes rows where no rows have been read for an index, and that index is not a primary key or a unique index. Tables in the `mysql` schema are excluded as you should not change the definition of any of those. The tables are ordered alphabetically according to the schema and table names.

File I/O Information

When the workload hits the disk, it can quickly become a bottleneck given that disk I/O is slower than memory I/O. It is thus useful to track which files are seeing the most file I/O. The tables and views are best used to determine what is causing the I/O once you have determined that the disk I/O is a bottleneck. You can then work backward to find the tables involved. From there you may determine if you can optimize queries using the tables or that you need to increase the I/O capacity.

The Performance Schema tables with file I/O information are

- **events_waits_summary_global_by_event_name:** This is a summary table grouped by the event names. By querying event names starting with `wait/io/file/`, you can get I/O statistics grouped by the type of I/O. For example, I/O caused by reading and writing the binary log files uses a single event (`wait/io/file/sql/binlog`). Note that events set to `wait/io/table/sql/handler` correspond to table I/O; including the table I/O allows you to easily compare the time spent on file I/O with the time spent on table I/O.

- **file_summary_by_event_name:** This is similar to the `events_waits_summary_global_by_event_name` table but just including file I/O and with the events split into reads, writes, and miscellaneous.

- **file_summary_by_instance:** This is a summary table grouped by the actual files and with the events divided into reads, writes, and miscellaneous. For example, for the binary logs, there is one row per binary log file.

The sys schema file I/O views include

- **io_by_thread_by_latency:** This view uses the events_waits_ summary_by_thread_by_event_name table to return the file I/O statistics grouped by the thread with the rows ordered by the total latency in descending order. The threads include the background threads which are the ones causing a large part of the write I/O.

- **io_global_by_file_by_bytes:** This view uses the file_summary_ by_instance table to return the number of read and write operations and the amount of I/O in bytes for each file. The rows are ordered by the total amount of read plus write I/O in bytes in descending order.

- **io_global_by_file_by_latency:** This view is the same as the io_ global_by_file_by_bytes view except it reports the I/O latencies.

- **io_global_by_wait_by_bytes:** This view is similar to the io_global_ by_file_by_bytes view except it groups by the I/O event names instead of file names and it uses the file_summary_by_event_name table.

- **io_global_by_wait_by_latency:** This view is the same as the io_ global_by_wait_by_bytes view except it reports the I/O latencies.

Error Information

Unlike transactions, statements, and waits, error events are only exposed through summary tables with aggregate data. The tables are

- **events_errors_summary_by_account_by_error:** The errors grouped by the account (username and hostname) and error number.

- **events_errors_summary_by_host_by_error:** The errors grouped by hostname and error number.

- **events_errors_summary_by_thread_by_error:** The errors grouped by thread and error number. Only threads that still exists are included.

- **events_errors_summary_by_user_by_error:** The errors grouped by username and error number.

- **events_errors_summary_global_by_error:** The errors grouped by error number. This table is also useful to map error numbers to the error name and SQL state.

Status Variables and InnoDB Metrics

The session and global status variables as well as the InnoDB metrics are useful to get a high-level overview of the activity in MySQL. The tables and view are

- **performance_schema.session_status:** The status variables for the session querying the table. This is mostly equivalent to SHOW SESSION STATUS.

- **performance_schema.global_status:** The global status variables. This is mostly equivalent to SHOW GLOBAL STATUS.

- **information_schema.INNODB_METRICS:** InnoDB-specific metrics similar to the global status variables.

- **sys.metrics:** A view that combines the global status variables and the InnoDB metrics plus a few other metrics.

InnoDB Monitor Sections

The InnoDB monitor report is created with the SHOW ENGINE INNODB STATUS statement. Alternatively, it can be written to the stderr (usually redirected to the error log) every 15 seconds by enabling the innodb_status_output option. The report itself is divided into several sections, including

- **BACKGROUND THREAD:** The work done by the main background thread.

- **SEMAPHORES:** Semaphore statistics. The section is most important in cases where contention causes long semaphore waits in which case the section can be used to get information about the locks and who holds them.

- **LATEST FOREIGN KEY ERROR:** If a foreign key error has been encountered, this section includes details of the error. Otherwise, the section is omitted.

- **LATEST DETECTED DEADLOCK:** If a deadlock has occurred, this section includes details of the two transactions and the locks that caused the deadlock. Otherwise, the section is omitted.

- **TRANSACTIONS:** Information about the InnoDB transactions. Only transactions with at least one exclusive lock on InnoDB tables are included. If the `innodb_status_output_locks` option is enabled, the locks held for each transaction are listed; otherwise, it is just locks involved in lock waits. It is in general better to use the `information_schema.INNODB_TRX` view to query the transaction information and for lock information to use the `performance_schema.data_locks` and `performance_schema.data_lock_waits` tables.

- **FILE I/O:** Information about the I/O threads used by InnoDB including the insert buffer thread, log thread, read threads, and write threads.

- **INSERT BUFFER AND ADAPTIVE HASH INDEX:** Information about the change buffer (this was formerly called the insert buffer) and the adaptive hash index.

- **LOG:** Information about the redo log.

- **BUFFER POOL AND MEMORY:** Information about the InnoDB buffer pool. This information is better obtained from the `information_schema.INNODB_BUFFER_POOL_STATS` view.

- **INDIVIDUAL BUFFER POOL INFO:** If `innodb_buffer_pool_instances` is greater than 1, this section includes information about the individual buffer pool instances with the same information as for the global summary in the previous section. Otherwise, the section is omitted. This information is better obtained from the `information_schema.INNODB_BUFFER_POOL_STATS` view.

- **ROW OPERATIONS:** This section shows various information about InnoDB including the current activity and what the main thread is.

The sections present in the report depend on the InnoDB configuration and what has happened before the report is generated.

MySQL Shell Module

Several of the examples in this book can be reproduced using the `concurrency_book.generate` MySQL Shell module that is available from this book's GitHub repository. The installation and basic usage instructions are available in Chapter 1 (but are also included here for completeness). Additionally, this appendix covers the structure of the module and provides instructions on how to add new test cases.

Prerequisites

The most important requirement to use the MySQL Shell module provided with this book is that you are using MySQL Shell 8.0.20 or later. This is a strict requirement as the module primarily uses the `shell.open_session()` method to create the connections needed for the test cases. This method was only introduced in release 8.0.20. The advantage of `shell.open_session()` over the `mysql.get_classic_session()` and `mysqlx.get_session()` is that `open_session()` works transparently with both the classic MySQL protocol and the new X protocol.

If you for some reason are stuck with an older version of MySQL Shell, you can update the test cases to include the `protocol` setting (see Defining Workloads later in this appendix) to explicitly specify which protocol to use.

It is also required that a connection already exists from MySQL Shell to MySQL Server as the module uses the URI of that connection when creating the additional connections required for the example.

The examples have been tested with MySQL Server 8.0.21; however, most of the examples will work with older releases, and some even with MySQL 5.7. That said, it is recommended to use MySQL Server 8.0.21 or later.

© Jesper Wisborg Krogh 2021
J. W. Krogh, *MySQL Concurrency*, https://doi.org/10.1007/978-1-4842-6652-6

Installation

To use the module, you need to download the files in the concurrency_book directory from this book's GitHub repository (the link can be found on the book's home page at www.apress.com/gp/book/9781484266519). The easiest is to clone the repository or to download the ZIP file with all the files using the menu shown in Figure B-1.

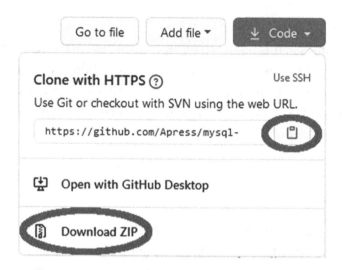

Figure B-1. *The GitHub menu for cloning or downloading the repository*

Click on the clipboard icon to copy the URL used to clone the repository using the Git software of your system, or use the *Download ZIP* link to download a ZIP file of the repository. You are free to choose any path as the location of the files as long as the structure below the concurrency_book directory is kept. For this discussion, it is assumed you have cloned the repository or unzipped the file to C:\Book\mysql-concurrency, so the generate.py file is in the directory C:\Book\mysql-concurrency\concurrency_book\.

To be able to import the module in MySQL Shell, open or create the mysqlshrc.py file. MySQL Shell searches in four places for the file. On Microsoft Windows, the paths are in the order they are searched:

1.   %PROGRAMDATA%\MySQL\mysqlsh\

2.   %MYSQLSH_HOME%\shared\mysqlsh\

3.   <mysqlsh binary path>\

4.   %APPDATA%\MySQL\mysqlsh\

On Linux and Unix

1. `/etc/mysql/mysqlsh/`

2. `$MYSQLSH_HOME/shared/mysqlsh/`

3. `<mysqlsh binary path>/`

4. `$HOME/.mysqlsh/`

All four paths are always searched, and if the file is found in multiple locations, each file will be executed. This means that the last found file takes precedence if the files affect the same variables. If you make changes meant for you personally, the best place to make the changes is in the fourth location. The path in step 4 can be overridden with the `MYSQLSH_USER_CONFIG_HOME` environment variable.

You need to ensure the `mysqlshrc.py` file adds the directory with the module to the Python search path, and optionally you can add an `import` statement to make the module available when you start MySQL Shell. An example of the `mysqlshrc.py` file is

```
import sys
sys.path.append('C:\\Book\\mysql-concurrency')
import concurrency_book.generate
```

The double backslashes are for Windows; on Linux and Unix, you do not need to escape the slashes that separate the path elements. If you do not include the `import` in the `mysqlshrc.py` file, you will need to execute it in MySQL Shell before you can use the module.

The help( ) and show( ) Methods

The module includes two methods that return information on how to use the module. First is the `help()` method which provides information on how to use the module as shown in Listing B-1.

Listing B-1. Obtaining help for the concurrency_book.generate module

```
mysql-py> concurrency_book.generate.help()
The following actions are supported:
======================================
```

* help()
    Display this help.

* load(schema_name=None)
    Load a schema. Optionally takes the name of the schema to be
    loaded. If no schema name or an invalid is given, you
    will be prompted to select one.

* show()
    List the available workloads. The function takes no arguments.

* run(workload_name=None)
    Execute a workload. Optionally the name of the workload can be
    specified. If no workload name or an invalid is given, you
    will be prompted to select one. You will also be required to
    enter the password.

The two main methods are load() and run(). The load() method can be used to
load the world, sakila, and employees sample databases, while the run() method is
used to execute one of the workloads.

There is also the show() method which lists the workloads that the run() method
can execute and the schemas that the load() method can load. The use of the show()
method is demonstrated in Listing B-2.

Listing B-2. Using the show() method to list tasks for run() and load()

```
mysql-py> concurrency_book.generate.show()
Available workloads:
====================
```

```
 # Name                 Description
-------------------------------------------------------------------------
 1 Listing  2-1         Example use of the metadata_locks table
 2 Listing  2-2         Example of using the table_handles table
```

```
Available Schema load jobs:
============================

  # Name                   Description
---------------------------------------------------------------------------
  1 employees              The employee database
  2 employees partitioned  The employee database with partitions
  3 sakila                 The sakila database
  4 world                  The world database
```

The workloads are named after the code listings in the book, for example, the workload named "Listing 6-1" implements the example in Listing 6-1.

Loading Test Data

The concurrency_book.generate module supports loading the employees, sakila, and world example databases into your MySQL instance. For the employees database, you can optionally choose a version with partitions. The world database is the most important for this book followed by the sakila database. The employees database is only used for the case study in Chapter 18. Each of the three schemas is described in more detail in Chapter 1.

Note   If the schema exists, it will be dropped as part of the load job. This effectively means that load() resets the schema.

You load a schema with the load() method which optionally takes the name of the schema you want to load. If you do not provide a schema name, then you will be prompted. Listing B-3 shows an example of loading the world schema.

Listing B-3. Loading the world schema

```
mysql-py> concurrency_book.generate.load()
Available Schema load jobs:
===========================

  # Name                      Description
--------------------------------------------------------------------

  1 employees                 The employee database
  2 employees partitioned     The employee database with partitions
  3 sakila                    The sakila database
  4 world                     The world database

Choose Schema load job (# or name - empty to exit): 4
2020-07-20 21:27:15.221340  0 [INFO] Downloading https://downloads.
mysql.com/docs/world.sql.zip to C:\Users\myuser\AppData\Roaming\mysql_
concurrency_book\sample_data\world.sql.zip
2020-07-20 21:27:18.159554  0 [INFO] Processing statements in world.sql
2020-07-20 21:27:27.045219  0 [INFO] Load of the world schema completed

Available Schema load jobs:
===========================

  # Name                      Description
--------------------------------------------------------------------

  1 employees                 The employee database
  2 employees partitioned     The employee database with partitions
  3 sakila                    The sakila database
  4 world                     The world database

Choose Schema load job (# or name - empty to exit):
```

The load() method downloads the file with the schema definition, if it does not already have it. The downloaded file is stored in %APPDATA\ mysql_concurrency_book\ sample_data\ on Microsoft Windows and in ${HOME}/.mysql_concurrency_book/ sample_data/ on other platforms. If you want the file re-downloaded, delete it from that directory.

Tip   As only relatively low-level network routines are available in MySQL Shell's Python, downloading the employees database may fail if you have a slow or unstable connection. One option – other than installing the schema manually – is to download `https://github.com/datacharmer/test_db/archive/master.zip` and save it in the `sample_data` directory. After that, the `load()` method will pick it up and not attempt to download it again.

If you only want to load a single schema, you can specify the name as an argument to `load()`. This can be particularly useful when initiating a schema load as a command given directly on the command line when invoking MySQL Shell, for example

```
shell> mysqlsh --user=myuser --py -e "concurrency_book.generate.
load('world')"
```

When you are done loading the schemas you need, you can reply with an empty answer to exit. You are now ready to execute the workloads.

Note   If the load process crashes complaining about the file, for example, that it is not a ZIP file, then it suggests the file is corrupted or incomplete. In that case, delete the file, so it is re-downloaded, or try to download the file manually using your browser.

Executing a Workload

You execute a workload with the `run()` method. If you specify the name of known workload, then that workload will be executed immediately. Otherwise, the available workloads are listed, and you are prompted for the workload. You can in this case specify the workload either by the number (e.g., 15 for Listing 6-1) or by the name. When using the name, the number of spaces between `Listing` and the listing number does not matter as long as there is at least one space. When you choose the workload using the prompt, you can choose another workload once the previous has completed.

After the workload has completed, for several of the workloads, you will be given a list of suggestions for investigations you can do. This can, for example, be to query the locks held by the connections used in the example. The investigations are meant as inspiration, and you are encouraged to explore the workload using your own queries. Some of the investigations are also used in the discussion of the example. Listing B-4 shows an example of executing a workload using the prompt.

Listing B-4. Executing a workload using the prompt

```
mysql-py> concurrency_book.generate.run()
Available workloads:
====================

 # Name                      Description
-----------------------------------------------------------------------
 1 Listing  2-1              Example use of the metadata_locks table
 2 Listing  2-2              Example of using the table_handles table
 3 Listing  2-3              Using the data_locks table
...
14 Listing  5-2              Example of obtaining exclusive locks
15 Listing  6-1              A deadlock for user-level locks
...

Choose workload (# or name - empty to exit): 15
Password for connections: ********
2020-07-20 20:50:41.666488  0 [INFO] Starting the workload Listing 6-1

***************************************************
*                                                 *
*    Listing 6-1. A deadlock for user-level locks  *
*                                                 *
***************************************************

-- Connection    Processlist ID   Thread ID    Event ID
-- ----------------------------------------------------
--           1             105          249           6
--           2             106          250           6

-- Connection 1
Connection 1> SELECT GET_LOCK('my_lock_1', -1);
```

```
+---------------------------+
| GET_LOCK('my_lock_1', -1) |
+---------------------------+
|                         1 |
+---------------------------+
1 row in set (0.0003 sec)

-- Connection 2
Connection 2> SELECT GET_LOCK('my_lock_2', -1);
+---------------------------+
| GET_LOCK('my_lock_2', -1) |
+---------------------------+
|                         1 |
+---------------------------+
1 row in set (0.0003 sec)

Connection 2> SELECT GET_LOCK('my_lock_1', -1);

-- Connection 1
Connection 1> SELECT GET_LOCK('my_lock_2', -1);
ERROR: 3058: Deadlock found when trying to get user-level lock; try rolling
back transaction/releasing locks and restarting lock acquisition.

Available investigations:
==========================

 # Query
-----------------------------------------------------
 1 SELECT *
     FROM performance_schema.metadata_locks
    WHERE object_type = 'USER LEVEL LOCK'
          AND owner_thread_id IN (249, 250)

 2 SELECT thread_id, event_id, sql_text,
          mysql_errno, returned_sqlstate, message_text,
          errors, warnings
     FROM performance_schema.events_statements_history
    WHERE thread_id = 249 AND event_id > 6
    ORDER BY event_id
```

```
3 SELECT thread_id, event_id, sql_text,
         mysql_errno, returned_sqlstate, message_text,
         errors, warnings
    FROM performance_schema.events_statements_history
   WHERE thread_id = 250 AND event_id > 6
   ORDER BY event_id

Choose investigation (# - empty to exit): 2
-- Investigation #2
-- Connection 3
Connection 3> SELECT thread_id, event_id, sql_text,
                     mysql_errno, returned_sqlstate, message_text,
                     errors, warnings
                FROM performance_schema.events_statements_history
               WHERE thread_id = 249 AND event_id > 6
               ORDER BY event_id\G
*************************** 1. row ***************************
        thread_id: 249
         event_id: 7
         sql_text: SELECT GET_LOCK('my_lock_1', -1)
      mysql_errno: 0
returned_sqlstate: NULL
     message_text: NULL
           errors: 0
         warnings: 0
*************************** 2. row ***************************
        thread_id: 249
         event_id: 8
         sql_text: SELECT GET_LOCK('my_lock_2', -1)
      mysql_errno: 3058
returned_sqlstate: HY000
     message_text: Deadlock found when trying to get user-level lock;
     try rolling back transaction/releasing locks and restarting lock
     acquisition.
           errors: 1
         warnings: 0
```

```
*************************** 3. row ***************************
        thread_id: 249
         event_id: 9
         sql_text: SHOW WARNINGS
       mysql_errno: 0
returned_sqlstate: NULL
     message_text: NULL
            errors: 0
          warnings: 0
3 rows in set (0.0009 sec)

Available investigations:
=========================

 # Query
-------------------------------------------------
 1 SELECT *
     FROM performance_schema.metadata_locks
    WHERE object_type = 'USER LEVEL LOCK'
          AND owner_thread_id IN (249, 250)

 2 SELECT thread_id, event_id, sql_text,
          mysql_errno, returned_sqlstate, message_text,
          errors, warnings
     FROM performance_schema.events_statements_history
    WHERE thread_id = 249 AND event_id > 6
    ORDER BY event_id

 3 SELECT thread_id, event_id, sql_text,
          mysql_errno, returned_sqlstate, message_text,
          errors, warnings
     FROM performance_schema.events_statements_history
    WHERE thread_id = 250 AND event_id > 6
    ORDER BY event_id

Choose investigation (# - empty to exit):
```

```
2020-07-20 20:50:46.749971  0 [INFO] Completing the workload Listing 6-1
-- Connection 1
Connection 1> SELECT RELEASE_ALL_LOCKS();
+---------------------+
| RELEASE_ALL_LOCKS() |
+---------------------+
|                   1 |
+---------------------+
1 row in set (0.0004 sec)

-- Connection 2
Connection 2> SELECT RELEASE_ALL_LOCKS();
+---------------------+
| RELEASE_ALL_LOCKS() |
+---------------------+
|                   2 |
+---------------------+
1 row in set (0.0002 sec)

2020-07-20 20:50:46.749971  0 [INFO] Disconnecting for the workload Listing 6-1
2020-07-20 20:50:46.749971  0 [INFO] Completed the workload Listing 6-1

Available workloads:
====================

 # Name                    Description
---------------------------------------------------------------------------
 1 Listing  2-1            Example use of the metadata_locks table
 2 Listing  2-2            Example of using the table_handles table
 3 Listing  2-3            Using the data_locks table
...

Choose workload (# or name - empty to exit):

mysql-py>
```

There are a few things to notice from this example. After choosing the workload, you are asked for a password. This is the password for the MySQL account that you are using. The other connection options are taken from the `session.uri` property in MySQL Shell, but for security reasons, the password is not stored. If you execute multiple workloads in one invocation of `run()`, you will only be prompted for the password once.

At the start of the execution of the workload, there is an overview of the process list ids (as from `SHOW PROCESSLIST`), the (Performance Schema) thread ids, and the last event ids before the start of the workload for each connection used for the workload:

```
-- Connection   Processlist ID   Thread ID   Event ID
-- ------------------------------------------------------

--          1              105         249          6
--          2              106         250          6
```

You can use these ids to execute your own investigative queries, and you can use the overview to identify listings that have been implemented as a workload in `concurrency_book.generate.run()`.

At the end of executing the workload, this example has three queries you can execute to investigate the issue the example demonstrates. You can execute one or more of these by specifying the number of the query (one query at a time). In the code listings in this book, the output of an investigation is preceded with a comment showing which of the investigations has been executed, for example

```
-- Investigation #2
```

The number of investigations per workload varies from none to more than ten. The listings in the book do not always include the result of all of the investigations as some are left as inspiration and further examination of the issue.

Once you are done with the investigation, submit an empty answer to exit from the workload. If you do not want to execute more workloads, submit an empty answer again to exit the `run()` method.

If you only want to execute a single workload, you can specify the name as an argument to `run()`. This can be particularly useful when executing a workload as a command given directly on the command line when invoking MySQL Shell, for example

```
shell> mysqlsh --user=myuser --py -e "concurrency_book.generate.
run('Listing 6-1')"
```

The remainder of this appendix describes the internals of the module.

Module Structure

The files included in the concurrency_book module can be divided into three categories depending on how they are used. The structure is shown in Figure B-2.

```
C:\BOOK\MYSQL-CONCURRENCY\CONCURRENCY_BOOK
    generate.py
    __init__.py

────libs
        innodb_buffer_pool.py
        innodb_monitor.py
        innodb_mutex.py
        load.py
        log.py
        metrics.py
        query.py
        util.py
        workloads.py
        __init__.py

────workloads
        listing_10-1.yaml
        listing_10-2.yaml
        listing_10-3.yaml
        listing_10-4.yaml
        listing_10-5.yaml
        listing_10-6.yaml
        listing_10-9.yaml
        listing_12-1.yaml
        listing_12-2.yaml
        listing_12-3.yaml
        listing_12-4.yaml
        listing_12-5.yaml
        listing_12-6.yaml
        listing_12-7.yaml
        listing_13-1.yaml
        listing_14-1.yaml
        listing_15-2.yaml
        listing_16-1.yaml
        listing_17-1.yaml
        listing_17-4.yaml
        listing_17_1.py
        listing_18-1.yaml
        listing_18_1.py
        listing_2-4.yaml
```

Figure B-2. *The structure of the* concurrency_book *module*

At the top level, there is the generate.py file which is the entry point and where the four public methods (help(), load(), show(), and run()) are implemented. The libs directory contains various libraries used by the module. Unless you plan on extending the functionality of the module, you will not need to modify these files, but some of the libraries are also useful if you want to implement your own workloads in Python.

The workloads directory contains the workload definitions of which all have a YAML file and two tests (for Chapters 17 and 18) also include a Python file. If you want to modify or add tests, this is where you need to edit the files.

Library Files

It is worth touching on the library files as some of them are useful for implementing complex workloads like those in Chapters 17 and 18.

Note   Because the module is written for use from within MySQL Shell, referencing other module is a bit different from normal Python modules. This section contains some examples, and you can look at some of the existing workloads for further examples.

---

innodb_buffer_pool.py

This module implements an interface to monitor the InnoDB buffer pool through the information_schema.INNODB_BUFFER_POOL_STATS view. You will need to provide a MySQL Shell session object that is connected to MySQL when you initialize the Stats class. An example usage is

```
# noinspection PyUnresolvedReferences
from concurrency_book import libs
# noinspection PyUnresolvedReferences
import concurrency_book.libs.innodb_buffer_pool

bp_stats = libs.innodb_buffer_pool.Stats(session)
bp_stats.collect()
...
bp_stats.collect()
young = bp_stats.delta('pages_made_young')
print(f'Made young ......: {young.value:6d} pages ' +
      f'({young.rate:8.2f} pages/s)')
```

The collect() method queries that view and stores the result, and the delta() method calculates the difference between two results (by default the first and last) for the column specified and returns a named tuple with the difference as well as the rate.

innodb_monitor.py

This module implements an interface to monitor the InnoDB monitor output with support to return the content of individual sections and for the SEMAPHORES section calculate some statistics that can be used to monitor when waits have happened. You will need to provide a MySQL Shell session object that is connected to MySQL when you initialize the InnodbMonitor class. An example usage is

```
# noinspection PyUnresolvedReferences
from concurrency_book import libs
# noinspection PyUnresolvedReferences
import concurrency_book.libs.innodb_monitor

innodb = libs.innodb_monitor.InnodbMonitor(session)
innodb.fetch()
semaphores = innodb.get_section('SEMAPHORES')
if semaphores.num_waits >= 2:
    print(r'mysql> SHOW ENGINE INNODB STATUS\G')
    print('...')
    print(semaphores.content)
    print('...')
```

innodb_mutex.py

The innodb_mutex.py module implements support for monitoring the output of SHOW ENGINE INNODB MUTEX. There is support for fetching the total waits and the delta compared to the previous output. You will need to provide a MySQL Shell session object that is connected to MySQL when you initialize the InnodbMutexMonitor class. An example usage is

```
# noinspection PyUnresolvedReferences
from concurrency_book import libs
# noinspection PyUnresolvedReferences
import concurrency_book.libs.innodb_mutex

mutex = libs.innodb_mutex.InnodbMutexMonitor(session)
mutex.fetch()

...
```

```
mutex.fetch()
delta = mutex.delta_by_file('dict'))
if delta['btr0sea.cc'] > 0:
    print(mutex.delta_by_file_line('report'))
```

The delta_by_file() and delta_by_file_line() group the waits by the file name and filename:line, respectively. They can return the result either as a dictionary or a report (using MySQL's table format). Additionally, there are three methods to return the number of waits as an integer, get_waits_by_name(), get_waits_by_file(), and get_waits_by_file_line(), each taking one argument with the value of what to filter by.

There are also four properties:

- **output_time:** A datetime.datetime object when the latest output was fetched.

- **total_waits:** The total waits across all names in the latest output.

- **waits_increased:** A Boolean reflecting whether the total number of waits increased between the two most recent measurements.

- **report:** The latest output printed similar to how MySQL returns a result in table format.

load.py

The load.py module is where the logic for loading test data is implemented. If you want to add support for loading a new schema, you will need to add it to KNOWN_SCHEMAS and URLS constants and add a method named _exec_<schema name>(), for example, for the world schema, the method is _exec_world(), and it has the following definition:

```
def _exec_world(self):
    """Execute the steps required to load the world schema."""
    file = self._download()
    with zipfile.ZipFile(file) as zip_fs:
        self._delimiter = ';'
        with zip_fs.open('world.sql') as world:
            self._sql_file(world, zip_fs)

    LOG.info('Load of the world schema completed')
    return True
```

Notice that the file downloaded with the SQL statements is never explicitly decompressed. Instead the `zipfile.ZipFile()` class is used to access the compressed files directly.

log.py

This module provides a logging functionality including support for printing under a lock for use in multi-threaded workloads. An example of using the module is

```
import threading

# noinspection PyUnresolvedReferences
from concurrency_book import libs
# noinspection PyUnresolvedReferences
import concurrency_book.libs.log

LOG = libs.log.Log(libs.log.INFO)

lock = threading.Lock()
LOG.lock = lock
LOG.level = libs.log.DEBUG
LOG.debug('Some debug informatiom.')
LOG.level = libs.log.INFO
LOG.info('Some informational content.')
LOG.warning('Something unexpected happened.')
LOG.error('An error occurred.')
LOG.lock = None
```

When initializing the `Log()` class, you provide the default log level which is one of `libs.log.DEBUG`, `libs.log.INFO`, `libs.log.WARNING`, or `libs.log.ERROR`. The log level can be changed later using the `level` property. If you set the lock property with an instance of the `threading.Lock()` class, then that lock will be acquired before each time the log object is used for logging, making it safe to log from multiple threads at the same time.

You may ask why the built-in `logging` module is not used. The reason is mainly the support for logging under a lock and that `log.py` also includes the logic for logging the SQL statements and their result.

metrics.py

The metrics.py module allows you to monitor the sys.metrics view. This is what was used for the test cases in Chapters 17 and 18 to generate CSV outputs of various metrics. You will need to provide a MySQL Shell session object that is connected to MySQL when you initialize the Metrics class. An example usage is

```
# noinspection PyUnresolvedReferences
from concurrency_book import libs
# noinspection PyUnresolvedReferences
import concurrency_book.libs.metrics

metrics = libs.metrics.Metrics(session)
for i in range(10):
    metrics.collect()
    sleep(1)

metrics.collect()

count_metrics = [
    'innodb_row_lock_current_waits',
    'lock_row_lock_current_waits',
]
delta_metrics = [
    'innodb_row_lock_time',
    'lock_deadlocks',
    'lock_timeouts',
]
print('-- Metrics reported by count collected during the test:')
metrics.write_csv(count_metrics)
print('')
print('-- Metrics reported by rate collected during the test:')
metrics.write_rate_csv(delta_metrics)
```

query.py

This module includes various tools related to executing the workload and investigation queries. Of most interest in this discussion is the `Formatter()` class which can be used to format queries including adding indentation for keeping the lines of the query aligned when adding a prompt and replacing parameter placeholders. You must provide three lists with the process list ids, thread ids, and last event id before the tests, respectively, when initializing the class. An example usage is

```
# noinspection PyUnresolvedReferences
from concurrency_book import libs
# noinspection PyUnresolvedReferences
import concurrency_book.libs.query

sql_formatter = libs.query.Formatter([6, 7], [12, 14], [6, 6])
sql = """
SELECT *
  FROM world.city""".strip()
print('mysql> ' + sql_formatter.indent_sql(sql, 7))
```

The supported placeholders will be discussed when covering how to implement your own tests.

Another interesting function of query.py is `get_connection_ids()` which takes a session as the argument and returns a list with the process list id, thread id, and latest event id for the connection. For example (using MySQL Shell interactively)

```
mysql-py> from concurrency_book import libs
mysql-py> import concurrency_book.libs.query
mysql-py> libs.query.get_connection_ids(session)
[
    8,
    28,
    18
]
```

util.py

The util.py module contains various utilities used throughout the concurrency_book module. For creating test cases, the most interesting functions are prompt_int() and prompt_bool() which are used in the case studies in Chapters 17 and 18 for asking questions on how the test should be executed. Example uses are

```
# noinspection PyUnresolvedReferences
from concurrency_book import libs
# noinspection PyUnresolvedReferences
import concurrency_book.libs.util

prompt = 'Specify the number of seconds to run for'
max_runtime = libs.util.prompt_int(1, 3600, 10, prompt)

prompt = 'Restart MySQL before executing the test?'
restart_mysql = libs.util.prompt_bool('No', prompt)
```

The prompt_int() function takes four arguments: the minimum value, maximum value, default value, and the text for the prompt. The prompt_bool() function takes two arguments: the default value as 'No'/'Yes' and the prompt text; the answer is returned as True/False.

If you implement a workload in Python, you can use the get_session() function to create a new session. The function takes the workload named tuple (see next) as an argument.

workloads.py

The final library module is workloads.py which implements the YAML parser used to convert the workload definitions to Workload named tuples which in turn contain Query, Completion, Investigation, and Implementation named tuples. The reason for implementing a custom parser instead of using a PyPi package is that it is not simple to add third-party packages to the Python shipped with MySQL Shell. Additionally, workloads.py includes validation of the workloads.

Caution   The YAML parser in workloads.py is not a full-fledged parser, but just enough to handle the supported workload features. Do not try to use it for general-purpose YAML files.

If you need to add new properties to one of the named tuples, then the definition is at the top of the file. They support optional and required keys which are tracked in constant dictionaries just after the definition of the named tuples. If you change the fields of the `Workload` tuple, you will also have to edit the `_dict_to_tuple()` function.

Workloads Directory

If you want to add a new workload, then you need to add a YAML file with the definition to the `workloads` directory. You can name the file as you wish as long as the file name extension is `.yaml` or `.yml`. Files with these extensions are automatically parsed when the `concurrency_book.generate` module is imported. The structure of the YAML files is discussed next.

Defining Workloads

The workloads are defined through a series of elements of which some are required, and some are optional. While there is some flexibility in the syntax, remember it is not a full YAML parser that reads the files, so you are encouraged to use a syntax that matches the existing workload definitions.

Tip If you have problems getting the parser to read your workload definitions, make sure you use the same structure as in one of the existing workloads.

At the top level, you define the global properties for the workload which include the name and a description, the number of connections to use, etc. Then follows a list of queries to execute and at the end optional queries to execute upon completion of the workload and investigations that can be executed. Listing B-5 shows an example utilizing most of the supported features.

Listing B-5. Example demonstrating the workload syntax

```
--- # Listing B-5. Example demonstrating the workload syntax
name:        Listing B-5
description: Example demonstrating the workload syntax
connections: 2
```

```
concurrent:  No
loops:       1
queries:
  - connection:  1
    sql:         SET SESSION innodb_lock_wait_timeout = 1
    silent:      No
    wait:        Yes
  - connection:  1
    sql:         START TRANSACTION
  - connection:  2
    sql:         START TRANSACTION
  - connection:  1
    sql:         SET @id = CEIL(RAND()*4079)
  - connection:  1
    sql: |
      SELECT *
        FROM world.city
       WHERE ID = @id
    format:      json
    store:       Yes
  - connection:  2
    sql: |
      UPDATE world.city
         SET Population = Population + 1
       WHERE ID = 130
  - connection:  1
    comment: This will cause a lock wait timeout
    sql: |
      UPDATE world.city
         SET Population = Population + 1
       WHERE Name = ?
    parameters:  [Name]
completions:
  - connection:  1
    sql:          ROLLBACK
```

```
 - connection:  2
   sql:         ROLLBACK
investigations:
 - sql: |
     SELECT thread_id, event_id, sys.format_statement(sql_text) AS 'SQL',
            mysql_errno, message_text
       FROM performance_schema.events_statements_history
      WHERE thread_id IN ({thread_ids})
            AND mysql_errno > 0
      ORDER BY thread_id, event_id
   format:      vertical
 - sql: |
     SELECT THREAD_ID, EVENT_ID, SQL_TEXT
       FROM performance_schema.events_statements_history
      WHERE thread_id = ? AND event_id > ?
      ORDER BY thread_id, event_id
   parameters:  [thread_id, event_id]
   format:      vertical
```

The remainder of this appendix goes through each of global, queries and completions, and investigations and discusses the supported keys.

Global Keys

The global keys that are supported are summarized in Table B-1 with the key name, data type, whether it is required, and a description.

Table B-1. *Global workload keys*

Key Name	Data Type	Required	Description
name	String	Yes	The name of the workload. This is used to select the workload.
description	String	Yes	A description of the workload. This is used when listing the available workloads.
connections	Integer	No	The number of connections to create in addition to the main connection. Not setting this key is only useful when the `implementation` key is set. The default is 0.
queries	List	No	The queries to execute for the workload. The "Queries and Completions" subsection includes more information. The default is an empty list.
completions	List	No	The queries to execute upon completion of the workload (after the investigations have been completed). The completions are identical to queries and are discussed at the same time. The default is an empty list.
investigations	List	No	The queries to make available as example investigations between executing the queries and the completions. The "Investigations" subsection includes more information.
implementation	List	No	The module, class name, and extra arguments for a Python class implementing the workload, for example `[workloads.listing_17_1, ForeignKeys, {}]`. This is used for Chapters 17 and 18. The default is None.
protocol	Enum	No	Whether to require the connection to use the `mysql` or `mysqlx` protocol. This is used for the `Listing 6-8` workload. The default is None which means either protocol is allowed.
loops	Integer	No	The number of times to execute the queries in the `queries` list. The default is 1.

In most of the workloads, the keys that are used are limited to `name`, `description`, `connections`, `queries`, `completions`, and `investigations`.

If you implement the workload in Python, then the class signature must consist of (`workload, session, log, ...`) where `workload` is the named tuple defining the workload, `session` is the global MySQL Shell session object, and log is an instance of the `libs.log.Log()`. The ellipses signify any additional arguments you require for the test and can be used to reuse the same class for different workloads.

Queries and Completions

The queries and completions are identical except for the time they are executed. There are a number of properties defining a query as summarized in Table B-2.

Table B-2. *Keys for queries and implementations*

Key Name	Data Type	Required	Description
connection	Integer	Yes	The connection that will execute the query. This is an integer between 1 and the number of connections for the workload.
sql	String	Yes	The SQL statement to execute.
format	Enum	No	The format to use when printing the result. The same formats as for `shell.dump_rows()` are supported: `table`, `tabbed`, `vertical`, `json`, `ndjson`, `json/raw`, `json/array`, `json/pretty`. The default is `table`.
wait	Boolean	No	Whether to wait for the query to complete before executing the next query. It is important to set this to No when executing a query that will block for more than 10 seconds.
comment	String	No	A comment to print before the query.
show_result	Boolean	No	Whether to print the result of the query. The default is Yes.

(*continued*)

Table B-2. (*continued*)

Key Name	Data Type	Required	Description
silent	Boolean	No	Whether to suppress printing the query and its result. The default is No.
store	Boolean	No	Whether to store the result of the first row of the result so it can be used as parameters in subsequent queries for the same connection. Note that this consumes the result, so it cannot be printed, and any previous stored result is discarded. The default is No.
parameters	List	No	A list of column labels from a previous query where the result was stored. The values for those columns will be used to replace the ? placeholders in the query. Note that the ? placeholder will still be visible when printing the query as the value of the parameter is not known in the part of the code that prints the query.
sleep	Integer	No	The number of seconds to sleep after executing the query before executing the next query. The default is 0.

By far the most commonly used keys are connection, sql, format, and wait. The SQL statement can be written either on the same line as the key or using | to start a multiline string:

```
- connection:  2
  sql:          START TRANSACTION
- connection:  2
  sql: |
    UPDATE world.city
      SET Population = Population + 1
    WHERE ID = 130
```

There is also support for a limited number of parameters that are written inline into the statement. These are

- **{processlist_ids}:** This parameter is replaced with a list of process list ids for all connections in the workload.

- **{thread_ids}:** This parameter is replaced with a list of thread ids for all connections in the workload.

- **{thread_ids_not_self}:** This parameter is replaced with a list of thread ids for all connections in the workload except the connection itself.

- **{(event|processlist|thread)_id_connection_<connection>+<adjust>}:** This group of parameters is replaced with either the event, process list, or thread id of a specific connection optionally adjusted with a positive integer. Examples are {event_id_2+1} for the last event id before the workload plus 1 for connection 2 and {thread_id_1} for the thread id of connection 1.

The most commonly used of these four queries is {thread_ids_not_self}, whereas the others are more useful for investigations.

Investigations

The investigations support a subset of the keys that are used by queries. These are listed in Table B-3.

Table B-3. *Keys for queries and implementations*

Key Name	Data Type	Required	Description
sql	String	Yes	The SQL statement to execute.
format	Enum	No	The format to use when printing the result. The same formats as for shell.dump_rows() are supported: table, tabbed, vertical, json, ndjson, json/raw, json/array, json/pretty. The default is table.
parameters	List	No	A list of parameters to replace the ? placeholders in the query. The supported parameters will be discussed shortly.

The sql and format keys work the same way as for queries, but there are some differences for the parameters key as the substitution is not based on a stored result but rather has a specific list of supported parameters:

- **processlist_id:** The process list id for a connection.

- **thread_id:** The thread id for a connection.

- **event_id:** The last event id before the workload for a connection.

- **thread_ids:** A list of all the thread ids for the workload.

For processlist_id, thread_id, and event_id, you can optionally add + and an integer to adjust the value (this is mainly useful for event ids), for example, event_id+2. For these parameters, it also applies that they trigger a loop of all the connections which expands one investigation definition into one per connection. For example, consider workload that was shown in Listing B-5 which has an investigation defined as

```
- sql: |
    SELECT THREAD_ID, EVENT_ID, SQL_TEXT
      FROM performance_schema.events_statements_history
    WHERE thread_id = ? AND event_id > ?
    ORDER BY thread_id, event_id
  parameters:  [thread_id, event_id]
  format:      vertical
```

This results in two investigation queries (the ids will differ from execution to execution):

```
2 SELECT THREAD_ID, EVENT_ID, SQL_TEXT
    FROM performance_schema.events_statements_history
  WHERE thread_id = 89 AND event_id > 6
  ORDER BY thread_id, event_id

3 SELECT THREAD_ID, EVENT_ID, SQL_TEXT
    FROM performance_schema.events_statements_history
  WHERE thread_id = 90 AND event_id > 6
  ORDER BY thread_id, event_id
```

This simplifies writing investigations that applies to one connection at a time.

Summary

In this appendix, you learned how you can reproduce the examples in this book using the `concurrency_book.generate` MySQL Shell module from this book's GitHub repository. The primary purpose of the module is to make it easy to try the same examples and provide inspiration on how to examine the available information for each case.

You may also be interested in modifying the examples or add new test cases. If you modify an existing example, it is recommended that you make a copy of it unless you just want to add more investigation queries; that way you can still reproduce the examples from the book. A good reason to add more workloads is to build up a library of issues you encounter in your work, so you can easily reproduce them and practice troubleshooting them.

This concludes *MySQL Concurrency: Locking and Transactions for MySQL Developers and DBAs*. I hope the book has inspired you and that you are better prepared to work with locks and transactions.

Index

A, B

ACID, see Atomicity, consistency, isolation, and durability
Atomicity, consistency, isolation, and durability, 193–196, 200, 295

C

CATS, *see* Contention-Aware Transaction Scheduling
concurrency_book.generate
  commands
    help(), 7
    load(), 7, 8
    run(), 7
    show(), 7
  executing (*see* concurrency_book. generate, commands, run())
  import (*see* concurrency_book. generate, install)
  install, 5–6, 338
  loading test data (*see* concurrency_ book.generate, commands, load())
  prerequisites, 4–5, 337
  source code files
    generate.py, 338, 352
    innodb_buffer_pool.py, 353
    innodb_monitor.py, 354
    innodb_mutex.py, 354, 355
    load.py, 355, 356
    log.py, 356
    metrics.py, 357
    query.py, 358
    util.py, 359, 360
    workloads.py, 360, 361
  workload keys
    protocol, 5, 337, 363
Configuration options
  autocommit, 70, 85, 89, 93, 158, 245
  binlog_group_commit_sync_delay, 200
  binlog_group_commit_sync_no_ delay_count, 200
  binlog_transaction_dependency_ tracking, 201
  foreign_key_checks, 69, 194
  gtid_next, 84
  innodb_adaptive_hash_index, 166, 168, 316, 317
  innodb_adaptive_hash_index_parts, 69, 166, 317
  innodb_autoinc_lock_mode, 132, 133
  innodb_buffer_pool_instances, 166, 335
  innodb_buffer_pool_size, 64
  innodb_concurrency_tickets, 69
  innodb_deadlock_detect, 153
  innodb_flush_log_at_trx_commit, 196
  innodb_lock_wait_timeout, 145, 146, 153, 277

T, U, V, W, X, Y, Z

Printed in the United States
By Bookmasters